START YOUR DAY WITH GOD

Daily meditation for your spiritual growth

Anthony Sanders

PRESS

Preface

In this day and age, we must seek the face of God more than ever. We must do this by rising early in the morning, as Jesus did, to commune, pray, and seek the counsel of God our heavenly Father for His life and guidance. If Jesus could take time out of His ministry to speak to the Father, we can do likewise. "And in the morning, long before daylight, He got up and went out to a deserted place, and there He prayed" (Mark 1:35). So get up out of the bed, rise while the dew is yet fresh on the green grass and the birds are stretching their wings and warming their voices to sing praises to the Lord. Watch closely as the sun begins to peek over the horizon and the farmer is plowing his field with a bag of seed (the Word of God) over his shoulder and hope in his heart, expecting a plenteous harvest in the fall. Commune with God and listen attentively for direction as you start your day with Him. Do not allow the farmer's labor to go in vain; get up speak to God. He will speak back to you in His Word, and the Spirit will give you a fresh revelation each morning as you yearn to work on your personal relationship with the Savior Jesus Christ, the only begotten Son of the Father, who died on the cross for your sins and mine.

Embark on this journey and grow in leaps and bounds, discovering more about yourself and your relationships (with Christ and others), as you start your day with the

Lord early in the morning. Each day you should be closer to the Lord, stronger and better able to make wise decisions. Above all, be a better disciple of Jesus Christ; in serving and knowing Jesus Christ better and showing and sharing His love to others, sheep beget sheep and disciples beget disciples. "Go then and make disciples of all the nations, baptizing them into the name of the Father and of the Son and of the Holy Spirit, teaching them to observe everything that I have commanded you, and behold, I am with you all the days (perpetually, uniformly, and on every occasion), to the [very] close and consummation of the age. Amen (so let it be)" (Matt. 28:19-20).

As you start your day with God, you will get a meal and a spirit (personal challenge) to grow in Christ.

Anthony Rodrigues Sanders

Dedication

First, I dedicate this book to the Lord God, who inspired me and told me to write, as the Holy Spirit provided revelation, in order that all may know Jesus Christ as their personal Savior.

To my wife and best friend Jennifer, who is the love of my life—thank you for your prayers and support. I love you more than words can express.

To our three children, Qiana, Zemariah, and Caleb —I love you guys very much; I often thank God for you and your encouragement each day for me to do my best to live up to God's standard, because you all are watching me.

Mom and Dad (Bobbie Jean Donald [James] and David Sanders)—I love you and thank God for you, raising me the way that you all did.

To my sister Lakeisha (Fred) and my brothers (William and Joseph)—I love you guys. Thank you for the laughs.

Mama Jan (Esther Bishop)—thank you for receiving me as your son and allowing me to take your eldest daughter as my wife.

To Karolyn and Allison—thank you for being the sisters.

To all of my nieces and nephews (Katura; Cayman; Malachi; Kameron; Taurus; Keba; William, Jr.; John; and Xavier)—I love you guys very much.

Thanks to all of my family and friends. Grandma Ida I love you. Lord, thank You for Nanny Ruth Hudson (Abe Beird) and Grandma Mattie Wright.

To my great Uncle Tommy and Aunt Thelma Booze—thank you for setting the example. My uncles and aunts, I love you guys so much.

Class of 1990 of Greenwood High School (including friends for twenty-five-plus years, LaTonya Washington; Dedric Griffin; John Jones, Jr.; and Teresa Strong).

To my navy family (navy chiefs, thanks for keep the navy running strong)—Otis and Vickie Tyner, Allard and Sandra Russell, Chris Williams, Elwood Agent, Brian Rice, Robert Best, Kelcy and Benita Parks, Sheilah Joseph, Anthony Cason, Phil White, Carla Anders, Anthony Sealy, Frank McCray, Tonja and Chester Spence, Carol and Randy Bell, Carrie and Donald Terry, George Odem, Becky and Yancy Davis, Nicole Gill, Steve Hunnicut, Alicia Barnes, Aleta Cason, Melvin and Faye Ridley, Carolyn and Bruce Coleman Timothy, and LaTonya Ferguson—thank you all for your encouragement and prayers.

My church family—Morris Chapel Baptist Church in Greenwood, SC, and MT Zion AME Church in Virginia Beach, VA. Pastor Lonnie (Betsy) McClain, Presiding Elder William (MaryAnn) Dyson, thank you for your love and support.

To all who serve in uniform—keep the faith and trust God.

To the crew of USS DWIGHT D. EISENHOWER where this all started (October 2007)—may God's richest blessings and peace fall on all of you.

Here are some questions that only you can answer. Start your day off with God will help you discover who you really are in the Lord.

1. How often do you spend time with God?

2. Do you know where you stand in your personal relationship with Jesus?
3. What do others say when they see you? Do they see Christ?
4. Are you willing to show unconditional love to all humankind?
5. How often do you share the Word of God with others?
6. Do you know what your spiritual gifts are?
7. Are you walking in the power and authority that God has given?

Day 1

I pray that your day was started with God. As I turned to step out of bed, I said, "Thank you, Lord," and proceeded to worship God by reading the Word, praying, and meditating. The more we worship God, the more inclined we become to desire to be in His presence and understand who He is to us, who we are to Him, and how to perfect our daily walk with Him. "O come, let us worship and bow down, let us kneel before God the Lord our Maker [in reverent praise and supplication]" (Ps. 95:6). Start your day off with God and watch how things will turn out for you.

> "Therefore God also has highly exalted Him and given Him the name which is above every name, that at the name of Jesus every knee should bow, of those in heaven, and of those on earth, and of those under the earth, and that every tongue should confess that Jesus Christ is Lord, to the glory of God the Father" (Phil. 2:9-11 NKJV).

Challenge of the day: Worship and meditate on the wonders of God throughout the day.

To God be the glory and many blessings, and may you rise with peace, daily thinking about the Lord.

Day 2

I pray that all is well with you and your family, and I pray that God's love is evident within your household. I pray that you are starting your day off with God, knowing that God will not go back on His Word. When God tells us something, it will happen. God keeps His promises, and He is very punctual. "So let us seize and hold fast and retain without wavering the hope we cherish and confess and our acknowledgement of it, for He Who promised is reliable (sure) and faithful to His word. And let us consider and give attentive, continuous care to watching over one another, studying how we may stir up (stimulate and incite) to love and helpful deeds and noble activities" (Heb. 10:23-24). So be encouraged this morning. God is not slack concerning His Word and His promises. Keep close to the Lord and watch the results manifest within your life.

"I have set watchmen upon your walls, O Jerusalem, who will never hold their peace day or night; you who [are His servants and by your prayers] put the Lord in remembrance [of His promises], keep not silence" (Isa. 62:6).

Challenge of the day: Be always watchful and put God in remembrance of His promises and Word, through knowing and understanding the Word and His promises for you.

To God be the glory and many blessings. May the Lord's promises be revealed to you and may you be receptive to His promises.

Day 3

I pray that all is well with you and your family. I also pray that you are starting your day with God, knowing that you must live to please God rather than trying to please man. You must strive daily to hold on to and live out the Word of God, serve and please Him in all that you do. God desires and yearns to hear from you daily through prayers and conversations. Also, He desires to see us witness for Him by sharing the gospel of Jesus Christ. "FURTHERMORE, BRETHREN, we beg and admonish you in [virtue of our union with] the Lord Jesus, that [you follow the instructions which] you learned from us about how you ought to walk so as to please and gratify God, as indeed you are doing, [and] that you do so even more and more abundantly [attaining yet greater perfection in living this life]" (1 Thess. 4:1). So be encouraged this morning and live and walk to please the Living God, and life will be satisfying unto you.

"When a man's ways please the Lord, He makes even his enemies to be at peace with him" (Prov. 16:7).

Challenge of the day: Please God with the way you live and what you say, and you will see the benefits of living right and pleasing the Lord in your life daily.

To God be the glory. Many blessings to you and have a powerful day and enjoy pleasing and serving the Lord with your whole heart.

Day 4

I pray that all is well with each of you and you are starting your day with God, knowing that you must work your faith. Believe in the impossible and trust God to be God. If God declares in His Word that you are healed from all diseases, then that is what you ought to believe. You must confess the promises of God on and in your life and have the faith to believe that all things are possible. You must work your faith in accordance with the Word of the Living God. "So faith comes by hearing [what is told], and what is heard comes by the preaching [of the message that came from the lips] of Christ (the Messiah Himself)" (Rom. 10:17). So be encouraged this morning, work your faith through knowing and understanding the Word of the Living God, believe the contents of the Word, and practice what you preach. Then see the results of God's hand on your life!

"[And I pray] that the participation in and sharing of your faith may produce and promote full recognition and appreciation and understanding and precise knowledge of every good [thing] that is ours in [our identification with] Christ Jesus [and unto His glory]" (Philem. 1:6).

Challenge of the day: Identify yourself with Christ through your lifestyle.

To God be the glory. Many blessings and have a powerful day, worshiping God through living for Him.

Day 5

May God's grace be received by you each day. You should be starting your day with God, knowing that you must never surrender your joy. The joy that the Lord gives cannot be taken away by the world. An attitude of joy starts within the mind and heart. You have to make up your mind that you are not going to give your joy away to anyone. A person or situation can take your joy, if and only if you give it to them. So do not give it away, but share the joy of Jesus with all you meet today. "As the Father loved Me, I also have loved you; abide in My love. If you keep My commandments, you will abide in My love, just as I have kept My Father's command-ments and abide in His love. These things I have spoken to you, that My joy may remain in you, and that your joy may be full" (John 15:9-11 NKJV). So be encouraged this morning and experience true joy in Jesus Christ, and neither let it go nor give it up, especially when things do not go your way.

"You will show me the path of life; in Your presence is fullness of joy; at Your right hand are pleasures forevermore" (Ps. 16:11 NKJV).

Challenge of the day: Follow the path of life that leads to everlasting joy in the presence of the Lord.

To God be the glory. Many blessings and have a powerful day full of the joy of the Lord; it will indeed strengthen you. Moreover, please do not ever give your joy away, but share it with others and leave bitterness in the desert where it belongs.

15

Day 6

I pray that all is well with each of you and that you are starting your day with God, knowing that it is good to be saved. It is good to have an established relationship with Jesus Christ. No matter what may be going on in or around your life, you are going to be all right. You already know the outcome. You will win. No matter who may try to be against you or plan crazy schemes to harm you, you are still going to win. Why? Because you are saved through the blood of Jesus Christ. "Because if you acknowledge and confess with your lips that Jesus is Lord and in your heart believe (adhere to, trust in, and rely on the truth) that God raised Him from the dead, you will be saved. For with the heart a person believes (adheres to, trusts in, and relies on Christ) and so is justified (declared righteous, acceptable to God), and with the mouth he confesses (declares openly and speaks out freely his faith) and confirms [his] salvation. The Scripture says, No man who believes in Him [who adheres to, relies on, and trusts in Him] will [ever] be put to shame or be disappointed. [No one] for there is no distinction between Jew and Greek. The same Lord is Lord over all [of us] and He generously bestows His riches upon all who call upon Him [in faith]. For everyone who calls upon the name of the Lord [invoking Him as Lord] will be saved. (Rom.10:9-13). So be encouraged this morning and forget about the past, embracing your future and knowing that it is good to live a saved lifestyle with Jesus Christ. However, we must work constantly on our relationship with Christ Jesus so we can better appreciate what it really means to be saved.

"Save now, we beseech You, O Lord; send now prosperity, O Lord, we beseech You, and give to us success!" (Ps. 118:25).

Challenge of the day: Cry unto the Lord for salvation (to be saved) and know what it means to live a successful life.

To God be the glory. Many blessings to you and have a powerful day experiencing the favor of God and true success in Christ Jesus as your personal Lord and Savior. Live it! Know it! Share it and experience it, a true relationship with Jesus Christ. It is indeed good to be saved! Hosanna.

Day 7

I pray that all is well with each of you and your family and that God's mercy is cherished within your lives. I pray that you are starting your day with God, knowing that we must forgive and experience freedom in Christ. "If you forgive anyone anything, I too forgive that one ; and what I have forgiven, if I have forgiven anything, has been for your sakes in the presence [and with the approval] of Christ (the Messiah)" (2 Cor. 2:10). So be encouraged this morning, experience true freedom, forgive those that need it (even yourself), and watch how your surroundings will be impacted and changed. Then you will feel a great burden lifted off you.

"For You, O Lord, are good, and ready to forgive [our trespasses, sending them away, letting them go completely and forever]; and You are abundant in mercy and loving-kindness to all those who call upon You" (Ps. 86:5).

Challenge of the day: Do not stand in the way of receiving all that God has for you by not seeking the Lord, who is standing by to forgive all who call on Him and ask to be forgiven, even forgiving someone who has trespassed against you. The Lord is ready to forgive. When will you forgive? Do not wait. Let it go and allow God to show you how it is done.

To God be the glory. Many blessings and have a powerful day serving the Lord and experiencing His liberties in your life.

Day 8

I pray you are starting your day off with God, knowing that it is your mind and heart that must be transformed into understanding and receiving the things of God. When you can think and receive the things of God, you will be able to operate better in the spiritual gifts that were given unto you. Think and move on the Word of God and witness the true transformation that is desired. "Do not be conformed to this world (this age), [fashioned after and adapted to its external, superficial customs], but be transformed (changed) by the [entire] renewal of your mind [by its new ideals and its new attitude], so that you may prove [for yourselves] what is the good and acceptable and perfect will of God, even the thing which is good and acceptable and perfect [in His sight for you]" (Rom. 12:2). So be encouraged this morning and feel the power of transformation happening in your life, as you allow your mind and heart to be renewed daily in the living Word of God through Jesus Christ.

"And be constantly renewed in the spirit of your mind [having a fresh mental and spiritual attitude]" (Eph. 4:23).

Challenge of the day: Strive to change your attitude daily to line up with the Word of God and witness a true change in your life.

To God be the glory. Many blessings and have a powerful day renewing your mind and heart toward the things of Christ Jesus.

Day 9

I pray that God's love rules in your hearts. Starting your day off with God means you must put on Christ. Your mind must be in alignment with the Word of God and the Spirit of Christ. You must excel in all that you do and have great compassion toward humanity and show and share the love of Jesus Christ. Our thought process must reflect the living Word of God. "But clothe yourself with the Lord Jesus Christ (the Messiah), and make no provision for [indulging] the flesh [put a stop to thinking about the evil cravings of your physical nature] to [gratify its] desires (lusts)" (Rom. 13:14). So be encouraged this morning. Put on Christ, guard against the lustful desires of the flesh, and consume yourself with the things of Christ and His characteristics.

"Delight yourself also in the Lord, and He will give you the desires and secret petitions of your heart" (Psalms 37:4).

Challenge of the day: Let your desires line up with the Word and not be that of the flesh.

To God be the glory. Many blessings and have a powerful day in the Lord. Remain focused on serving Him and living up to His standards. Be blessed in all that you all do for the living Lord.

Day 10

I pray that you are starting your day off with God, knowing that you must live holy lives. You must be willing to separate yourself from the things of the world and lay hold of the things of God. Holiness is not just a word that stands out, but also one that requires action on your part. You must bear the characteristics of Jesus Christ. It is not about how we dress or speak only, but it is about living a lifestyle for Christ. "And put on the new nature (the regenerate self) created in God's image, [Godlike] in true righteousness and holiness" (Eph. 4:24). So be encouraged this morning and wear your holy lifestyle as if it is near and dear to you. Grow into it and develop it daily.

> "For in the time being no discipline brings joy, but seems grievous and painful; but afterwards it yields a peaceable fruit of righteousness to those who have been trained by it [a harvest of fruit which consists in righteousness—in conformity to God's will in purpose, thought, and action, resulting in right living and right standing with God]" (Heb. 12:11).

Challenge of the day: Accept discipline; in fact, learn to discipline your life and watch how holiness and right living will become a habit.

To God be the glory. Many blessings and have a powerful day living a holy and upright life before the Lord Jesus Christ.

Day 11

I pray that the peace of God rest within your homes. Knowing that you must give honor unto the Lord, reverence Him, and lift Him up in every area of your life is a great way to start your day. Let us magnify the Lord in all that we do, share in the love of Christ, and give honor to that which honor is due. Do not be afraid to honor God in all that you do. Remember Him because the Lord will never forget you. "This is in keeping with my own eager desire and persistent expectation and hope, that I shall not disgrace myself nor be put to shame in anything; but that with the utmost freedom of speech and unfailing courage, now as always heretofore, Christ (the Messiah) will be magnified and get glory and praise in this body of mine and be boldly exalted in my person, whether through (by) life or through (by) death" (Phil. 1:20). So be encouraged this morning, lift up, honor, and magnify the Lord this morning, regardless of the circumstances which life may present you. Be persistent in glorifying and honoring the Lord Jesus Christ.

> "Let those who favor my righteous cause and have pleasure in my uprightness shout for joy and be glad and say continually, Let the Lord be magnified, Who takes pleasure in the prosperity of His servant" (Ps. 35:27).

Challenge of the day: Feel and search for God's presence and seek to live in His righteousness for His cause. Move toward a continuous praise and magnification of the Lord in all that you aspire to accomplish on a day-to-day basis.

To God be the glory. Many blessings and have a powerful day in the Lord, honoring Him and those who serve the Lord with a righteous and glad heart.

Day 12

It is good to start your day with God, knowing you must release the pains and circumstances of life over to the Lord. Give your pains and circumstances all to the Lord and do not take them back or talk yourself out of receiving what God has in store for you. God's desire is to bless us, take care of us, and teach us His ways daily. "Cast your burden on the Lord [releasing the weight of it] and He will sustain you; He will never allow the [consistently] righteous to be moved (made to slip, fall, or fail)" (Ps. 55:22). So be encouraged this morning and get up and give your problems (even your church pains) to the Lord, and He will deal with them. Do not hinder your growth in the Lord by remaining in the same circumstances from which God Himself is trying to release you. Give it up and grow in the grace and loving arms of the almighty and everlasting God through Jesus Christ and the Holy Spirit. Listen and hearken unto the voice of God, and He will give you a clear and concise way to move forward.

"Are not the angels all ministering spirits (servants) sent out in the service [of God for the assistance] of those who are to inherit salvation?" (Heb. 1:14).

Challenge of the day: Know that we are not alone in the kingdom-building process, so do not carry the burdens of life without prayer. Release them and learn to tend to and to minister to others. Release the stress of life. God's commands are not burdensome (1 John 5:3).

To God be the glory. Many blessings and have a powerful day serving the Lord and give glory always. Release your praise unto the Lord.

Day 13

You must know where you stand with God as you start each day. You must understand your relationship with God; live out His promises in His Word, while you have the opportunity. "Seek, inquire for, and require the Lord while He may be found [claiming Him by necessity and by right]; call upon Him while He is near" (Isaiah 55:6). In your relationship with God, you will know His presence and understand the urgency to worship Him and relate to His Word, because of the closeness that you have. You must know the connection of the Word in your life and the connection that is strong and will sustain life itself. So be encouraged this morning, seek the Lord Jesus, and develop your relationship with the Lord daily.

> "But seek (aim at and strive after) first of all His kingdom and His righteousness (His way of doing and being right), and then all these things taken together will be given you besides. So do not worry or be anxious about tomorrow, for tomorrow will have worries and anxieties of its own. Sufficient for each day is its own trouble" (Matt. 6:33, 34).

Challenge of the day: Seek the Lord and work on your relationship daily. Do not fret about troubles of tomorrow, for God holds tomorrow in His hand as well. Just work on your relationship and you will see God actively moving in every area of your life.

To God be the glory. Many blessings and have a powerful day in the Lord trusting and relying on Him!

Day 14

Surrendering your thoughts and your heart to the Lord is an excellent way to start your day with God. Sometimes your thoughts are not aligned with the Word of God, and those thoughts can turn into actions. Use wise counsel and carefully consider the very thoughts that you think. "[Inasmuch as we] refute arguments and theories and reasonings and every proud and lofty thing that sets itself up against the [true] knowledge of God; and we lead every thought and purpose away captive into the obedience of Christ (the Messiah, the Anointed One)" (2 Cor. 10:5). So be encouraged this morning and think the thoughts of the Lord. Refresh your minds. Change your thoughts and heed the words of the Lord so that your life may be changed day by day.

"I considered my ways; I turned my feet to [obey] Your testimonies" (Ps. 119:59).

Challenge of the day: Consider the route you are taking and who you are representing (the Lord Jesus Christ) and ensure that you are walking and living up to His standards.

To God be the glory. Many blessings and have a powerful day surrendering even your thoughts to the Lord.

Day 15

As you start this day, know that you should recognize God in all that you do. You can no longer afford to hold back your praises unto the Lord when it is the Lord moving you through life. You must lift up holy hands and shout with a voice of triumph unto the Lord. You must give God glory in spite of what is going on within your lives, and we must seek and acknowledge God's presence always. "And I will give them a heart to know (recognize, understand, and be acquainted with) Me, that I am the Lord; and they will be My people, and I will be their God, for they will return to Me with their whole heart" (Jer. 24:7). So be encouraged this morning and know with great understanding that God still moves in your life, even during the challenging times. It is during these times you must—now more than ever—recognize and praise Him even more and indeed look toward the Lord Jesus for guidance and direction.

"I am the Good Shepherd ; and I know and recognize My own, and My own recognize Me" (John 10:14).

Challenge of the day: God recognizes and knows us completely, so why is it sometimes difficult (when we are so busy) for us to know and recognize God? Get to know the Lord Jesus personally and without fear, but with reverence and pure satisfaction. It is the Lord God who rules and runs everything.

To God be the glory. Many blessings and have a powerful day serving the Lord and feeling His presence as you worship and magnify Him.

Day 16

In truly serving God, you must live beyond what you see with your natural eyes. You must possess a strong and bold walk of faith. Now more than ever you must have faith to move the mountains in your life, regardless of how huge those mountains may be or how rough and rugged the sides may be. You must have faith and walk in strength and boldness there. When you walk in faith and see things beyond your natural sight, you will not be concerned about what you are facing because you will rely on the Lord for deliverance and salvation. "Without having seen Him, you love Him; though you do not [even] now see Him, you believe in Him and exult and thrill with inexpressible and glorious (triumphant, heavenly) joy. [At the same time] you receive the result (outcome, consummation) of your faith, the salvation of your souls" (1 Pet. 1:8). So be encouraged, see Jesus in all that you do, and watch the mountains of life move because of your faith, according to the power and will of the living God. Allow the same faith that was used to believe in Jesus grow and do His will in your life.

"Now FAITH is the assurance (the confirmation, the title deed) of the things [we] hope for, being the proof of the things [we] do not see and the conviction of their reality [faith perceiving as real fact what is not revealed to the senses]" (Heb. 11:1).

Challenge of the day: Know and understand the power of the faith you possess and use it to glorify God! Do not be fearful of what you do not see or even what you do see. Stand on the promises of God by faith; regardless of what the natural eye is viewing, go with the revelation of the Holy Spirit.

To God be the glory. Many blessings and have a powerful day full of faith, knowing that your salvation is secured through Jesus Christ and you have the faith to see beyond your natural sight.

Day 17

When starting your day with God, you must be willing to receive God's mercy. You must know that you are forgiven once you've asked the Lord Jesus, who died on the cross for your sins and the world's sins, to forgive you and not hold any grudges against you. In order for you to move forward in life, you must not limit yourself because of your past misfortunes, but lean forward with God's unlimited mercy and love. "Let us then fearlessly and confidently and boldly draw near to the throne of grace (the throne of God's unmerited favor to us sinners), that we may receive mercy [for our failures] and find grace to help in good time for every need [appropriate help and well-timed help, coming just when we need it]" (Heb. 4:16). So be encouraged this morning and know with a clear heart that God's mercy and love supersedes your past mistakes.

"For His mercy and loving-kindness are great toward us, and the truth and faithfulness of the Lord endure forever. Praise the Lord! (Hallelujah!)" (Ps. 117:2).

Challenge of the day: Walk in the power of God's mercy, love, faithfulness, and truth, because they will outlast anything that you are facing.

To God be the glory. Many blessings and have a powerful day in the Lord and move according to the beat that the Lord provides for you.

Day 18

Start this day with God, knowing that you must prepare your heart to hear and receive the Word of the Lord. You must be attentive to His Word and receive understanding. To understand is to receive and apply what you know or have knowledge of. Pray for understanding as your receive the Word of God and observe how your life will change. "Then opened he their understanding, that they might understand the scriptures, and said unto them, Thus it is written, and thus it behooved Christ to suffer, and to rise from the dead the third day: And that repentance and remission of sins should be preached in his name among all nations, beginning at Jerusalem. And ye are witnesses of these things" (Luke 24:45-48 KJV). So be encouraged this morning, seek to understand what you know about the Word of God, and apply it to everyday living.

"Get wisdom, get understanding: forget it not; neither decline from the words of my mouth. Forsake her not, and she shall preserve thee: love her, and she shall keep thee. Wisdom is the principal thing; therefore get wisdom: and with all thy getting get understanding" (Prov. 4:5-7 KJV).

Challenge of the day: Do not cease seeking wisdom from the Lord. Get it and gain understanding in all that you do.

To God be the glory. Many blessings and have a powerful day understanding the power of the Word of God

Day 19

As you start this day with God, know that you must draw close to Him daily. Daily you must strive to draw closer toward God in your personal relationship. You should constantly communicate your thoughts and prayers unto the Lord to ensure that you are aligned with His Word. You must draw closer to Him in order to gather the details needed for the day-to-day living in Christ. The Spirit of the Lord will indeed reveal unto you what it is you should do once you seek His guidance daily. "But what does it say? The Word (God's message is Christ) is near you, on your lips and in your heart ; that is, the Word (the message, the basis and object) of faith which we preach" (Rom. 10:8). The Word of God will make you closer to the living God as you ponder, study, and speak His Word, so be encouraged this morning, feed on the Word of God, and walk closer to the Lord daily.

"The Lord is near to all who call upon Him, to all who call upon Him sincerely and in truth" (Ps. 145:18).

Challenge of the day: Draw near unto the Lord with a sincere heart and know Him like never before. Come clean before the Lord with clean hands and a pure heart. Fix your eyes and motives upon the Lord and observe the changes of life that God will give you.

To God be the glory. Many blessings and have a powerful week in the Lord studying, fasting, praying, and basking in His presence.

Day 20

As you start this beautiful day with God, know that you must live out the Word of God by faith and with great expectation. The Word of God is living and powerful. You must live it out to the fullest and not be afraid of hearing from the Lord. The Lord will speak to you through His Word, and the Holy Spirit will give you revelation as needed. Hear the Word of God with distinction and operate according to the will of God. "So Jesus said to those Jews who had believed in Him, If you abide in My word [hold fast to My teachings and live in accordance with them], you are truly My disciples" (John 8:31). So be encouraged this morning and allow your life to be transformed by the Word of God and live it out daily with great expectation of seeing the Word made manifest in your walk with Christ.

"As for God, His way is perfect! The word of the Lord is tested and tried; He is a shield to all those who take refuge and put their trust in Him" (Ps. 18:30).

Challenge of the day: The Word of God has been proven. Try it and see great things happen in your life.

To God be the glory. Many blessings and have a powerful day meditating on the powerful Word of God and examining your life through the living Word of God.

Day 21

Knowing and accepting that you must give an account to the Lord for your life is a powerful way to begin this day. In everything that you do as a believer, you must be accountable to your Lord. You must respond to the issues of life by first going to the Lord and seeking His guidance and direction. Make sure that whatever you do is for His glory and not for your fame. God knows your heart, and your heart must be sincere in what you do for Him. Be very careful about how you respect and treat one another. Are you your brother's keeper? Without question, you must be accountable to and for one another. "And so each of us shall give an account of himself [give an answer in reference to judgment] to God" (Rom. 14:12). So be encouraged this morning and know what you are responsible and accountable for in the Lord. Hold on to the Lord's hand and trust in Him to guide you to make the right decisions.

"Lord, what is man that You take notice of him? Or [the] son of man that You take account of him?" (Ps. 144:3).

Challenge of the day: God notices what we do and what we say, so strive to live in a well-pleasing manner unto the Lord daily.

To God be the glory. Many blessings and have a powerful day living up to the standards of God through Christ Jesus.

Day 22

It is a beautiful day to start off knowing that God's wisdom is available to you and that His wisdom is like none other. God's wisdom is perfect, sound, and precise. "But it is from Him that you have your life in Christ Jesus, Whom God made our Wisdom from God, [revealed to us a knowledge of the divine plan of salvation previously hidden, manifesting itself as] our Righteousness [thus making us upright and putting us in right standing with God], and our Consecration [making us pure and holy], and our Redemption [providing our ransom from eternal penalty for sin]" (1 Cor. 1:30). God's wisdom provided a way for you to be righteous through Christ Jesus, so be encouraged this morning and seek God's wisdom in your daily walk and decision-making process. With His wisdom, things will make sense to you in due time.

"But to man He said, Behold, the reverential and worshipful fear of the Lord—that is Wisdom; and to depart from evil is understanding" (Job 28:28).

Challenge of the day: Look up and, within your surroundings, worship the Lord with a reverent heart, mind, and spirit. Get away from the evil things of the world and gain much understanding in your daily dealings with others and even yourself.

To God be the glory. Many blessings and have a safe and powerful day discovering more about who you are in the Word of God.

Day 23

Today is the day to start your day knowing that God's love is stronger than any crisis that you may face. His love will carry you through the many trials and tribulations of life. His love will guarantee that you will have eternal life in Jesus Christ, if only you believe and trust in Him. "Love bears up under anything and everything that comes, is ever ready to believe the best of every person, its hopes are fadeless under all circumstances, and it endures everything [without weakening]" (1 Cor. 13:7). God's love will never fail, and His love for you and me will carry us beyond our greatest imagination. His love will cause you to be strengthened during any and every crisis you may face in life. So be encouraged this morning and hold on to God's love, because His love for you is real and everlasting.

"Surely or only goodness, mercy, and unfailing love shall follow me all the days of my life, and through the length of my days the house of the Lord [and His presence] shall be my dwelling place" (Ps. 23:6).

Challenge of the day: Understand the power of God's love and yearn to be in His presence all the days of your life.

To God be the glory. Many blessings and have a powerful day sharing in and experiencing the love of God.

Day 24

God gave His children gifts, and today as you start your day, recognize the gifts God has given you. God desires that we use the gifts that are within and not be fearful of the gifts or calling. Fear will keep us from doing all that God has us to do. Accept the gifts and your call, and use them according to the will of God. "I wish that all men were like I myself am [in this matter of self-control]. But each has his own special gift from God, one of this kind and one of another" (1 Cor. 7:7). Do not say that you are not worthy of the gifts or call from God or allow the "I am not's" to hinder you from accepting the gift from God. So be encouraged this morning, stay close to God, use the gifts, and walk in the call that is upon your life.

> "For God's gifts and His call are irrevocable. [He never withdraws them when once they are given, and He does not change His mind about those to whom He gives His grace or to whom He sends His call]" (Rom. 11:29).

Challenge of the day: Do not run from the call and the gift. Accept them because God will not take them back or change His mind. Serve Him to the fullest in all that He has given unto you. Be who God called you to be and do not concern yourself with what others will say nor think. It is God who qualifies and not others.

To God be the glory. Many blessings and have a powerful day serving the Lord as He has called you to do.

Day 25

I pray that all is well with you and your family. Start your day with God, knowing that you must adore the Lord, reverence Him, and lift His name up in all that you do, so that He will get the glory. "And I, if and when I am lifted up from the earth [on the cross], will draw and attract all men [Gentiles as well as Jews] to Myself" (John 12:32). When we lift up the name of Jesus daily, regardless of what is going on in our lives and even in our very surroundings, God will get the glory. Adore the name of the Lord, because there is power in the name of Jesus Christ. So be encouraged this morning and give God glory from the time you get up, throughout the workday and everywhere you go. God's name must be praised, and you must have peace and joy in lifting up the name of Jesus in your daily living.

"Lift up your heads, O you gates; and be lifted up, you age-abiding doors, that the King of glory may come in. Who is the King of glory? The Lord strong and mighty, the Lord mighty in battle" (Ps. 24:7, 8).

Challenge of the day: Look at God and for God in all of your situations, and He will show you just how strong He really is in your life. Remember the battles of life are not ours, but they indeed belong to the Lord. We must focus on God and not the situations and issues of life.

To God be the glory. Many blessings and have a powerful day serving the Lord, lifting up His name, and allowing God, the King of Glory, to come in and reign on all of your issues of life. AMEN.

Day 26

I pray that God's light is shining brightly in each of your lives. Start your day off with God knowing that you must experience the joy of the Lord. God's joy runs deep and is forever. You must have a joyful heart while serving the Lord Jesus. "But none of these things move me; neither do I esteem my life dear to myself, if only I may finish my course with joy and the ministry which I have obtained from [which was entrusted to me by] the Lord Jesus, faithfully to attest to the good news (Gospel) of God's grace (His unmerited favor, spiritual blessing, and mercy)" (Acts 20:24). When serving the Lord, you will have many encounters, but you must not fear what you face; rather, hold true to the joy of the Lord that is your strength. So be encouraged this morning and have the joy of the Lord resting upon you.

> "And the ransomed of the Lord shall return and come to Zion with singing, and everlasting joy shall be upon their heads; they shall obtain joy and gladness, and sorrow and sighing shall flee away" (Isa. 35:10).

Challenge of the day: Prepare your mind to be restored and receive the joy of the Lord.

To God be the glory. Many blessings and expect the joy of the Lord in your life; regardless of what you are facing, God can bring you out.

Day 27

I pray that all is well with you and your family. Start your day off with God, knowing that you must believe that there is indeed nothing too hard for God to do and accomplish in our lives. God commands that we believe in the impossible and trust in His ability to get those impossible things accomplished. We must have faith and know that God can do all things, and He gives us strength to do all things in and through His only Son Jesus Christ. "Is anything too hard or too wonderful for the Lord? At the appointed time, when the season [for her delivery] comes around, I will return to you and Sarah shall have borne a son." (Gen. 18:14). So be encouraged this morning and receive the notion that there is indeed nothing to hard for God; no matter what is going on in your life, God can handle it. Trust and believe that He can and will.

"You have a mighty arm; strong is Your hand, Your right hand is soaring high" (Ps. 89:13).

Challenge of the day: Lean on God's strong arm; He will never let you down.

To God be the glory. Many blessings and have a powerful day in the Lord trusting in Him who gave us the ability to dream big and accomplish the impossible in His Son, Jesus the Christ.

Day 28

I pray that all is well with each of you and your family and that God's unconditional love is received. Start your day off with God, knowing that you must pray in an effective manner. Pray the Word of God, recall Scripture, pray by the leading of the Holy Spirit, pray with a sincere and earnest heart, and feel the closeness of God when connecting with Him through prayer. "Confess to one another therefore your faults (your slips, your false steps, your offenses, your sins) and pray [also] for one another, that you may be healed and restored [to a spiritual tone of mind and heart]. The earnest (heartfelt, continued) prayer of a righteous man makes tremendous power available [dynamic in its working]. Elijah was a human being with a nature such as we have [with feelings, affections, and a constitution like ours]; and he prayed earnestly for it not to rain, and no rain fell on the earth for three years and six months. [I Kings 17:1] And [then] he prayed again and the heavens supplied rain and the land produced its crops [as usual]. [I Kings 18:42-45]" (James 5:16-18). So be encouraged this morning and pray with a sincere and earnest heart, pray with power; but make sure you pray the Word of God through faith by the leading of the Holy Spirit.

"I desire therefore that in every place men should pray, without anger or quarreling or resentment or doubt [in their minds], lifting up holy hands" (1 Tim. 2:8).

Challenge of the day: Pray with reverence unto the Lord, lift up your holy hands and hearts unto Him as He receives the word of faith from you.

To God be the glory. Many blessings and have a power-packed day praying and praising God.

Day 29

I pray that all is well with each of you and your family. Start your day off with God knowing that you must always pray; pray with a sincere heart and with the leading and guiding of the Holy Spirit. Never stop praying for your family, your friends, other believers, those who are lost (who do not know or have not received Jesus Christ as their Lord and Savior), and pray for our nation, Israel, and the world. When we pray with power, a sincere heart, and under the direction of the Spirit of God, all we have to do is have faith and believe that God will make a change around us, in everything and everywhere we go. "Pray at all times (on every occasion, in every season) in the Spirit, with all [manner of] prayer and entreaty. To that end keep alert and watch with strong purpose and perseverance, interceding in behalf of all the saints (God's consecrated people)" (Eph. 6:18). So be encouraged this morning—always pray and expect God to answer your prayers according to His will and in His way.

> "HEAR THE right (my righteous cause), O Lord ; listen to my shrill, piercing cry! Give ear to my prayer, that comes from unfeigned and guileless lips" (Ps. 17:1).

Challenge of the day: Pray with a pure and sincere heart and undefiled lips. Pray with power and faith and wait expectantly for God's answer.

To God be the glory. Many blessings and have a powerful day praying without ceasing.

Day 30

I pray that all is well with you and your family. Start your day off with God knowing that He will protect you from all hurt, harm, and even dangers. When we are under the arm of God's protection, we can know safety like never before. God protects His own, like a shepherd protecting his sheep. "Happy are you, O Israel, and blessing is yours! Who is like you, a people saved by the Lord, the Shield of your help, the Sword that exalts you! Your enemies shall come fawning and cringing, and submit feigned obedience to you, and you shall march on their high places" (Deut. 33:29). God's protection is like a shield blocking the attacks and will help you in the midst when things come against you. So be encouraged this morning and do not fret when things get hard and the attacks seems heavy. God is your Shield, He has you covered by the blood of Jesus Christ.

> "For You, Lord, will bless the [uncompromisingly] righteous [him who is upright and in right standing with You]; as with a shield You will surround him with goodwill (pleasure and favor)" (Ps. 5:12).

Challenge of the day: Live upright and know the protection of the Lord, and the Lord will surround you with His favor.

To God be the glory. Many blessings and have a powerful day receiving the Lord as your Shield.

Day 31

I pray that all is well with each of you and your family. Start your day off with God knowing that you must be covered in the entire armor of the Lord. You cannot fight a spiritual fight in the physical; we must use the spiritual equipment prepared and given unto us. Often we may attempt to fight this fight without coming to the fight in spiritual shape and end of being knocked down. Come ready and armed with the Word, faith, peace, righteousness, and prayer. "Therefore put on God's complete armor, that you may be able to resist and stand your ground on the evil day [of danger], and, having done all [the crisis demands], to stand [firmly in your place]" (Eph. 6:13). So be encouraged this morning and come dressed for the spiritual battles that we face on a daily basis and stand and see the salvation of the Lord.

> "The night is far gone and the day is almost here. Let us then drop (fling away) the works and deeds of darkness and put on the [full] armor of light" (Rom. 13:12).

Challenge of the day: Come from the darkness, rid yourself of the bad habits of life, and dress yourself completely in the light of the Lord.

To God be the glory. Many blessings and have a powerful day in the Lord, serving God and walking in the Light that shines ever so brightly.

Day 32

I pray that all is well with you and your family. Start your day off with God knowing that you must pursue your dreams constantly and never allow your dreams to fall by the wayside. When God gives us a dream or vision, we must go forward and see God's plan through and fear neither success nor the path we must travel to get where God requires us to be. Feel the dreams inside and move by the grace and Spirit of the Living God. "[One may hear God's voice] in a dream, in a vision of the night, when deep sleep falls on men while slumbering upon the bed" (Job 33:15). So be encouraged this morning and fulfill the dreams and visions given unto you by the Lord. If God revealed it to you, He will see you through it all; trust and rely on God to be God and for Him alone to bring you through.

"And He said, Hear now My words: If there is a prophet among you, I the Lord make Myself know to him in a vision and speak to him in a dream" (Num. 12:6).

Challenge of the day: When God speaks, listen, heed His words, and gain understanding for what it is you are to do in life.

To God be the glory. Many blessings, have a powerful day in the Lord, and receive the dreams He has for you in your life. Let us keep the dream of hope and change alive and live a life that is pleasing unto the Lord.

Day 33

I pray that all is well with you and your house. Start your day off with God knowing that you must worship Him. In spite of your circumstances and status in life, allow God to have complete control over your life. We sometimes give things to God and then take them back. Go with faith this morning and leave everything up to God; begin to worship Him first for who He is and He will make His presence known in and around your life. "Again, the devil took Him up on a very high mountain and showed Him all the king-doms of the world and the glory (the splendor, magnificence, preeminence, and excellence) of them. And he said to Him, These things, all taken together, I will give You, if You will prostrate Yourself before me and do homage and worship me. The Jesus said to him, Begone, Satan! For it has been written, You shall worship the Lord your God, and Him alone shall you serve." (Matt. 4:8-10; see also Deut. 6:13). So be encouraged this morning and surrender those things that may hinder your worship to God. Whether material or situational, do not allow those things to hinder your worship experience with God. Do not give in to the pressures of this world; give in to the Lord Jesus Christ and watch how your life will begin to turn around.

"O come, let us worship and bow down, let us kneel before the Lord our Maker [in reverent praise and supplication]" (Ps. 95:6).

Challenge of the day: Worship the Lord in spite of what is going on in your life; worship Him because of who He is and how much He adores and loves.

To God be the glory. Many blessings and have a powerful day serving the Lord with a glad heart.

Day 34

I pray that all is well with each of you and your family and may God's blessings flow like a river. Start your day off with God knowing that it is God who covers you; His protection and love are like none other. "They shall not hurt or destroy in all My holy mountain, for the earth shall be full of the knowledge of the Lord as the waters cover the sea" (Isa. 11:9). Knowledge about God and His desire to cover us is throughout the Bible; we must tune in to His Word and seek understanding and divine protection as we walk this walk of faith. So be encouraged this morning and lift up your head; God's got you covered everywhere you go.

> "[Then] He will cover you with His pinions, and under His wings shall you trust and find refuge; His truth and His faithfulness are a shield and a buckler" (Ps. 91:4).

Challenge of the day: Remove yourself from a false shield (an "I can do things on my own" mentality), get under God's wings of protection, and love—because He always will remain faithful throughout life.

To God be the glory. Many blessings and have a powerful day seeking the knowledge of God.

Day 35

I pray that all is well with you and your family and that God's presence is ever so radiant in your lives. Start your day off with God knowing that you must resist the devil. Do not give way to him or give in to your fleshly desires. Resist temptation and stand on the promises of God. "So be subject to God. Resist the devil [stand firm against him], and he will flee from you" (James 4:7). So be encouraged this morning; pray, watch, and give no room to the devil. Pray over your spouse, children, parents and relatives, and friends and coworkers. Go throughout your house and anoint it with oil. Read the Word aloud; be spiritually combat ready.

"Put on God's whole armor [the armor of a heavy-armed solider which God supplies], that you may be able successfully to stand up against [all] the strategies and the deceits of the devil" (Eph. 6:11).

Challenge of the day: Dress appropriately for this spiritual warfare. God already has supplied the hardware; we just have to know and understand how to wear it right.

To God be the glory. Many blessings and have a powerful day in the Lord being subject unto Him and not giving into your flesh. Stay focused on what God would have you to do for Him. No bad attitudes or grudge-holding; the battle has been won, just give God the glory.

Day 36

I pray that all is well with each of you and your family and that God's grace is received and appreciated by all. Start your day off with God knowing that you must open your heart and mind to receive the Word of God. The Word is transforming and is strong and compassionate enough to change the lives of those who are willing to feast upon it. "So Jesus said to those Jews who had believed in Him, If you abide in My word [hold fast to My teachings and live in accordance with them], you are truly My disciples" (John 8:31). So be encouraged this morning, allow the Word of God to abide with you in your mind and heart, and be transformed by it through your daily living for Jesus Christ.

"And now, little children, abide (live, remain permanently) in Him, so that when He is made visible, we may have and enjoy perfect confidence (boldness, assurance) and not be ashamed and shrink from Him at His coming" (1 John 2:28).

Challenge of the day: Come clean and let your lifestyle (make it a habit to live for) speak of Jesus Christ with a boldness and assurance that Jesus is coming back again.

To God be the glory. Many blessings and have a powerful day serving and living for Christ Jesus with a fresh boldness.

Day 37

I pray that all is well with each of you. Start your day off with God knowing that you must love in spite of what is going on in and around our lives. Let love prevail over everything. We must walk in love and allow God to move in our hearts to show and share the love of Jesus Christ. Not everyone will always agree in life, but everyone needs love, regardless of what is going on in his or her personal lives. "And may the Lord make you to increase and excel and overflow in love for one another and for all people, just as we also do for you, so that He may strengthen and confirm and establish your hearts faultlessly pure and unblamable in holiness in the sight of our God and Father, at the coming of our Lord Jesus Christ (the Messiah) with all His saints (the holy and glorified people of God)! Amen, (So be it)!" (1 Thess. 3:12-13). So be encouraged this morning and love others, and even yourself, because God's love for you is unconditional and too deep to refuse, being demonstrated on the cross with Jesus Christ giving up His spirit and dying for the entire world's sins.

"Your testimonies have I kept [hearing, receiving, loving, and obeying them]; I love them exceedingly!" (Ps. 119:167).

Challenge of the day: Testify about the goodness and love of the Lord and walk in His precepts.

To God be the glory. Many blessings and have a powerful day serving the Lord, sharing, and receiving His unconditional love.

Day 38

I pray that all is well with you and your family and that God's favor will rest on each of you. Start your day off with God knowing that you must understand that you live out the Word of God in your life. You must activate your faith walk and watch the Word be made manifest within your life. Neither hold back, nor be afraid of what may transpire, but welcome a constant transformation within your life as you live out the Word of the living God. "But be doers of the Word [obey the message], and not merely listeners to it, betraying yourselves [into deception by reasoning contrary to the Truth]" (James 1:22). So be encouraged this morning, do what the Word declares, live out your life for Jesus, and see the fruit of your labor for the Lord.

"Your words were found, and I ate them; and Your words were to me a joy and the rejoicing of my heart, for I am called by Your name, O Lord God of hosts" (Jer. 15:16).

Challenge of the day: Allow the living Word of God to consume you and rest within your heart and be glad about it. That which consumes you will keep you and occupy 90 percent of your time.

To God be the glory. Many blessings and have a blessed day, glorifying the living God, for He is worthy to be praised. Know His Word and His Word will know you.

Day 39

I pray that all is well with each of you. Start your day off with God knowing that you must never stop expecting miracles to happen in and around your life. Believe always in the impossible, because there is nothing too hard for the God that we serve. Many think that miracles happened only back in the early church days; well, God's Word has not changed, and God still performs and displays miracles daily. We must continue to believe, and we will see them in our lives. "Now by the hands of the apostles (special messengers) numerous and startling signs and wonders were being performed among the people. And by common consent they all met together [at the temple] in the covered porch (walk) called Solomon's" (Acts 5:12). So be encouraged this morning and dare to still believe in miracles, because God is still performing them daily. We just have to trust and believe in the Lord of life and the Lord of all, Jesus Christ.

"To Him Who alone does great wonders, for His mercy and loving-kindness endure forever" (Ps. 136:4).

Challenge of the day: God has not changed; believe in Him who can do great things, even still performs wonders in your life.

To God be the glory. Many blessings and have powerful day in the Lord, believing that God can do all things.

Day 40

I pray that all is well with you and your family. Start your day off with God knowing that you must show love always. You must even love your neighbors, enemies, and those folks who are hard to love for some unknown reason. God desires that all experience His love, and we must not be afraid to love and share in His love. "You shall not take revenge or bear any grudge against the sons of your people, but you shall love your neighbor as yourself. I am the Lord" (Lev. 19:18). So be encouraged and show love to all that you come across; neither hold grudges nor be afraid to ask for forgiveness.

"Love one another with brotherly affection [as members of one family], giving precedence and showing honor to one another" (Rom. 12:10).

Challenge of the day: Love like it is your last time to see your neighbor or family member—regretting nothing.

To God be the glory. Many blessings, have a blessed day, and enjoy being in the presence of the Lord; love always, not just on special days.

Day 41

I pray that all is well with you and your family and that the knowledge of God rests within your hearts. Start your day off with God knowing that you must have a clear conscience and use godly wisdom when making decisions. God will never lead us wrong; He knows our beginning and ending, so we must trust Him to guide us directly down the path He desires for us to take. We stray when we want to do our own thing. Follow God and have that assurance of what your end will be. "The beginning of Wisdom is: get Wisdom (skillful and godly Wisdom)! [For skillful and godly Wisdom is the principal thing.] And with all you have gotten, get understanding (discernment, comprehension, and interpretation)" (Prov. 4:7). So be encouraged this morning and seek wisdom, and you will not go wrong when God is guiding you on this journey we call life.

"If any of you is deficient in wisdom, let him ask of the giving God [Who gives] to everyone liberally and ungrudgingly, without reproaching or fault-finding, and it will be given him. Only it must be in faith that he asks with no wavering (no hesitating, no doubting). For the one who wavers (hesitates, doubts) is like the billowing surge out at sea that is blown hither and thither and tossed by the wind" (James 1:5-6).

Challenge of the day: Seek and ask for wisdom; do not hesitate or doubt when asking God for it, just have faith and believe, and you will see it in your action and know within your heart what God's response will be.

To God be the glory. Many blessings, have a powerful day, and share in the love of Jesus Christ daily.

Day 42

I pray that all is well with each of you and your family and that you all experience God's strength in all that you all do for the Lord. Start your day off with God knowing that God can handle anything. It does not matter what is going on in and around your life, God can handle it. If there is a need for healing, God can do it; if there is a need for deliverance, God can do it. When there is a need for any miracle, God can and will perform it. Our part is trusting God to be God, knowing and understanding His Word and walking by faith. "Is anything too hard or too wonderful for the Lord? At the appointed time, when the season [for her delivery] comes around, I will return to you and Sarah shall have borne a son" (Gen. 18:14). So be encouraged this morning and know that God can handle anything and everything simultaneously; we simply must try God and see. Do not hold on to things you have no control over; release it and let it go for your sake and enjoy life with the Lord Jesus Christ. There is no time to be stressing when God is blessing; look for those blessings and recognize God in them.

"By [the help of] God I will praise His word; on God I lean, rely and confidently put my trust; I will not fear. What can man, who is flesh, do to me?" (Ps. 56:4).

Challenge of the day: Praise God for who He is and do not worry about someone or some situation, allowing them to unnerve you. Just put your trust in God; He can help you through the trials of life.

To God be the glory. Many blessings and have a powerful day serving the Lord and observing God handling your issues of life.

Day 43

I pray that you are doing well. Start your day off with God, knowing that you must be totally committed to serving the Lord—mind, body, and spirit aligned with the living Word of God. We must have that balance in life in order to stand totally on the promises of God. We cannot be tossed off the horse as easily if something comes across that we were not expecting. We must be totally committed to serving the Lord, regardless of what comes our way. "Therefore, those who are ill-treated and suffer in accordance with God's will must do right and commit their souls [in charge as a deposit] to the One Who created [them] and will never fail [them]" (1 Pet. 4:19). So be encouraged this morning and be sold out for Christ, totally regardless of your situation or circumstances or even the trials and tribulations you face. Trust and rely on God totally and see His salvation for your life.

> "Roll your works upon the Lord [commit and trust them wholly to Him; He will cause your thoughts to become agreeable to His will, and] so shall your plans be established and succeed" (Prov. 16:3).

Challenge of the day: Be committed to the Lord totally, yes even your thoughts, and watch how your life will fall into alignment with the will of the Lord.

To God be the glory. Many blessings and have a powerful worship experience with great expectation, knowing that God will do a new thing in your life. Purge us, wash us over again, Lord, afresh. Renew us in You totally and make us committed to serving You, Lord.

Day 44

I pray that all is well with each of you and your family; may God's wisdom rest within your souls. Start your day off with God knowing that you are not in this race of life alone. We are supposed to encourage one another and lift one another up in prayer. Not only this, but also remember God is always available; He is ever present and is indeed concerned about our welfare. "Therefore encourage (admonish, exhort) one another and edify (strengthen and build up) one another, just as you are doing" (1 Thess. 5:11). So be encouraged this morning and build up and encourage others around you, because one never knows what others are going through. Just a simple smile, hug, handshake, or solid word of encouragement can make all the difference in a person's life. Keep the faith and watch God move as we lift up Christ in all that we do.

"For just as Christ's [own] sufferings fall to our lot [as they overflow upon His disciples, and we share and experience them] abundantly, so through Christ comfort (consolation and encouragement) is also [shared and experienced] abundantly by us" (2 Cor. 1:5).

Challenge of the day: Be encouraged by what you know Christ Jesus went through for us all and share His love through how you live for Christ and serve others.

To God be the glory. Many blessings to you and have a powerful day experiencing Christ in all that you do and sharing it with someone else.

Day 45

I pray that all is well with each of you. Start your day off with God knowing that you must keep the faith in God. No matter what things may look like or seem to be now, with faith in God, things can and will change. Moving forward in life with God will put the heart at ease, because of the faith we possess in God. Without faith, it is impossible to please God, so we must keep the faith in God and allow God to take control of our lives and the situations we face on daily basis. "And Jesus answered them, Truly I say to you, if you have faith (a firm relying trust) and do not doubt, you will not only do what has been done to the fig tree, but even if you say to this mountain, Be taken up and cast into the sea, it will be done. And whatever you ask for in prayer, having faith and [really] believing, you will receive" (Matt. 21:21-22). So be encouraged this morning—walk by faith and do not give up because things do not look like you want. Trust God and keep the faith.

> "Look at the proud; his soul is not straight or right within him, but the [rigidly] just and the [uncompromisingly] righteous man shall live by his faith and in his faithfulness" (Hab. 2:4).

Challenge of the day: Live by faith and do not be fearful of the challenges that are before you. Trust God and reap the benefits that God has prepared for the righteous.

To God be the glory. Many blessings and have a powerful day serving God and others through faith in God. Be blessed in all that you do for the kingdom of God.

Day 46

I pray that all is well with each of you and your family and that the joy of the Lord is truly residing within your hearts this morning. Start your day off with God, knowing that you must have a humble heart, attitude, and spirit. We must be willing to live in peace and harmony with others and within ourselves. We cannot afford to be puffed up, arrogant, or even prideful in this faithful lifestyle in Christ Jesus. We must rely on the Lord and be humble; if we are not willing to humble ourselves, then it would be a hurtful thing to be humbled by the hand of God. "Live in harmony with one another; do not be haughty (snobbish, high-minded, exclusive), but readily adjust yourself to [people, things] and give yourselves to humble tasks. Never overestimate yourself to be wise in your own conceits" (Rom. 12:16). So be encouraged this morning and live with a humbled mind and heart, serving the Lord and others and not lifting up your own agenda.

"The reverent fear and worshipful awe of the Lord [includes] hatred of evil; pride, arrogance, the evil way, and perverted and twisted speech I hate" (Prov. 8:13).

Challenge of the day: Move away from a prideful and arrogant attitude and humble yourself before they Lord. If not, then you leave God no choice but to humble you.

To God be the glory. Many blessings and have a powerful day serving the Lord with a glad heart and a humble spirit.

Day 47

I pray that all is well with each of you and your family. Start your day off with God, knowing you must recognize the power of the blood of Jesus Christ. We must embrace the fact that Jesus gave up His blood for our sins and faultiness; He did this out of love for the Father and for us. What a powerful and personal statement Jesus made on the cross the day of His crucifixion: "And Jesus prayed, Father, forgive them, for they know not what they do. And they divided His garments and distributed them by casting lots for them" (Luke 23:34). So be encouraged this morning and know with a full heart that it is because of the blood given up and the prayer spoken by Jesus that we are forgiven of our sins. We can live again with power and love and show others just how much Jesus loves us.

"For every time you eat this bread and drink this cup, you are representing and signifying and proclaiming the fact of the Lord's death until He comes [again]" (1 Cor. 11:26).

Challenge of the day: How often do you remember and reflect on the death of Jesus Christ for you? Move away from being self-centered and focused on being Christ-centric, being about the business of Jesus—representing Him and reflecting and remembering His death until He comes again. He is coming back. Will you be ready?

To God be the glory. Many blessings and have a powerful day reflecting on the life, death, and resurrection of Jesus Christ. Celebrate Jesus daily.

Day 48

I pray that all is well with each of you. Start your day off with God knowing that you can walk in God's grace. His grace will carry us through the troubled days of life. We should not look back on what is keeping us from moving forward, but simply leave the past in the past and walk in God's amazing grace. "For the Lord God is a Sun and Shield; the Lord bestows [present] grace and favor and [future] glory (honor, splendor, and heavenly bliss)! No good thing will He withhold from those who walk uprightly" (Ps. 84:11) So be encouraged this morning and walk in the grace and favor of God, knowing that God is not slack concerning His promise that He will not withhold any good thing to those who walk uprightly with Him. So walk uprightly, receive, and enjoy the blessings of God.

> "[All] are justified and made upright and in right standing with God, freely and gratuitously by His grace (His unmerited favor and mercy), through the redemption which is [provided] in Christ Jesus" (Rom. 3:24).

Challenge of the day: God's grace is free in and through Christ Jesus; receive Him and live a righteous life.

To God be the glory. Many blessings to you and have a powerful day trusting in the Lord and living uprightly before Him.

Day 49

I pray that all is well with each of you and that you all have peace. Start your day off with God, knowing you must call on the name of the Lord constantly and seek His counsel concerning the day-to-day issues of life. The more we call on the name of the Lord, the more we will realize that it is in the power and name of Jesus that we have the strength to get things done in our lives. We must humble ourselves; submit unto the Lord our mind, body, and soul; and watch how the Lord will mold and shape us. Constantly communicate with the Lord—not just during the good times, mind you, but all the time. God wants to hear from us and He wants us to take His Word and live it out. "He shall call upon Me, and I will answer him; I will be with him in trouble, I will deliver him and honor him. With long life will I satisfy him and show him My salvation" (Ps. 91:15, 16). So be encouraged and know that God will hear our cry when we call upon Him, and He will respond with a heart of compassion. Never cease from calling on the Lord and observe just how powerful the living God really is in our lives.

"My eye grows dim because of sorrow and affliction. Lord, I have called daily on You; I have spread forth my hands to You" (Ps. 88:9).

Challenge the day: Surrender to the Lord all of life's issues daily. No matter how great or small they may be, allow God to give you guidance and direction.

To God be the glory. Many blessings and have a powerful worship experience and serve the Lord willing with a glad and receptive heart.

Day 50

I pray that all is well with each of you. Start your day off with God knowing you must receive His grace. God's grace will carry us and sustain us through the many trials of life. We must tune into receiving His grace and walk in it. "[All] are justified and made upright and in right standing with God, freely and gratuitously by His grace (His unmerited favor and mercy), through the redemption which is [provided] in Christ Jesus" (Rom. 3:24). So be encouraged this morning and know that you are justified and made right by the grace of God. So live and walk in His grace.

"For the Lord God is a Sun and Shield; the Lord bestows [present] grace and favor and [future] glory (honor, splendor, and heavenly bliss)! No good thing will He withhold from those who walk uprightly" (Ps. 84:11).

Challenge of the day: With God's grace comes promises that only God can complete. So walk uprightly and receive the promises of the Lord.

To God be the glory! Many blessings to you and have a powerful worship service. Expect to know God better.

Day 51

I pray that all is well with each of you. Start your day off with God knowing that you must learn to forgive in order to be forgiven. True healing of past pain will come when we learn to release the hurt and forgive ourselves and those who have transgressed against us. Our souls and spirit will then be at ease and will know comfort and peace. "And whenever you stand praying, if you have anything against anyone, forgive him and let it drop (leave it, let it go), in order that your Father Who is in heaven may also forgive you your |own| failings and shortcomings and let them drop. But, if you do not forgive, neither will your Father in heaven forgive your failings and shortcomings" (Mark 11:25, 26). The power of forgiving someone is crucial to our walk with Christ; let it drop, leave it, let it go, and receive true forgiveness from the inside out. So be encouraged this morning, walk, and live in the freedom from your past through forgiving yourself and others in the power name and love of Jesus Christ.

> "Bless (affectionately, gratefully praise) the Lord, O my soul, and forget not |one of| all His benefits— Who forgives |every one of| all your iniquities, Who heals |each one of| all your diseases, Who redeems your life from the pit and corruption, Who beautifies, dignifies, and crowns you with loving-kindness and tender mercy; Who satisfies your mouth |your necessity and desire at your personal age and situation| with good so that your, renewed, is like the eagle's |strong, overcoming, soaring|!" (Ps. 103:2-5).

Challenge of the day: Learn to forgive because the Lord yearns and desires to bless you and forgive you. Do not miss out on the benefits of being forgiven through Jesus Christ.

To God be the glory! Many blessings to you and have a powerful day forgiving someone from your past or even present, so you can love and enjoy the future that is waiting for you with Jesus Christ.

Day 52

I pray that all is well with each of you and your family. Start your day off with God knowing that you must never forget to worship God. We must bring back the worship in our services and in our personal time with God. We must honor Him and magnify His name. We must never be so busy to stop and just worship God for who He is. Lift up holy hands, lay prostrate before God, call unto Him, and reverence the one and only living God. Do not let the distractions of today cause us to forget about what our true purpose is, which is to worship God. "The Jesus said to him, Begone, Satan! For it has been written, You shall worship the Lord your God, and Him alone shall you serve" (Matt 4:10). So be encouraged this morning and make time to worship God and wait with an expectant heart for His glory to be revealed unto you.

"O come, let us worship and bow down, let us kneel before the Lord our Maker [in reverent praise and supplication]" (Ps. 95:6).

Challenge of the day: Position yourself to worship God and make room in your heart to receive His presence.

To God be the glory! Many blessings to you, have a blessed day, and prepare yourself to meet the Spirit of the Lord in your personal sanctuary.

Day 53

I pray that all is well with you and your family. Start your day off with God, knowing that you must maintain a godly character. Do not fall in agreement with the things of the world or hold back your righteousness in order to fit in. Shine bright before the Lord, be the salt of the earth. Replenish the goodness in others by living an upright life before God and humankind. "Do not therefore let what seems good to you be considered an evil thing [by someone else]. [In other words, do not give occasion for others to criticize that which is justifiable for you.]" (Rom. 14:16). So be encouraged this morning, hold on to that which is good, and walk in righteousness, being unconcerned with what others are saying about you. Live up to God's standards and experience His liberty for living.

"Repay no one evil for evil, but take thought for what is honest and proper and noble [aiming to be above reproach] in the sight of everyone" (Rom. 12:17).

Challenge of the day: It is not your job to get even with someone. Be honest and focus on living a godly life for Jesus Christ. Imitate Christ and give no room for the flesh.

To God be the glory! Many blessings to you and have a powerful day in the Lord, looking unto Him for constant guidance.

Day 54

I pray that all is well with each of you. Start your day off with God knowing that you must surrender every issue you have unto the Lord. Let it go and give it up. When you hold on to things, it means you no good; it is like extra baggage or unnecessary junk on your journey in this life. Let those things go; clear out your baggage carriage, if you will, and give those things to the Lord. I am positive He can handle all things. "Cast your burden on the Lord [releasing the weight of it] and He will sustain you; He will never allow the [consistently] righteous to be moved (made to slip, fall, or fail)" (Ps. 55:22). So be encouraged this morning and lean on God to help you surrender the dead weight or excess baggage in your life. Trust Him and allow Him to handle your issues of life.

> "Casting the whole of your care [all your anxieties, all your worries, all your concerns, once and for all] on Him, for He cares for you affectionately and cares about you watchfully" (1 Pet. 5:7).

Challenge of the day: Stop all of your worries and give your cares and concerns to the Lord. He is aware of your issues of life, but you must present them to Him and allow the Lord Jesus to deal with them and to give you peace about life.

To God be the glory! Many blessings to you, have a powerful day, and enjoy giving up and releasing the things that hinder you from coming closer to the Lord.

Day 55

I pray that all is well with each of you. Start your day off with God knowing that we must give our hearts to the Lord. Fret not about what is going on around you and do not let the things in your life consume you. We must depend on the Lord for deliverance and wisdom to hold on to His unchanging hand. Regardless of what is going on in our "sphere," God can deliver and strengthen us as we give Him our hearts and be content with what He is doing in our lives. "Peace I leave with you; My [own] peace I now give and bequeath to you. Not as the world give do I give to you. Do not let your hearts be troubled, neither let them be afraid. [Stop allowing yourself to be agitated and disturbed; and do not permit yourselves to be fearful and intimidated and cowardly and unsettled.] You heard Me tell you, I am going away and I am coming [back] to you. If you [really] loved Me, you would have been glad, because I am going to the Father; for the Father is greater and mightier than I am. And now I have told you [this] before it occurs, so that when it does take place you may believe and have faith in and rely on Me" (John 14:27-29). So be encouraged this morning and put your hearts at ease and give them to the Lord. Fear not and be completely happy in Lord; He knows your heart, but you must relax your heart and give it to Him, along with all your issues and concerns. He's got this for you!

"Examine me, O Lord, and prove me; test my heart and my mind" (Ps. 26:2).

Challenge of the day: Live according to the Word of the Lord and take notice how He will review what is really in your heart.

To God be the glory! Many blessings to you and have a powerful day expecting great things with a grateful heart unto the Lord.

Day 56

I pray that all is well with each of you. Start your day off with God knowing we must learn to forgive. If we cannot forgive, then how do we expect God the Father to forgive us? When we forgive, it is twofold: we are released from the past hurt and the one who offended us is released as well. Live now to be healed and restored; it will be a refreshing moment in our lives once we are released from all anxieties and from our past. "Judge not [neither pronouncing judgment not subjecting to censure], and you will not be judged; do not condemn and pronounce guilty, and you will not be condemned and pronounced guilty; acquit and forgive and release (give up resentment, let it drop), and you will be acquitted and forgiven and released" (Luke 6:37). So be encouraged this morning and be released from the past by forgiving those who mistreated us and meant to hurt us. We must now move forward and receive what God has in store for us and our future. Know also that all things have worked together for our good and for you and me to bring glory and honor unto the living Lord Jesus Christ.

"And become useful and helpful and kind to one another, tenderhearted (compassionate, understanding, loving-hearted), forgiving one another [readily and freely], as God in Christ forgave you" (Eph. 4:32).

Challenge of the day: Learn to forgive and love one another, move forward and leave your past behind you. As you move forward in life, bring someone else along with you through showing them how to live a life that is pleasing to the Lord.

To God be the glory! Many blessings to you and have a powerful day in the Lord, trusting and believing in Him and knowing that He did bring you to this point in your life not to leave you but to strengthen you and shape you for His glory.

Day 57

I pray that all is well with each of you. Start your day off with God knowing you must never stop praising the Lord! We must lift up the name of Jesus Christ at every opportunity; we must never stop singing the praises of the Lord and calling on the name of the living God, through Jesus Christ. Let everything that has breath praise the Lord. Though tough times may be present for a moment, still praise the Lord. Though pain may try to persist, keep praising the Lord. Though it may be a time of loneliness, yet praise the Lord; because we are never alone, God always is near us. "Praise Him for His mighty acts; praise Him according to the abundance of His greatness!" (Ps. 150:2). So be encouraged this morning and praise God through your situations and experience the greatness of God in your life.

"Let them praise and exalt the name of the Lord, for His name alone is exalted and supreme! His glory and majesty are above earth and heaven! He has lifted up a horn for His people [giving them power, prosperity, dignity, and preeminence], a song of praise for all His godly ones, for the people of Israel, who are near to Him. Praise the Lord! (Hallelujah!)" (Ps. 148:13, 14).

Challenge of the day: Neither be afraid to lift up the name of the Lord, nor forget to praise Him in all circumstances of life. He has not forgotten you, and He is indeed near you; just trust and believe and expect and receive when you praise the Lord for who He is.

To God be the glory! Many blessings to you and have a powerful day in the Lord and lift up the name of Jesus at all times and in whatever you do.

Day 58

I pray that all is well with each of you. Start your day off with God knowing that it is God's love that will prevail in the end. Regardless of what others will attempt to do to us, we must rely solely on God's love and protection. God's love is so real and unconditional that it will prevail against any and everything. "The Lord opens the eyes of the blind, the Lord lifts up those who are bowed down, the Lord loves the [uncompromisingly] righteous (those upright in heart and in right standing with Him)" (Ps. 146:8). So be encouraged this morning knowing that you are loved beyond your greatest imagination, because you serve the awesome Wonder, God Almighty. God's love even will cause miracles to happen in your life—as you believe in Him, so shall it be unto you.

"And He said to him, Go, wash in the Pool of Siloam—which means Sent. So he went and washed, and came back seeing" (John 9:7).

Challenge of the day: God's love is so great that when He commands us to do something, we must be obedient and watch how an immediate change will come upon us; even if it is life-changing physically, it will be an immediate noticeable change. Do not run away from the love of God and His ability to change the things that will bring Him glory from your life.

To God be the glory! Many blessings to you and have a powerful day believing and expecting God's love to change your life according to the will of God, even if it is for healing or deliverance. Whatever your case may be, let it be known unto the living Lord Jesus Christ, the One who loves you most.

Day 59

I pray that all is well with each of you. Start your day off with God, knowing that we must establish a solid and intimate relationship with God. Our relationship with God deserves daily attention—not just a relationship with the church or even a denomination, but with Jesus Christ our risen Savior. Daily communication with Him occurs through reading and studying the Word and a constant and solid prayer life. How much time are we willing to spend with God? Are we too busy during this season? Let us relish the time with God in order to draw closer to Him and with one another. "Now these [Jews] were better disposed and more noble than those in Thessalonica, for they were entirely ready and accepted and welcomed the message [concerning the attainment through Christ of eternal salvation in the kingdom of God] with inclination of mind and eagerness, searching and examining the Scriptures daily to see if these things were so" (Acts 17:11). So be encouraged this morning and search the Word of God and find out for yourself who you are and what God's purpose is for your life through the established personal and intimate relationship with Jesus Christ.

"[The Servant of God says] The Lord God has given Me the tongue of a disciple and of one who is taught, that I should know how to speak a word in season to him who is weary. He wakens Me morning by morning, He wakens my ear to hear as a disciple [as one who is taught]. The Lord God has opened My ear, and I have not be rebellious or turned backward" (Isa. 50:4, 5).

Challenge of the day: Draw closer to God and learn from Him as one who is being taught as a disciple to speak and represent God. Know when to say something and how to say it from the living Word of God, also by the direction of the Holy Spirit. Study the Word and be amazed at how your life will change to bring glory and honor to the Lord as one of His disciples.

To God be the glory! Many blessings to you and have a powerful day in the Lord as you pursue to serve the Lord through knowing who He is to you.

Day 60

I pray that all is well with each of you. Start your day off with God, knowing you can survive anything because God is our help. No matter what we are going through in life, God can and will deliver us. We must zoom into the trust factor and rely heavily on God's ability to deliver and heal. It will be only then that we will realize that we are survivors. Better yet, we are victors and not victims of circumstances of life, because we solely rely on the almighty and everlasting God. "O God, be not far from me! O My God, make haste to help me!" (Ps. 71:12). So be encouraged this morning and know that when God is on the scene, we must surrender to Jesus Christ as Lord over our lives. Allow God to be God and take care of us and our needs as He deems necessary.

> "IN YOU, O Lord, do I put my trust and confidently take refuge; let me never be put to shame or confusion! Deliver me in Your righteousness and cause me to escape; bow down Your ear to me and save me!" (Ps. 71:1, 2).

Challenge of the day: Listen to God's direction, and He will deliver and save you as you put your trust in Him completely—not just when you need Him, but every day. And you will survive life's challenges.

To God be the glory! Many blessings to you and have a great day in the Lord, knowing that you already are delivered from whatever it is you need God's help with.

Day 61

I pray that all is well with each of you. Start your day off with God, knowing that it is God who will provide you the courage you need to make the changes in your life and environment. We must not be afraid of change; in fact we must embrace it and approach it with a courageous heart. Whenever change comes about, it normally sends folk running in the opposite direction, but in this junction in our lives we must embrace that which God has ordained for us to do. We may not understand it at that moment, but in time we will begin to appreciate the guidance afforded to us by God during the moments in which we did not understand clearly what was taking place. "Also David told Solomon his son, Be strong and courageous, and do it. Fear not, be not dismayed, for the Lord God, my God, is with you. He will not fail or forsake you until you have finished all the work for the service of the house of the Lord" (1 Chron. 28:20). So be encouraged this morning and neither fear what is next for your life nor be afraid of the challenges ahead. Be strong and courageous; God is with you and He is on your side, so do not fight against God's purpose for your life. Serve Him and be glad.

"Yet now be strong, alert, and courageous, O Zerubbabel, says the Lord; be strong, alert, and courageous, O Joshua son of Jehozadak, the high priest; and be strong, alert, and courageous, all you people of the land, says the Lord, and work! For I am with you, says the Lord of hosts" (Hag. 2:4).

Challenge of the day: Be ready when the challenge comes. Be alert and courageous; neither back down nor be afraid. Be humble that the Lord is with you.

To God be the glory! Many blessings to you and have a great day knowing that God is with you.

Day 62

I pray that all is well with each of you. Start your day off with God knowing that it is important to fellowship with other believers. You cannot walk this walk of faith alone; we must have folk that are like-minded in our company. Folk that will pray with us and for us, even while it seems as we are going through trials and tribulations. We need folk around us, who will not judge us but who will encourage us as we go through. We need folk who will sharpen our spiritual intellect. We need folk who will tell us the truth, regardless of whether we will accept it or not. My brothers and sisters, we need true believers in our company at all times. "Iron sharpens iron; so a man sharpens the countenance of his friend [to show rage or worthy purpose]" (Prov. 27:17)... So be encouraged and pray and ask God to surround you with the right people at the right time, people who will be honest with you. So walk well, brothers and sisters, and know and respect the company you keep.

> "Again I tell you, if two of you on earth agree (harmonize together, make a symphony together) about whatever [anything and everything] they may ask, it will come to pass and be done for them by My Father in heaven. For wherever two or three are gathered (drawn together as My followers) in (into) My name, there I AM in the midst of them" (Matt. 18:19, 20).

Challenge of the day: When believers come together and agree, powerful things can and will happen, so are things happening in your life with the people you come together and agree with?

To God be the glory! Many blessings to you and have a powerful day of fellowship with people you can agree with in the Lord.

Day 63

I pray that all is well with each of you. Start your day off with God knowing that you must be glad in the Lord. Have a sense of peace in the midst of the fiery trials of life. No matter what we are facing this morning, God will see us through; we must know this without a shadow of doubt. Rejoice in the fact that God has everything under control. Rejoice knowing that we are alive and well. Rejoice and be glad that God cares enough about us that He will never leave us alone. "So rejoice in the LORD and be glad, all you who obey Him! Shout for joy, all you whose hearts are pure!" (Ps. 32:11 NLT). So be encouraged this morning and be glad that GOD IS GOD and He has our best interests at heart. We must appreciate the fact that God loves us in spite of our past—and even our present—condition. God's love is boundless and unconditional and that's enough for us to be glad in the Lord.

> "The humble will see their God at work and be glad. Let all who seek God's help be encouraged" (Ps. 69:32 NLT).

Challenge of the day: Be glad and encouraged that God is at work in your life; trust and believe that all is in God's hands.

To God be the glory! Many blessings to you and have a powerful day in the Lord. Move forward, leave the past in the past, and trust God to deliver you from your past and take you to a great future.

Day 64

I pray that all is well with each of you. Start your day off with God knowing we can trust that God's Word is true and powerful. Certainly we cannot live without it. God's Word will sustain us in the midst of trials and tribulation. His Word and love will keep us from all hurt and unseen danger. God's Word will protect us from making faulty decisions. His Word will bring restoration to a broken relationship. God's Word will teach us how to have that unspeakable joy and peace, and about unconditional love. God's Word will teach us how to survive what may seem to be unbearable moments in our lives. "Yes, he humbled you by letting you go hungry and then feeding you with manna, a food previously unknown to you and your ancestors. He did it to teach you that people do not live by bread alone; rather, we live by every word that comes from the mouth of the LORD" (Deut. 8:3 NLT). So be encouraged this morning and stay close to the living Word of God, because it will keep you through every situation and circumstances that may come your way. It will energize you to go beyond your expectation. God's Word is powerful — use it and apply it and live in it. Stay close and stay hungry for the living Word of God.

"Make them holy by your truth; teach them your word, which is truth" (John 17:17 NLT).

Challenge of the day: Know the Word of God and live in truth and holiness. Have enough passion for the Word that it may cause you to be compassionate toward others in the love of Jesus Christ.

To God be the glory! Many blessings to you and have a powerful week in the Lord through operating and living in His Word.

Day 65

I pray that all is well with each of you. Start your day off with God knowing that you need God more now than ever; you cannot make it without God and certainly you cannot do anything without the Spirit of the Lord in your life. We must recognize that we are blessed because we acknowledge the need for God to be in and around our lives. "God blesses those who are poor and realize their need for him, for the Kingdom of Heaven is theirs" (Matt. 5:3 NLT). So be encouraged this morning, sisters and brothers, knowing we can survive the storms of life with God in control, because we have need of Him to be there for us. Pastor Marvin Sapp said it best in his song, "I Never Would Have Made It Without You, Lord." This is indeed a testimony that we need God daily in our lives.

> "Praise the LORD! Blessed is the man who fears the LORD, who delights greatly in His commandments" (Ps. 112:1 NKJV).

Challenge of the day: We must delight ourselves in the Lord and be obedient unto His Word.

To God be the glory! Many blessings to you and have a powerful day in the Lord, full of faith and great expectations.

Day 66

I pray that you all had a great evening. Start your day off with God, knowing you must worship Him in all that you do. God must get the glory—not from lip service, but through action. "Honor the LORD, you heavenly beings; honor the LORD for his glory and strength. Honor the LORD for the glory of his name. Worship the LORD in the splendor of his holiness" (Ps. 29:1, 2 NLT). The Lord is awesome and we must worship Him for who He is. He is God; His greatness and holiness is above any king or super power. His very presence and voice will cause the mountains to move. So be encouraged this morning, brothers and sisters, and worship the Lord because He deserves all of our attention. We must not allow the things of this world to distract us from worshipping the living God.

> "Just think how much more the blood of Christ will purify our consciences from sinful deeds so that we can worship the living God. For by the power of the eternal Spirit, Christ offered himself to God as a perfect sacrifice for our sins" (Heb. 9:14 NLT).

Challenge of the day: Live in such a manner that others will know that you have been in the presence of God and understand that true worship will come about as your mind, body, and spirit are purified by the blood of Jesus Christ.

To God be the glory! Many blessings to you and yearn to experience true worship with God.

Day 67

I pray that all you are well. Start your day off with God knowing that you must rely on Him as the source of your strength. He will give us the strength to make it through the tough times of life—the times when we do not think we can make. It is during these tough times that we need to lean even more on the almighty and everlasting God. "For who is God except the LORD? Who but our God is a solid rock? God arms me with strength, and he makes my way perfect. He makes me as surefooted as a deer, enabling me to stand on mountain heights. He trains my hands for battle; he strengthens my arm to draw a bronze bow" (Ps. 18:31-34 NLT). So be encouraged this morning and understand that when God is in the midst we will be strength and be the victors in any tough situation.

> "I am the LORD, there is no other God. I have equipped you for battle, though you don't even know me" (Isa. 45:5 NLT).

Challenge of the day: The battles we fight are not physical but spiritual, and we must be ready at all times. We are constantly under attack, and we must not get frustrated when we are attacked but we must stand strong and be strengthened in our character by the one and only living God, because He is the true Source.

To God be the glory! Many blessings to you and have a powerful experience in the Lord.

Day 68

I pray that all of you had a peaceful rest. Start your day off with God, knowing it is God who will grant us the deliverance and peace that we need. It will be through our faith that it will happen. When God delivered the people of Israel, they were delivered, no-ifs-ands-or-buts-about-it, and God sustained them, just like He will do for us. He is the same God who does not change. We change, but the living God will never change. "When Pharaoh finally let the people go, God did not lead them along the main road that runs through Philistine territory, even though that was the shortest route to the Promised Land. God said, 'If the people are faced with a battle, they might change their minds and return to Egypt.' So God led them in a roundabout way through the wilderness toward the Red Sea. Thus the Israelites left Egypt like an army ready for battle" (Ex. 13:17, 18 NLT). So be encouraged this morning, sisters and brothers, knowing that the route to our deliverance is in God's hands. He knows the beginning and the ending; we may not understand why or even how, but we must trust God's way of doing things and be at peace about it.

"He rescued me from my powerful enemies, from those who hated me and were too strong for me" (Ps. 18:17 NLT).

Challenge of the day: When God delivers you, you will know it and recognize that His power is stronger than any enemy you may face. Even if the enemy (of sickness) is within you, God can deliver (and heal) you from anything and anyone!

To God be the glory! Many blessings to you and have a powerful and peaceful day in the Lord, knowing YOU CAN BE DELIVERED IN THE POWERFUL NAME OF JESUS CHRIST.

Day 69

I pray that all is well with each of you. Start your day off with God knowing that we must trust Him at all costs, no matter what is going on around us and how things may seem to appear. Yet we must trust God with a reverent heart. "They do not fear bad news; they confidently trust the LORD to care for them" (Ps. 112:7 NLT). Oftentimes we fear what the situations or circumstances appear to be and sometimes seem to panic when we are unsure of the outcome. But we must understand the fact that God will take care of us. So be encouraged this morning, resting on the fact that we can trust in the one and only true and living God. At all times and in all places we can trust Him to be God, Lord over our lives, and to take really good care of us.

> "I praise God for what he has promised. I trust in God, so why should I be afraid? What can mere mortals do to me?" (Ps. 56:4 NLT).

Challenge of the day: Fear God not people; trust God and praise Him because His promises are true!

To God be the glory! Many blessings to you and have a powerful day in the Lord.

Day 70

I pray that all is well with each of you. Start your day off with God knowing that you must demonstrate your faith walk daily. When things get challenging, walk in faith; in the midst of uncertainty, walk in faith; and even in the midst of afflictions, walk in faith. "'You don't have enough faith,' Jesus told them, 'I tell you the truth, if you had faith even as small as a mustard seed, you could say to this mountain, 'Move from here to there,' and it would move. Nothing would be impossible" (Matt. 17:20 NLT). Brothers and sisters, we have to act on the faith that God has given us and use it daily. The very mountains around will move because of our faith; the mountains will not have a choice in the matter, because our faith in God is stronger than the mountains we face daily. So be encouraged this morning and move the mountains. See and receive the healing; see and receive the deliverance; receive the help and watch your life improve because of the faith that you demonstrate daily. Walk by faith and act upon the living Word of God.

"Then he touched their eyes and said, 'because of your faith, it will happen'" (Matt. 9:29 NLT).

Challenge of the day: If you want something to happen in your life, then walk by faith and see it come to pass.

To God be the glory! Many blessings to you and have a powerful day in the Lord.

Day 71

I pray that all is well with each of you. Start your day off with God knowing that you must praise the Lord at all times. Praise Him every chance you get. We must lift up the name of the Lord, shouting with a triumphant voice. No matter what we are going through, we must give praises to the Lord. "Let all that I am praise the LORD; with my whole heart, I will praise his holy name. Let all that I am praise the LORD; may I never forget the good things he does for me. He forgives all my sins and heals all my diseases" (Ps. 103:1-3 NLT). When we begin to praise the Lord with our entire being—from the inside out—we also can experience being complete in the Lord. David understood how to get his breakthrough, through praising the Lord anyhow, anywhere, and at all times. So be encouraged this morning and praise the Lord. Regardless of what circumstances or situations you may be facing in your life, praise the Lord.

"Let the godly sing for joy to the LORD; it is fitting for the pure to praise him" (Ps. 33:1 NLT).

Challenge of the day: Praise God with a pure heart and receive the breakthrough you need or desire.

To God be the glory! Many blessings to you and have a powerful time praising the Lord.

Day 72

I pray that you all had a grand evening. Start your day off with God knowing that you must not try to fix things or people on your own. Let God handle it. We tend to give things to God, but then reach for them back. Allow God to handle the day-to-day bundles of frustration that seem to overwhelm us. We must trust God and not be concerned about not being able to handle things. Give it to God. He will give us wisdom to do what we need to do and He will handle what He needs to handle. "What does God know? They ask. 'Does the Most High even know what's happening?'" (Ps. 73:11 NLT). If you've asked or pondered on that question concerning things and people in your life, no worries, God knows exactly what He is doing and can handle all things and all people. Just live a righteous life and all will be well. So be encouraged this morning and understand for certain that God knows every-thing and everybody on the face of this earth. So do not fear or fret; God will take care of the righteous.

"Please God, rescue me! Come quickly, LORD, and help me" (Ps. 70:1 NLT).

Challenge of the day: God will answer our cry and will rescue us; be ready for His response.

To God be the glory and many blessings to you. Have a blessed day.

Day 73

I pray that all had a great evening. Start your day off with God knowing we must come and talk with Him. You must yearn to build your personal relationship with Him every day, as King David did. David understood that he could not make without the Lord. He yearned to be in His holy presence. Even when he made a mistake, he knew how to repent and come and talk with the Lord. "The one thing I ask of the LORD — the thing I seek most — is to live in the house of the LORD all the days of my life, delighting in the LORD's perfections and meditating in his Temple. For he will conceal me there when trouble comes; he will hide me in his sanctuary. He will place me out of reach on a high rock. Then I will hold my head high above my enemies who surround me. At his sanctuary I will offer sacrifices with shouts of joy, singing and praising the LORD with music. Hear me as I pray, O LORD. Be merciful and answer me! My heart has heard you say, 'Come and talk with me.' And my heart responds, 'LORD, I am coming' (Ps. 27:4-8 NLT). So be encouraged and come close to God and build your relationship and truly enjoy the company of the almighty and everlasting God.

> "Turn and answer me, O LORD my God! Restore the sparkle to my eyes, or I will die" (Ps. 13:3 NLT).

Challenge of the day: Come at the calling of God and watch your life be restored and the flames of excitement resonate over you.

To God be the glory and many blessings to each of you on your journey to discovering God more each day, one-on-one.

Day 74

I pray that all had a grand evening. Start your day off with God, knowing that you must stand boldly and firmly be outfitted with God's war gear during the testing times of life. We cannot falter or be timid when we are faced with the trials of life and the attacks of wickedness. We must stand boldly and represent Jesus Christ in all that we do, especially during trying times and when no one else is looking. Boldness is a key element in our walk with the Lord. "Therefore take up the whole armor of God that you may be able to withstand in the evil day, and having done all, to stand. Stand therefore, having girded your waist with truth, having put on the breastplate of righteousness, and having shod your feet with the preparation of the gospel of peace; above all, taking the shield of faith with you which you will be able to quench all the fiery darts of the wicked one. And take the helmet of salvation, and the sword of the Spirit, which is the word of God; praying always with all prayer and supplication for all the saints" (Eph. 6:13-18). So be encouraged this morning and stand boldly; in spite of what is going on around you, fear not—God is in control.

"Watch, stand fast in the faith, be brave, be strong" (1 Cor. 16:13 NKJV).

Challenge of the day: Be ready to stand always as a warrior for Christ.

To God be the glory! Many blessings to you and have a powerful worship experience in the Lord. Worship the Lord with gladness.

Day 75

I pray that you all had a peaceful evening. Start your day off with God, knowing it is not for us to be judgmental, but to build others up in the love of Jesus Christ. Sometimes it is so easy to say negative things about folk before we even get to know them. We automatically judge them from jump, instead of spending time getting to know them. What if the shoe was on the other foot, how would you feel? "Do not judge others, and you will not be judged. For you will be treated as you treat others. The standard you use in judging is the standard by which you will be judged" (Matt. 7:1, 2 NLT). So be encouraged this morning, treat everyone the way you want to be treated, love everyone the way you want to be loved, and be mindful if and when you judge others, because you will be judged the same way.

> "You may think you can condemn such people, but you are just as bad, and you have no excuse! When you say they are wicked and should be punished, you are condemning yourself, for you who judge others do these very same things" (Rom. 2:1 NLT).

Challenge of the day: Be careful who and how we judge, because in reality we are judging ourselves. Look in the minor and see your faults before pointing out others. Self examination is critical in our spiritual walk; we have to ensure we do what is right and pleasing in the sight of the Lord, regardless of who is around us. God is the final Judge and we all desire to get His seal of approval as we walk this life on this side of heaven.

To God be the glory! Many blessings to you and have a powerful day. Show someone different the love of Jesus Christ in your life.

Day 76

I pray that all is well with each of you. Start your day off with God knowing that you must never give God's glory to someone or something else, no matter what is going on in your life or what your circumstances may be. He desires and deserves all of the glory and honor due to Him, because He is Lord and God of all. "I am the Lord; that is My name! And My glory I will not give to another, nor My praise to graven images. Behold, the former things have come to pass, and new things I declare; before they spring forth I tell you of them" (Isa. 42:8, 9). So be encouraged, and in every area of your life ensure that God gets the glory. When we glorify God in all that we do, it pleases Him.

"Behold, I have refined you, but not as silver; I have tried and chosen you in the furnace of affliction. For My own sake, for My own sake, I do it [I refrain and do not utterly destroy you]; for why should I permit My name to be polluted and profaned [which it would be if the Lord completely destroyed His chosen people]? And I will not give My glory to another [by permitting the worshipers of idols to triumph over you]" (Isa. 48:10-11).

Challenge of the day: As we go through the fires of life, let us not hold on to the situations that we may face. Let us glorify God as He delivers us for His name's sake.

To God be the glory! Many blessings to you and have a powerful day in the Lord.

Day 77

I pray that all is well with each of you. Start your day off with God knowing that you need the freshness of God's presence daily in your life. Not only when we have extreme challenges in our lives, but especially during those times. We need to hear God clearly for direction to get us through the challenging times. "What joy for those who can live in your house, always signing your praises? What joy for those whose strength comes from the LORD, who have set their minds on a pilgrimage to Jerusalem. When they walk through the Valley of Weeping, it will become a place of refreshing springs. The autumn rains will clothe it with blessings. They will continue to grow stronger, and each of them will appear before God in Jerusalem" (Ps. 84:4-7 NLT). So be encouraged this morning: draw closer toward God and yearn to feel His presence, even in the midst of our daily struggles. God's presence will consume us.

> "In that day, when your enemies are slaughtered and the towers fall, there will be streams of water flowing down every mountain and hill. The moon will be as bright as the sun, and the sun will be seven times brighter—like the light of seven days in one! So it will be when the LORD begins to heal his people and cure the wounds he gave them" (Isa. 30:25, 26 NLT).

Challenge of the day: Today we'll have a battle to face, but it will come to an end and there in the midst we'll know the freshness of God's presence. It is He who will bring us through it and heal us spiritually, physically, emotionally, and mentally, as needed.

To God be the glory! Many blessings to you and look for the freshness of God's presence today.

Day 78

I pray that you are happy today. Start your day off with God, knowing it is time to understand balance, time to understand change, and time to operate above the norms of life. You see, God desires that we keep evolving and growing each and every day. If we stay the same, we can expect the same results in life. If we were to study Abraham's life, we would notice how God constantly challenged him to evolve and grow, adjust and adapt to the changes of life—even to the point of being told to sacrifice his only son. This is significant to the sacrifice God made with Jesus. "Some time later, God tested Abraham's faith. 'Abraham!' God called. 'Yes,' he replied. 'Here I am.' 'Take your son, your only son—yes, Isaac, whom you love so much—and go to the land of Moriah. Go and sacrifice him as a burnt offering on one of the mountains, which I will show you" (Gen. 22:1-2 NLT). Had Abraham not gone through many trials previously, he would not have received this instruction from God. Abraham trusted God to move him from a known land to an unknown land into a better life. (Refer to Gen. 12-14.) Abraham continued to evolve, and we also must constantly evolve, change, move above the norms, and live a greater life of faith in God. So be encouraged and walk, live, and love above the norms of life.

> "Then the LORD said to Moses, 'Look, I'm going to rain down food from heaven for you. Each day the people can go out and pick up as much food as they need for that day. I will test them in this to see whether or not they will follow my instructions" (Ex. 16:4 NLT).

Challenge of the day: Follow God's instructions in life and live each day to the fullest, through your constant growth in Him with a sense of purpose in life.

To God be the glory! Many blessings to you and have a great week in the Lord. Always focus on what God would have you to be doing. It is essential that we understand our mission in life.

Day 79

I pray that all is well with each of you. Start your day off with God knowing that you must be willing to move forward in your life. Move with a sense of purpose and existence. Do not be willing to deviated from the plans of God, but be willing to live them out in our lives. Seeking to discover all that God has for us to do and accomplish as His personal creation. "For in him we live and move and exist. As some of your own poets have said, 'We are his offspring'" (Acts 17:28 NLT). So be encouraged this morning and do not be stuck in a rut, but spring forth with a new excitement for living and existing in God—with a sense of purpose.

"But as for me, I will sing about your power. Each morning I will sing with joy about your unfailing love. For you have been my refuge, a place of safety when I am in distress" (Ps. 59:16 NLT).

Challenge of the day: When moving through life, understand that you are safe in the arms of God and you must rejoice knowing that God's love will never fail you.

To God be the glory! Many blessings to you and have a powerful day in the Lord.

Day 80

I pray that all is well with each of you. Start your day off with God, knowing that you must never forget God in all that you do and in all that will happen to you. God is sovereign; He is Lord over all. "Remember now your Creator in the days of your youth, before the difficult days come, and the years draw near when you say, 'I have no pleasure in them'" (Eccles. 12:1 NKJV). So be encouraged this morning and remember God in all that you do and accomplish; remember that He is Lord, He is great, and He is awesome. He is love. Remember that God will always see us through tough times, even when we can see them coming our way; God is just that sovereign, knowing all things concerning our lives. We must never forget God!

"Some trust in chariots, and some in horses; but we will remember the name of the LORD our God" (Ps. 20:7 NKJV).

Challenge of the day: Trust God and remember He is stronger and more powerful, yet loving, than any existing thing or event in your life.

To God be the glory! Many blessings to you and have a powerful day trusting in the Lord.

Day 81

I pray that all is well with each of you. Start your day off with God knowing that you can conquer the things that hold you back from maturing in Christ. If you hold on to those things, you will never grow spiritually as you should in the things of God. Let go of the old and capture and embrace the new things that are ahead of you. "Since you have heard about Jesus and have learned the truth that comes from him, throw off your old sinful nature and your former way of life, which is corrupted by lust and deception. Instead, let the Spirit renew your thoughts and attitudes. Put on your new nature, created to be like God—truly righteous and holy" (Eph. 4:21-24 NLT). So be encouraged this morning and walk and live in the newness of life with our risen Savior Jesus Christ. He will help us overcome all that is keeping us from coming closer to Him.

> "So get rid of all the filth and evil in your lives, and humbly accept the word God has planted in your hearts, for it has the power to save your souls" (James 1:21 NLT).

Challenge of the day: Rid yourself of those things that will keep the Word of God from growing and spreading in your life.

To God be the glory! Many blessings to you and have a powerful day in the Lord. Walk by faith and not by sight.

Day 82

I pray that all is well with each of you. Start your day off with God knowing that faith without works is dead. We must allow our faith to merge with the works that we do. Our faith must produce the action that God is requiring of us. There are mountains to be moved and people to be healed, delivered, and set free from their current mind-set. Also, there are folk waiting on us to bring the gospel to them—not only in word, but also in how we really live for Jesus Christ. We must be ready to apply our faith and works. "You say you have faith, for you believe that there is one God. Good for you! Even the demons believe this, and they tremble in terror. How foolish! Can't you see that faith without good deeds is useless?" (James 2:19, 20 NLT). So be encouraged this morning, through applying your faith and works together, to accomplish God's purpose and plan in our lives.

"Faith is the confidence that what we hope for will actually happen; it gives us assurance about things we cannot see" (Heb. 11:1 NLT).

Challenge of the day: Move by faith and do good works, because without faith we cannot please God (Heb. 11:6). Have faith and watch God's hand move throughout your life.

To God be the glory! Many blessings to you and have a powerful day in the Lord and move by faith.

Day 83

I pray that all is well with each of you. Start your day off with God knowing that your faith in God can calm the rough waters of life and heal all of your ailments. We must have faith and believe in the impossible happening, when all things in our surrounding circumference say otherwise. "After Jesus left the girls' home, two blind men followed along behind him, shouting, 'Son of David, have mercy on us!' They went right into the house where he was staying, and Jesus asked them, 'Do you believe I can make you see?' 'Yes, Lord,' they told him, 'we do.' Then he touched their eyes and said, 'Because of your faith, it will happen.'" (Matt. 9:27-29 NLT). So be encouraged this morning and please exercise your faith and believe that God can make all things happen through faith in Him throughout your life.

> "Don't you remember that our ancestor Abraham was shown to be right with God by his actions when he offered his son Isaac on the altar? You see, his faith and his actions worked together. His actions made his faith complete" (James 2:21, 22 NLT).

Challenge of the day: Your faith and your actions will cause God to respond to your needs and desires.

To God be the glory! Many blessings to you and have a great day, full of your faith moving the heart of God to respond to your needs.

Day 84

I pray that all is well with each of you. Start your day off with God knowing you must release your fears. We must not be afraid of the things of this world. We must learn all the more to walk in the power and authority given unto us by the almighty and living God. "So we can say with confidence, 'The LORD is my helper, so I will have no fear. What can mere people do to me?'" (Heb. 13:6 NLT). So be encouraged this morning, brothers and sisters. God has our best interests at heart. We must know that He is our helper and not concern ourselves with the threats of others, but only trust, fear, and serve Him.

"For God has not given us a spirit of fear and timidity, but of power, love, and self-discipline" (2 Tim. 1:7 NLT).

Challenge of the day: Do not be afraid of the challenges that life brings us; hold on and use the power that has been given unto you.

To God be the glory! Many blessings to you and have a powerful day in the Lord.

Day 85

I pray that all had a great evening. Start your day off with God, knowing that you must acknowledge the power of God working in and around your life. When things begin to just happen and blessings are overtaking you, acknowledge God. Acknowledge God at every opportunity possible. "Everyone who acknowledges me publicly here on earth, I will also acknowledge before my Father in heaven" (Matt. 10:32 NLT). God desires and deserves our acknowledgement of Him in our lives. So be encouraged this morning, sisters and brothers, and be proud to call on God all the time. He yearns to hear His name come from His creation.

> "I will sacrifice a voluntary offering to you; I will praise your name, O LORD, for it is good" (Ps. 54:6 NLT).

Challenge of the day: Willingly call on and acknowledge God in every area of your life.

To God be the glory! Many blessings to you and have a powerful day in the Lord.

Day 86

I pray that each of you had a grand day. Start your day off with God knowing that you must surrender your thoughts to God. Thoughts can become actions, and if our thoughts are not aligned with the living Word of God, then our thoughts can be hazardous to our spiritual health. "For the Word that God speaks is alive and full of power [making it active, operative, energizing, and effective]; it is sharper than any two-edged sword, penetrating to the dividing line of the breath of life (soul) and [the immortal] spirit, and of joints and marrow [of the deepest parts of our nature], exposing and sifting and analyzing and judging the very thoughts and purposes of the heart" (Heb. 4:12). So be encouraged this morning, sisters and brothers, and know that when our thoughts are aligned with the living Word of God, our souls are protected from the wickedness of the enemy.

"For as the heavens are higher than the earth, so are My ways higher than your ways and My thoughts than your thoughts" (Isa. 55:9).

Challenge of the day: When you have your thoughts set on heavenly things, you will be able to be more in tune with the things of heaven and ensure that the living God is pleased with your thoughts.

To God be the glory! Many blessings to you and have a blessed day and keep your thoughts on the Lord.

Day 87

I pray that all is well with each of you. Start your day off with God, knowing that He holds the future in His hands and knows the outcome of our lives. So why fight with God about what it is you are supposed to be doing? God has a plan for us, and we must discover what it is and not be afraid of it or run from it. We must walk and live like we have purpose and understand that our destiny has been determined by God. "Everything has already been decided. It was known long ago what each person would be. So there's no use arguing with God about your destiny" (Eccles. 6:10 NLT). So be encouraged, brothers and sisters, that God's plan for our lives will not fail. It already has been determined what the end shall be. We must tap into the Source (God) and find out for ourselves what it is we are supposed to be doing and how we are to live an upright life that is pleasing unto God our Creator.

"Do you still want to argue with the Almighty? You are God's critic, but do you have the answers?" (Job 40:2 NLT).

Challenge of the day: We will not have all of the answers to life's problems and situations, but we must trust the One who does. Trust God, He knows exactly what He is doing in your life.

To God be the glory! Many blessings to you and have a powerful day in the Lord.

Day 88

I pray that all is well with each you. Start your day off with God knowing that trouble does not last always. We must know that God is with us during hard times; we must keep the faith and know that trouble is but for a short time. "And the patriarchs, becoming envious, sold Joseph into Egypt. But God was with him and delivered him out of all his troubles, and gave him favor and wisdom in the presence of Pharaoh, king of Egypt; and he made him governor over Egypt and all his house" (Acts 7:9, 10 NKJV). So be encouraged this morning, sisters and brothers; joy is right around the corner waiting to embrace us and keep us in God's perfect peace during the times of trouble.

"For in the time of trouble, He shall hide me in His pavilion; in the secret place of his tabernacle He shall hide me; He shall set me high upon a rock" (Ps. 27:5 NKJV).

Challenge of the day: In the face of trouble, know that you are not alone; God will shield you and raise you up at the appropriate time.

To God be the glory, many blessings, and have an awesome day in the Lord.

Day 89

I pray that all is well with each of you. Start your day off with God knowing that God is a just God. He loves all of us and He truly cares about what is happening in our lives. "He is the Rock; his deeds are perfect. Everything He does is just and fair. He is a faithful God who does no wrong; how just and upright he is!" (Deut. 32:4 NLT). So be encouraged and keep the faith; God is a just and a loving God.

> "You thrill me, LORD, with all you have done for me! I sing for joy because of what you have done" (Ps. 92:4 NLT).

Challenge of the day: God knows exactly what He is doing in your life; trust Him because He is faithful and just.

To God be the glory! Many blessings to you and have a joyful day in the Lord.

Day 90

I hope and pray that all is well with each of you. Start your day off with God knowing you must know how to discern the times and seasons in our lives. We may not always understand everything we go through, but know the various seasons. "To EVERYTHING there is a season, and a time for every matter or purpose under heaven" (Eccles. 3:1). "I said in my heart, God will judge the righteous and the wicked, for there is a time [appointed] for every matter and for every work" (Eccles. 3:17). So be encouraged this morning, sisters and brothers; there are many seasons we must go through in life, how we go through them will determine the outcome. If we do not get what we need out of a season, we may find ourselves repeating that season over again until we grasp the lesson that was intended for us.

"Show Your marvelous loving-kindness, O You Who save by your right hand those who take refuge in You from those who rise up against them" (Ps. 17:7).

Challenge of the day: God's loving-kindness will outlast our troubles in this life, as we journey through our various seasons and trust God to bring us through each period, leading all the way.

To God be the glory! Many blessings to you and have a powerful day, loving one another.

Day 91

I pray that all is well with each of you all. Start your day off with God, knowing it is God who gives us wisdom and strength to make sound decisions in life. When we do not think we are strong enough to complete assignments or tasks or when challenges become overwhelming, God will give us the wisdom and strength to go on just a little bit further. "Using a dull ax requires great strength, so sharpen the blade. That's the value of wisdom; it helps you succeed" (Eccles. 10:10 NLT). So be encouraged this morning, sisters and brothers. We must sharpen ourselves, using the wisdom and strength of God to do the things He has called and chosen us to do. Be not afraid; trust and believe that God will see us through.

"As iron sharpens iron, so a friend sharpens a friend" (Prov. 27:17 NLT).

Challenge of the day: Sharpen yourself through the wisdom of God to choose the right friends and people to be around— people who will challenge you to do that which is right and will cause you to think outside the normalcy of life. The results will cause all to be sharpened and live a life that will be pleasing unto God.

To God be the glory! Many blessings to you and have a peaceful day in the Lord, sharpening one another.

Day 92

I hope and pray that all is well with each of you. Start your day off with God, knowing that it is God who has called your name and it is He who has created you in His image. It is God who has redeemed us and protected us throughout our lives. We are His personal possession, and we were made for His glory. No one can take us from the Lord God almighty; no matter how hard one may try, they never will succeed. "Everyone who is called by My name, whom I have created for My glory; I have formed him, yes, I have made him" (Isa. 43:7 NKJV). So be encouraged this morning, sisters and brothers; we have the greatest supporting cast ever—GOD! What can be more satisfying than knowing how much God loves us? He created us in His image and called us by name! And, yes, we certainly must represent Him well in all that we do in life.

> "You are My witnesses, says the Lord, and My servant whom I have chosen, that you may know Me, believe Me and remain steadfast to Me, and understand that I am He. Before me there was no God formed, neither shall there be after Me" (Isa. 43:10).

Challenge of the day: Understand the power and responsibility of being chosen by God to serve Him and others.

To God be the glory! Many blessings to you and have a powerful worship experience.

Day 93

I pray that all is well with each of you. Start your day off with God knowing that you must move forward in life with God. We must not allow our past to hold us back from our future or allow our past to hinder our gifts within us. "Brethren, I do not count myself to have apprehended; but one thing I do, forgetting those things which are behind and reaching forward to those things ahead, I press toward the goal for the prize of the upward call of God in Christ Jesus" (Phil. 3:13-14 NKJV). So be encouraged this morning, sisters and brothers; go with God forward in your life, use your talents, and discover more about yourself each day in the Lord. Rest not until God's will is fulfilled and your purpose is completed. Do not give up, but press forward!

"But You, O Lord, are a shield for me, my glory, and the lifter of my head" (Ps. 3:3).

Challenge of the day: When it seems like your past is closing in on you, remember God has forgotten the past and it is He who will lift up your head and cause you to move forward in life as your guide and protector.

To God be the glory! Many blessings to you and have a powerful day in the Lord. Always strive to move closer to God through trusting His judgments and counsel.

Day 94

I pray that all is well with each of you. Start your day off with God knowing that you must learn to love people in spite of what has happened in your life. Hatred is not the Christ-like characteristic to possess; we must love in an unconditional manner. The power of love can and will change people's lives, hearts, and even change their destination. "But the other criminal protested, 'Don't you fear God even when you have been sentenced to die? We deserve to die for our crimes, but this man hasn't done anything wrong.' Then he said, 'Jesus, remember me when you come into your Kingdom.' And Jesus replied, 'I assure you, today you will be with me in paradise'" (Luke 23:40-43 NLT). Jesus showed the criminal beside Him on the cross love, in spite of his faults, failures, or other conditions. So be encouraged and mindful that we possess the ability to love people like Jesus does.

"Love never gives up, never loses faith, is always hopeful, and endures through every circumstance" (1 Cor. 13:7 NLT).

Challenge of the day: The power of love will never give up on life or people, and it will hold its own ground in and around every situation in life.

To God be the glory! Many blessings to you and have a powerful day in the Lord and do not give up on love.

Day 95

I pray that all is well with each of you. Start your day off with God, knowing that God places us strategically in certain positions at certain times in our lives. We must know and understand our destination and assignments. We must not waste time through idleness; we must maximize our potential, influence, and God-given gifts. Mordecai put a challenge to Esther the queen to use her influence to change the king's mind about destroying all of the Jews. "If you keep quiet at a time like this, deliverance and relief for the Jews will arise from some other place, but you and your relatives will die. Who knows if perhaps you were made queen for just such a time as this?" (Esther 4:14 NLT). So be encouraged this morning and understand the position and influence you may have. Know that it is God who places us all in different positions and seasons at the right time and in the right place, so that He will get all of the glory and honor. Know your season, position, and influence, because it may be life-saving to someone unknown to you. Know that you are where you are for such a time as this; no one else can do what you are doing or be where you are.

"O nations of the world recognize the LORD; recognize that the LORD is glorious and strong" (Ps. 96:7 NLT).

Challenge of the day: Recognize the Lord for who He is and know He is too wise to make any mistakes. Recognize His influence all throughout your life and your doings.

To God be the glory! Many blessings to you and have an exciting day in the Lord.

Day 96

I pray that you all are well. Start your day off with God knowing you must understand your purpose in this life. Our main purpose is to worship God, and through this we will discover what our earthly assignments are and know that we always must keep growing and living for God. We must be willing to be obedient to God and accomplish His will in our lives. No matter what things may seem like or what we are going through in life, when we follow God's will first, everything else will fall in place. "So they camped or traveled at the LORD's command, and they did whatever the LORD told them through Moses" (Num. 9:23 NLT). The children of Israel followed God as they traveled on their journey to the Promised Land, although it was a cloud that was given as a sign to help them remain faithful during this time. (Refer to Num. 9:15-23.) So be encouraged this morning and journey on through your purpose and to your own particular promised land. We may not always understand everything that we go through, but know that it is for the glory of God and for His will and purposed to be completed in our lives.

"The instructions of the LORD are perfect, reviving the soul. The decrees of the LORD are trustworthy, making wise the simple" (Ps. 19:7 NLT).

Challenge of the day: Follow the instructions of the Lord and live beyond your greatest imagination.

To God be the glory! Many blessings to you and have a powerful day in the Lord. Stay close to the Lord.

Day 97

I hope all is well with each of you. Start your day off with God knowing that you must exercise self-control and self-discipline. We must learn how to control our emotions and attitude toward life and doing the things of God. It is not always easy to examine our own actions. Sometimes it may be difficult or challenging at best to look in the mirror; however, in reality it is a must in order that we may strive to see more of Christ in us than we see ourselves. "So think clearly and exercise self-control. Look forward to the gracious salvation that will come to you when Jesus Christ is revealed to the world" (1 Pet. 1:13 NLT). So be encouraged this morning, brothers and sisters, and live to serve Christ and others through having a better understanding of self-control and not allowing your feeling or emotions to get the best of you.

> "Be the Holy Spirit produces this kind of fruit in our lives: love, joy, peace, patience, kindness, goodness, faithfulness, gentleness, and self-control. There is no law against these things!" (Gal. 5:22, 23 NLT).

Challenge of the day: Learn to bear the fruit of the spirit through understanding clearly who you are in God.

To God be the glory! Many blessings to you and have a powerful day in the Lord, being fruitful.

Day 98

I pray that all is well with each of you. Start your day off with God knowing that God is available to help us when we feel overwhelmed with the issues of life. It is vital that we understand that we do not have to deal with the crises of life by ourselves. God is willing, able, and ready to assist us in whatever we may need assistance with in life. We must call on His name, trust, and believe that He will hear and answer our prayers. "From the depths of despair, O LORD, I call for your help. Hear my cry, O LORD. Pay attention to my prayer" (Ps. 130:1, 2 NLT). So be encouraged this afternoon, sisters and brothers, no matter how deep we may have fallen in this life or what may have come upon us; when we call on God, we must know that He will respond and because He loves us!

"I am counting on the LORD; yes, I am counting on him. I have put my hope in his word" (Ps. 130:5 NLT).

Challenge of the day: Believe and know that we can count on God, even in the midst of disparity. God has everything under control.

To God be the glory, many blessing, and have a powerful day resting in God's help.

Day 99

I pray that all is well with each of you. Start your day off with God, knowing that it is not about us, you and I, it is about God. When we take self out of everything we do and have an attitude of serving God in and through our tribulations, which strengthens our character, then we will gain a better understanding of how to truly serve God and others. I've often heard, "What about me, what do I gain from doing this or that?" If we are doing something for someone with the intentions of getting something out of it, then maybe we should reconsider. Jesus died with the purpose of restoring humankind back to God the Father as a family, with no personal intention other than to do the will of the Father. "Be exalted, O God, above the highest heavens! May your glory shine over all the earth" (Ps. 57:5 NLT). So be encouraged this morning, sisters and brothers, exalt God in all that we do and take notice that it is not about us, it is about God.

"For you, O LORD, are supreme over all the earth;
you are exalted far above all gods" (Ps. 97:9 NLT).

Challenge of the day: Exalt God and not yourself; because it is not about you and me, it is indeed and will forever be about God. All that we do it is about God.

To God be the glory! Many blessings to you and have a powerful day lifting up the matchless name of Jesus Christ.

Day 100

I pray that all is well with each of you. Start your day off with God, knowing that you must learn the ways of God. We may not always understand everything, but we must know that God is in control. When we strive to live totally surrendered to God, we will not wrestle with why this or that happens. We will live in the confidence and understanding that in God we trust, and that is all that matters. We must learn the ways of God and enjoy His blessings—spiritually, physically, emotionally, mentally, and even financially. "Teach me your ways, O LORD, that I may live according to your truth! Grant me purity of heart, so that I may honor you" (Ps. 86:11 NLT). So be encouraged this morning, sisters and brothers; live and learn the ways of God—they are true and fulfilling. Our lives will never be the same; each and every day we must strive to move closer toward God. Be at peace; God is not done with us yet.

"Lead me by your truth and teach me, for you are the God who saves me. All day long I put my hope in you" (Ps. 25:5 NLT).

Challenge of the day: Follow God's leading through His Word and the Holy Spirit, and we will learn and know His ways.

To God be the glory! Many blessings to you and have a powerful week in the Lord. Be strengthened in the Lord; He knows what you are facing each and every day.

Day 101

I pray that all is well with each of you. Start your day off with God, knowing you can overcome any situation or circumstance that may come your way. Why? It is because of our faith and love in Jesus Christ: Jesus Himself is greater than anything we may face or anything that may come upon us. We must have faith that we can overcome anything at any time in our lives. If we do not believe, then we will be overcome by that which we fear. "Little children, you are of God [you belong to Him] and have [already] defeated and overcome them [the agents of the antichrist], because He Who lives in you is greater (mightier) than he who is in the world" (1 John 4:4). So be encouraged this morning, sisters and brothers; God is greater than what we are facing each day. We must know and understand that because of Jesus we are overcomers. We can and will overcome any and all situations in life, by faith and love in Jesus Christ.

> "I have told you these things, so that in Me you may have [perfect] peace and confidence. In the world you have tribulation and trials and distress and frustration; but be of good cheer [take courage; be confident, certain, undaunted]! For I have overcome the world. [I have deprived it of power to harm you and have conquered it for you.]" (John 16:33).

Challenge of the day: Be confident in the fact that Jesus has overcome the world and we belong to Him. We do not have to fret about what others will try to do to us or say about us; we must live in perfect peace, as Jesus desires us to live. Fret not; only have faith and confidence in Jesus Christ!

To God be the glory! Many blessings to you and have a blessed and powerful day in the perfect peace of Jesus Christ.

Day 102

I pray that all is well with each of you. Start your day off with God knowing that we must have endurance to run this race we call life. We must understand how to outlast the things that come upon us—not complaining about life or giving up on it, but enduring the things that life may bring us. "THEREFORE THEN, since we are surrounded by so great a cloud of witnesses [who have borne testimony to the Truth], let us strip off and throw aside every encumbrance (unnecessary weight) and that sin which so readily (deftly and cleverly) clings to and entangles us, and let us run with patient endurance and steady active persistence the appointed course of the race that is set before us" (Heb. 12:1). So be encouraged this morning, sisters and brothers, and run your race with endurance and let go of the things that you do not need. Give them to God and keep running your race of life. Your course is set before you; you cannot run someone else's life.

"For His anger is but for a moment, but His favor is for a lifetime or in His favor is life. Weeping may endure for a night, but joy comes in the morning" (Ps. 30:5).

Challenge of the day: When we make it through the night season of our lives, we will receive the joyous blessing of a new day in the morning. Then we truly can be able to understand that God's favor is for a lifetime when we endure life.

To God be the glory! Many blessings to you and have a powerful day, knowing that you have complete joy in Christ Jesus.

Day 103

I pray that you and your family experience the joy of the Lord this morning. Start your day with God by giving thanks unto the Lord for His everlasting kindness. God's kindness will outlast everything you may be facing. No matter how great the circumstance may be, God will be gracious enough to bring you out . . . as you believe in Him to do so. Sticky situations will come and go, but the love of God is everlasting. Give thanks unto the Lord for delivering you out of life's hard times. Give thanks unto the Lord for being the God with a kind heart. "Oh, give thanks to the LORD! Call upon His name; make known His deeds among the peoples!" (1 Chron. 16:8 NKJV). So be encouraged this morning and thank God for showing you kindness and bringing you through every situation in life. His mercies are new every day, so thank God for giving you another chance at life. Live on purpose and serve the Lord Jesus with a kind heart--after all He's been too kind to you, so run and tell someone how good Jesus is to you.

> "Praise, the LORD, all you Gentiles! Laud Him, all you peoples! For His merciful kindness is great toward us, and the truth of the LORD endures forever. Praise the LORD!" (Ps. 117 NKJV).

Challenge of the day: Lift up the name of the Lord with a thankful heart. Praise Him while you have another opportunity to do so. Call upon the Lord because His mercy is great and everlasting. Regardless of what you are going through, praise the Lord all the way through your situation. Praise Him and give Him thanks and see what will transpire during your praise.

To God be the glory! Many blessings to you and have a powerful day giving thanks unto the Lord; He deserves to hear praises from you.

Day 104

I pray that all is well with each of you. Start your day off with God knowing you must serve God and others more than yourself. It is a blessing to be a blessing, serving one another with a true and sincere heart. "For you, brethren, have been called to liberty; only do not use liberty as an opportunity for the flesh, but through love serve one another" (Gal. 5:13 NKJV). So be encouraged this afternoon and serve with a glad heart and love one another.

"Serve the LORD with fear, and rejoice with trembling" (Ps. 2:11 NKJV).

Challenge of the day: When serving God, we must be mindful of how we serve one another.

To God be the glory! Many blessings to you and have a blessed day and serve others well.

Day 105

I pray that all is well with each of you. Start your day off with God, knowing that it is God who protects and guide us through the fiery trials of life. You may not always understand what is happening, but know that it is God who delivers comfort and brings us through these trials of life, always on time. "Yea, though I walk through the valley of the shadow of death, I will fear no evil; for You are with me; Your rod and Your staff, they comfort me" (Ps. 23:4 NKJV). So be encouraged this morning; in spite of being pressed on every side, God will comfort and protect us through it all. We must remain faithful! Yes, we must remain faithful, trusting and leaning upon Him and His steadfast Word, which is readily available to each of us. No matter what is going on in and around our lives, God is aware of it; we must be submissive to Him in order to understand and receive the good that always comes out of bad circumstances.

"Lord, how long will You look on? Rescue me from their destructions . . ." (Ps. 35:17 NKJV).

Challenge of the day: God always is watching and waiting for an opportunity to show how strong and mighty He really is. We must learn to call on Him and expect Him to be God and Lord; yes, even over our personal circumstances.

To God be the glory! Many blessings to you and know that God is expecting to hear from you.

Day 106

I pray that all is well with each of you. Start your day off with God knowing that God desires to communicate with us. You must get in alignment with Him and be ready to serve Him with your whole heart. You must draw closer to God in order to understand and know what is desired of you. It will be through the communication of prayer, understanding, and reading the living Word of God. "I have followed your commands, which keep me from following cruel and evil people. My steps have stayed on your path; I have not wavered from following you. I am praying to you because I know you will answer, O God. Bend down and listen as I pray" (Ps. 17:4-6 NLT). So be encouraged today knowing that God has our best interests at heart; we must never give up, but draw closer to God.

"You have made a wide path for my feet to keep them from slipping" (Ps. 18:36 NLT).

Challenge of the day: Stay on course with God and do not forget about Him. He yearns to be close with you.

To God be the glory! Many blessings to you and have a blessed day.

Day 107

I pray that all is well with each of you. Start your day off with God, knowing that it is He who will calm the storms in our lives and provide us peace in their midst. You must not be fearful or worry. You must only trust and believe. Believe in the impossible and expect it to happen in and around your life. "Look at those who are honest and good, for a wonderful future awaits those who love peace" (Ps. 37:37 NLT). No matter how heavy the storms may be in your life, God will calm them and give you peace. Be encouraged and walk in the love of God.

"I will praise the LORD at all times. I will constantly speak his praises" (Ps. 34:1 NLT).

Challenge of the day: Praise God anyhow. No matter the size of the storms in your life, praise God all day and watch for Him to give you peace in your life.

To God be the glory! Many blessings to you and have a powerful day serving the Lord with your life.

Day 108

I pray that all is well with each of you. Start your day off with God knowing that you must rely on Him; it is He who will carry us through this journey we call life. Though trials of life may be heavy at times, rest assured that we can rely on God. "The LORD is my shepherd; I have all that I need" (Ps. 23:1 NLT). The Lord is so reliable—He is all that we need in order to get through day-to-day living. So be encouraged and keep on relying on God; He is the best help available.

"He renews my strength. He guides me along right paths, bringing honor to his name" (Ps. 23:3 NLT).

Challenge of the day: God will guide us and renew our strength throughout the day when we rely on and trust in Him.

To God be the glory! Many blessings to you and have a blessed day. Be renewed in the Lord.

Day 109

I hope and pray that all is well with each of you. Start your day off with God knowing that His way is perfect. There is no better way than to live in the perfect will of God. As we travail to live under His loving arms of protection, we must know that God is solid. He is strong and powerful, yet loving and caring at the same time. God cares more about us than we do ourselves. "God's way is perfect. All the LORD's promises prove true. He is a shield for all who look to him for protection. For who is God except the LORD? Who but our God is a solid rock?" (2 Sam. 22:31, 32 NLT). So be encouraged this morning knowing that God's way is perfect and we must strive to do His will daily.

"Your promises have been thoroughly tested; that is why I love them so much" (Ps. 119:140 NLT).

Challenge of the day: God's promises are true, try them and see them come to pass in and around your life daily!

To God be the glory! Many blessings to you and have a powerful day living in God's promises.

Day 110

I pray that all had a grand day. Start your day off with God knowing you can accomplish anything with God leading the way. You are more than conquerors. You do not have to live a defeated life; in fact, you are not supposed to live in such a manner, you are supposed to live victoriously through Christ Jesus, no matter what is going on in and through your life. "Yet in all these things we are more than conquerors through Him who loved us" (Rom. 8:37 NKJV). So be encouraged this morning and declare that you are more than a conqueror in Christ Jesus and move forward in life. Do not look back; just go with God as a victor and not a victim. No matter what—God knows all, sees all, and understands all!

> "These things I have spoken to you, that in Me you may have peace. In the world you will have tribulation; but be of good cheer, I have overcome the world" (John 16:33 NKJV).

Challenge of the day: Jesus has overcome the world so that you and I have inner peace, knowing we can do anything through Him.

To God be the glory! Many blessings to you and have a blessed day living in victory.

Day 111

I pray that all is well with each of you. Start your day off with God knowing that you must be mindful to be joyful always. No matter what we are going through in life, you must find the good in it and be joyful. Oftentimes we may find ourselves complaining about the smallest of things; in reality, we need not complain, but be joyful and thankful unto God for allowing us to live another day. "Always be joyful. Never stop praying. Be thankful in all circumstances, for this is God's will for you who belong to Christ Jesus" (1 Thess. 5:16-18 NLT). So be encouraged this morning, be joyful always, and smile often. God is leading the way.

"Always be full of joy in the Lord. I say it again—rejoice!" (Phil. 4:4 NKJV).

Challenge of the day: Allow the joy of the Lord to strengthen your heart and move your mind to a constant state, being able to rejoice no matter what may come your way.

To God be the glory! Many blessings to you and have a blessed day in the Lord living a joyful life.

Day 112

I pray that all is well with each of you. Start your day off with God, knowing that you must stand the test of time, regardless of what is going on in your life. Do not be afraid of what is before you, but hold on to that which is true. God's Word is powerful and living; we must surround ourselves with it at every opportunity we get. We must capture the essence of God's living Word and live daily. "But we have this treasure in earthen vessels, that the excellence of the power may be of God and not of us. We are hard-pressed on every side, yet not crushed; we are perplexed, but not in despair; persecuted, but not forsaken; struck down, but not destroyed" (2 Cor. 4:7-9 NKJV). So be encouraged as we stand on the living Word of God; we can face any problem and go through any and all circumstances in this life, with God leading us all the way through, and we will not be destroyed. In fact, we will be lifted up through the living Word of God. Hold on—God is not done with us yet!

"Commit your way to the LORD, Trust also in Him,
and He shall bring it to pass" (Ps. 37:5 NKJV).

Challenge of the day: When challenges come, trust God and stand on His Word!

To God be the glory! Many blessings to you and have a blessed day and trust in the Lord.

Day 113

I pray that all is well with each of you. Start your day off with God knowing that you need to appreciate God for who He is and be thankful. No matter where you are in life or what is going on in your life, first acknowledge, then appreciate and adore God for who He is. "Know that the Lord, He is God; it is He who has made us, and not we ourselves; we are His people and the sheep of His pasture. Enter into His gates with thanksgiving, and into His courts with praise. Be thankful to Him, and bless His name" (Ps. 100:3-4 NKJV). It is vital to our relationship that we maintain a true since of connection and realization that God is God. We must stay grounded in this fact or we will lose focus on what must be accomplished in and around our lives. So be encouraged this morning, sisters and brothers. God's got the helm; allow Him to lead the way.

"For the Lord is the great God, and the great King above all gods, in His hand are the deep places of the earth; the heights of the hills are His also" (Ps. 95:3-5).

Challenge of the day: God is greater than anything on and above the earth, and we must recognize that!

To God be the glory! Many blessings to you and have a blessed day, knowing that God is greater than your issues in life.

Day 114

I pray that all is well with each of you. Start your day off with God, knowing that you neither can fight against God, nor should you resist Him. He is the potter and we are the clay. No matter what we are going through in life, something old is going to fall off and something new is going to come into places, as we go through the fiery trials of life. We must not resist the trials, but withstand them as God leads us through them. It is our character that will stand the test of times. "But now, O LORD, You are our Father; we are the clay, and You our potter; and all we are the work of Your hand" (Isa. 64:8 NKJV). So be encouraged this morning—no matter the trial, remember God is at work in our lives.

"Save me, O God, by Your name, and vindicate me by your strength" (Ps. 54:1 NKJV).

Challenge of the day: God will save us, once we decide not to resist Him but surrender to Him.

To God be the glory! Many blessings to you and have a blessed and powerful day in the Lord.

Day 115

I pray that all is well with each of you. Start your day with God knowing you must serve with a glad heart. Serving others is what Jesus does; He takes care of everyone that comes into contact with Him. He turns no one away. He has a heart for people. Taking care of one another is a blessing within itself; whether small or large, it's that fact of being willing to take care of someone else other than yourself. "Just as the Son of Man did not come to be served, but to serve, and to give His life a ransom for many" (Matt. 20:28 NKJV). So be encouraged this morning, sisters and brothers, and serve well where you are. Take care of those people that God sends your way; whether you like them or not does not matter; it is about who you are really serving in the first place.

> "If anyone serves Me, let him follow Me; and where I am, there My servant will be also. If anyone serves Me, him My Father will honor" (John 12:26 NKJV).

Challenge of the day: Serve, follow, and honor God.

To God be the glory! Many blessings to you and have a blessed day following the Lord Jesus Christ.

Day 116

I pray that all is well with each of you. Start your day off with God knowing you can experience God's amazing grace daily. God's grace is available to you as you move throughout each day. In unfamiliar territory, God's grace and favor will be right there and will never miss a beat. His amazing grace will never lead us astray; it will keep us safe from all hurt, harm, and danger. "For the Lord God is a Sun and Shield: the Lord bestows [present] grace and favor and [future] glory (honor, splendor, and heavenly bliss)! No good thing will He withhold from those who walk uprightly" (Ps. 84:11). So be encouraged this morning as you experience God's grace and favor; as you move about the day, notice it and cherish it and even appreciate it. Ask for God's favor when you move in unfamiliar territory.

"And the king loved Esther more than all the women, and she obtained grace and favor in his sight more than all the maidens, so that he set the royal crown on her head and made her queen instead of Vashti" (Esther 2:17).

Challenge of the day: God's grace and favor will move a king's heart to bless His people and fulfill His purpose. Be in the right place at the right time to receive your blessings.

To God be the glory! Many blessings to you and have a blessed day living in God's grace and receiving His mercy.

Day 117

I pray that all is well with each of you. Start your day off with God knowing that He is a forgiving and loving God. The moment God forgives us, it is finished and forgotten about. So why must we hold on to it? The enemy loves to bring up what we used to do and used to be; leave it alone and let it be in the past. Live in the now and live for the mercy of a new today. "O GIVE thanks to the Lord, for He is good; for His mercy and loving-kindness endure forever! Let the redeemed of the Lord say so, whom He has delivered from the hand of the adversary" (Ps. 107:1, 2). So be encouraged this morning, sisters and brothers; we have been delivered from our past. Even so, shout about it and give thanks unto the Lord for His mercy today.

"The Lord is merciful and gracious, slow to anger and plenteous in mercy and loving-kindness" (Ps. 103:8).

Challenge of the day: God's mercy will outlast your past, so move out of your past and live in His mercy and grace.

To God be the glory! Many blessings to you and have a blessed and powerful worship experience.

Day 118

I pray that all is well with each of you. Start your day off with God knowing that you must live out the promises of God. If God said it in His Word, it will come to pass. You must have faith in God that things will happen in your lives, according to His will and His way. We must live out the Word in our lives. "So faith comes by hearing [what is told], and what is heard comes by the preaching [of the message that came from the lips] of Christ (the Messiah Himself)" (Rom. 10:17). When we begin to live out the Word of God, from what we hear and know of it, the enemy cannot hinder God's promises from happening in and around our lives. So be encouraged this morning, sisters and brothers, and watch the promises of God unfold in your life—for healing, for deliverance, for complete wholeness or whatever the personal promises from God may be to you. It can and will happen, when you live out His Word through Jesus Christ in your life.

"But You, O Lord, are a shield for me, my glory, and the lifter of my head" (Ps. 3:3).

Challenge of the day: When God lifts up your head, there is no need for it to ever fall down again. Know God, know His Word, and know His promises.

To God be the glory! Many blessings and have a powerful day in the Lord. Be safe and know where you stand in the Lord.

Day 119

I pray that all is well with each of you. Start your day off with God knowing forgiveness must start within. You must learn to forgive yourself of your past. Let the past be the past. No longer do you have to be bitter and live in pain. You must release all of the bitterness and pain and forgive yourself. "Judge not [neither pronouncing judgment nor subjecting to censure], and you will not be judged; do not condemn and pronounce guilty and you will not be condemned and pronounced guilty; acquit and forgive and release (give up resentment, let it drop), and you will be acquitted and forgiven and released" (Luke 6:37). So be encouraged this morning, sisters and brothers; release the pain, frustration, and bitterness. Forgive yourselves first, in order that you may forgive others and God may forgive you through Jesus Christ. What a wonderful way to begin the healing process, by releasing everything to Jesus Christ, the one who loves and adores us more than we know and understand.

"You are a hiding place for me; You, Lord, preserve me from trouble, You surround me with songs and shouts of deliverance. Selah [pause, and calmly think of that]!" (Ps. 32:7). (Read Ps. 32.)

Challenge of the day: The Lord desires to deliver us from our past and propel us into a great future. Regardless of where we are now in our lives, God desires to move us into our future, which must start in the inner person. David understood his personal relationship with the Lord. We must do the same.

To God be the glory! Many blessings and have a great day, full of peace and serenity in God.

Day 120

I pray that all had a grand evening. Start your day off with God, knowing that it is He who made us and not we ourselves. Know that it is God who will defend us, and we need not be concerned about defending ourselves or how or when God will defend us. Why should we even be concerned about the number of hairs on our head? "Who is this that darkens counsel by words without knowledge? Gird up now your loins like a man, and I will demand of you, and you declare to Me. Where were you when I laid the foundation of the earth? Declare to Me, if you have and know understanding" (Job 38:2-4). (Also refer to Job 35:16.) Who are we to question how God handles things? He will handle things according to His will and His way; we must be encouraged, knowing that He will take care of business as God, and we must trust Him to do just that. In the midst of being God, He will defend us at all costs. Certainly in the process He will set us straight and on the correct path, particularly when we fall. God desires that we fail not; He will be there to guide us through the process as we surrender our will to the will of Jesus Christ. So be encouraged this morning, sisters and brothers. Have that unmovable faith today more than ever, with a deep understanding that God made us and we did not make ourselves; no matter our position or authority, God made us. (Truth be told, God can take us out if we become too prideful.)

> "Show Your marvelous loving-kindness, O You Who save by Your right hand those who trust and take refuge in You from those who rise up against them" (Ps. 17:7).

Challenge of the day: God will take care of His own.

To God be the glory! Many blessings to you and have a blessed day knowing that God cares for you.

Day 121

I pray that all had a grand evening. Start your day off with God knowing that through disappointment you must remain faithful unto God. Disappointments are not God's way of showing disapproval or dismissing anything. How will we respond to the situation reveals how will respond to God during our time of disappointment. Will we walk away and never speak to God again, or just not for awhile? Or will we do like David did when he lost his son after fasting and praying for seven days. David got up, washed, changed his clothes, anointed himself, and went to the house of the Lord and worshipped. (Refer to 2 Sam. 12: 15-20.) Disappointment will come on this journey we call life, but it must not break our stride with God. Hold on to the hand that changes not. "Jesus Christ is [always] the same, yesterday, today [yes] and forever (to the ages)" (Heb. 13:8). So be encouraged this morning, sisters and brothers. No matter what is going on in your life, rely on, lean on, and trust in Jesus Christ. He never changes, and we must be faithful to Him, in spite of the situations that surround us.

> "Be still and rest in the Lord; wait for Him and patiently lean yourself upon Him; fret not yourself because of him who prospers in his way, because of the man who brings wicked devices to pass" (Ps. 37:7).

Challenge of the day: Rest in the Lord, remain faithful unto the Lord, and remember the Lord never changes.

To God be the glory! Many blessings and have a blessed and powerful day, remaining faithful unto the Lord.

Day 122

I pray that all of you had a great day. Start your day off with God, knowing that the freshness of God is like a brand new day. There are new opportunities available and new adventures and (spiritual) levels to explore. Starting over for some folk can be easy and for others very challenging, to say the least. Starting fresh with God is like a clean slate, a new start, and a new record. New beginnings are not bad; each day we have a chance to see God do something new within us, so discover the freshness of God in our personal relationship with Him in each new day. "And have clothed yourselves with new [spiritual self], which is [ever in the process of being] renewed and remolded into [fuller and more perfect knowledge upon] knowledge after the image (the likeness) of Him Who created it" (Col. 3:10). So be encouraged this morning, sisters and brothers; the process of perfection is in constant motion as we surrender to Christ Jesus daily.

"In the morning You hear my voice, O Lord; in the morning I prepare [a prayer, a sacrifice] for You and watch and wait [for You to speak to my heart]" (Ps. 5:3).

Challenge of the day: Rise early in the morning on a new day and take a chance at a fresh start, to reflect the image of Christ Jesus.

To God be the glory! Many blessings to you and have a blessed and powerful day starting afresh.

Day 123

I pray that all are doing well. Start your day off with God knowing that you must live for Jesus. We are His ambassadors, and certainly we represent Him in all that we do. Your actions speak volumes, whether you are doing something or not. Representing Christ Jesus on all levels means there will be times when we will have to stand tall and there will be times we will have to observe quietly, listen, and minister. There will be plenty of times to be bold (I'm of sure it), and there will be times where we'll have to gut check ourselves. "So we are Christ's ambassadors, God making His appeal as it were through us. We [as Christ's personal representatives] beg you for His sake to lay hold of the divine favor [now offered you] and be reconciled to God" (2 Cor. 5:20). So be encouraged this morning, brothers and sisters, and represent Christ Jesus. He holds the key to eternity.

"A wicked messenger falls into evil, but a faithful ambassador brings healing" (Prov. 13:17).

Challenge of the day: As an ambassador for Christ, restore the virtue, love, healing, peace, and forgiveness to those who need it. Represent Christ by doing that which is right.

To God be the glory! Many blessings to you and have a great and safe day. Keep Christ first and expect the best: expect healing and restoration.

Day 124

I pray that all is well with each of you. Start your day off with God knowing that He is faithful and just. God is faithful unto us, even when we make mistakes, are unfaithful, and just can't seem to get things right. He will be faithful to us, guiding us toward the right path. "If we are unfaithful, he remains faithful, for he cannot deny who he is" (2 Tim. 2:13 NLT). Jesus cannot deny who He is, nor will He deny the role He plays in our lives (the Bridge that brings us together through His death on the cross). We must strive to be faithful unto Him. So be encouraged this morning, brothers and sisters, and know that God is faithful. No matter what we are facing in this life this morning, God is faithful. He will see us through; yes, even to end of the world, He will see us through!

"But the Lord is faithful; he will strengthen you and guard you from the evil one" (2 Thess. 3:3 NLT).

Challenge of the day: Be strong in the Lord, knowing that the Lord is faithful and that it is He who keeps us from all harm, guarding constantly against the enemy.

To God be the glory, many blessings, and have powerful day in the Lord and be strong.

Day 125

I greet you all with God's great joy this morning, praying that all is well with each of you. Start your day off with God knowing that God's grace is immeasurable through salvation. It is unlimited and boundless and will take us beyond that which we can even see or imagine. God's grace will even cover us in our times of uncertainties. God's grace is restoring, and we are saved by and through His grace. "For it is by free grace (God's unmerited favor) that you are saved (delivered from judgment and made partakers of Christ's salvation) through [your] faith. And this [salvation] is not of yourself [of your own doing, it came not through your own striving], but it is the gift of God" (Eph. 2:8). So be encouraged this morning, sisters and brothers; God's grace is available always and will carry us through whatever we are going through. There is nothing we can do about this free gift of salvation in and through Jesus Christ, because His love is that wonderful and that strong. So walk in the love and free gift of grace and salvation this morning.

> "For the Lord God is a Sun and Shield: the Lord bestows [present] grace and favor and [future] glory (honor, splendor, and heavenly bliss)! No good thing will He withhold from those who walk uprightly" (Ps. 84:11).

Challenge of the day: There is no good thing God will keep back from those who walk and live uprightly before Him. His grace will expand beyond the imagination of those who follow after Him.

To God be the glory! Many blessings to you and walk in the grace of God.

Day 126

I pray that all is well with each of you and your family. Start your day off with God, knowing that we must release all pains and fears. We must no longer hold things in. If someone has hurt us in the past, or in the present for that matter, we must let it go and release. If we have to tell a friend in confidence or write it out, we must release that stress and aggravation from within. "Casting the whole of your care [all your anxieties, all your worries, all your concerns, once and for all] on Him, for He cares for you affectionately and cares about you watchfully" (1 Pet. 5:7). So be encouraged this morning, brothers and sisters; do not stress. God has got His catcher's mitt on and is waiting on us to throw all of our concerns, cares, hurts, pains, burdens, and even frustrations His way. He can handle them all. We just have to give them up in the name of Jesus Christ, release them all, and let our hearts be free of pain and frustration.

"Cast your burden on the Lord [releasing the weight of it] and He will sustain you: He will never allow the [consistently] righteous to be moved (made to slip, fall or fail)" (Ps. 55:22).

Challenge of the day: Release the pains and burdens from your heart and live in freedom. "Now the Lord is the Spirit; and where the Spirit of the Lord is, there is liberty" (2 Cor. 3:17 NKJV).

To God be the glory! Many blessings to you and let this day be a day that you release everything over to Jesus Christ.

Day 127

I pray that all is well with each of you. Start your day off with God knowing that we must never forget to be thankful. You must be thankful unto God at all times and in all situations and for all things. Yes, even the small or minute things in life; be thankful for family, work, and even our country. We must be thankful and at the same time pray for better days ahead. "O give thanks to the Lord, for He is good; for His mercy and loving-kindness endure forever!" (Ps. 118:1). We must render a thankful heart unto the Lord always and never forget to appreciate life and the love of God. So be encouraged this morning, sisters and brothers. With thanksgiving in our hearts, let us rejoice knowing that God is alive and on the throne. In Jesus' name, Amen!

"You are my God, and I will confess, praise, and give thanks to You; You are my God, I will extol You" (Ps. 118:28).

Challenge of the day: No matter what we are going through, we must acknowledge God and give thanks and praise unto Him always.

To God be the glory! Many blessings and have a blessed and powerful day in the Lord, giving Him praise at all times.

Day 128

I pray that all had a grand day. Start your day off with God, knowing that you should not fear, but have faith. "For God did not give us a spirit of timidity (of cowardice, of craven and cringing and fawning fear), but [He has given us a spirit] of power and of love and of calm and well balanced mind and discipline and self control" (2 Tim. 1:7). We must not be afraid of what is next, but walk by faith, knowing that God has "The Next" thing in line for us. We just have to avail ourselves and be ready when the opportunity comes. Fret not, but be ready. So be encouraged this morning, brothers and sisters; stay on the correct path of life and do not get off of it.

"You who [reverently] fear the Lord, trust in and lean on the Lord! He is their Help and their Shield" (Ps. 115:11).

Challenge of the day: Fear the Lord only; He can and will help and protect you in all situations and circumstances.

To God be the glory! Many blessings and have a powerful day and be not fearful.

Day 129

I pray that all is well with each of you. Start your day off with God, knowing we must have a mindset to pray always. We must intercede for all that God places before our faces. The power of prayer will change and direct the things that God deems so. We must be in tune with the Holy Spirit in order to know when, how, and for whom to pray. "I urge you, first of all, to pray for all people. Ask God to help them; intercede on their behalf, and give thanks for them" (1 Tim. 2:1 NLT). So be encouraged this morning, sisters and brothers; stay "prayed up," focus on what God would have you to say, do not use idle words, but pray with power and sincerity.

> "Confess your sins to each other and pray for each
> other so that you may be healed. The earnest prayer
> of a righteous person has great power and produces
> wonderful results" (James 5:16 NLT).

Challenge of the day: The power of your prayers will be determined by your lifestyle. Live right, pray right, and see the results of your prayers, right. God bless!

To God be the glory, many blessings and have a powerful day praying always.

Day 130

I pray that all is well with each of you this morning. Start your day off with God knowing you must express love to all of humankind always. Love is the key ingredient, if you will, that will spice up everyone's life. Without true love from God, how can we express love toward one another? Many are displaced or detached from society because of the lack of love. "For this is the message (the announcement) which you have heard from the first, that we should love one another" (1 John 3:11). So this morning, sisters and brothers, for the love of God, always observe your surroundings and pray for and love on those who may feel displaced or detached.

"See what [an incredible] quality of love the Father had given (shown, bestowed on) us, that we should [be permitted to] be named and called and counted the children of God! and so we are! The reason that the world does not know (recognize, acknowledge) Him"

(1 John 3:1).

Challenge of the day: The same quality of love that the Father God has shown toward us, we must as His children show others.

To God be the glory. Many blessings to you and have a great day full of love.

Day 131

I pray that all had a grand evening. Start your day off with God knowing that you must seek godly counsel in all things that you do. Many seek advice from outside the realm of godly counsel, like calling those hotline numbers. Not good or godly advice at all. "But only with God are [perfect] wisdom and might; He alone has [true] counsel and understanding" (Job 12:13). So be encouraged this morning, sisters and brothers; friends who know God truly will understand how to give godly counsel in your time of need.

"Oil and perfume rejoice the heart; so does the sweetness of a friend's counsel that comes from the heart" (Prov. 27:9).

Challenge of the day: Godly counsel from godly friends put the heart and mind at ease.

To God be the glory! Many blessings to you and have and powerful day full of peace. In Jesus' name, Amen.

Day 132

I pray that all is well with you and your family. Start your day off with God knowing that God's peace will cause you to be at ease in the midst of a stormy situation. You must learn never to be afraid or uneasy when storms come your way. Pray and let God's peace be your blanket. "These things I have spoken to you, that in Me you may have peace. In the world you will have tribulation; but be of good cheer, I have overcome the world" (John 16:33 NKJV). So be encouraged this morning and be at peace. God is watching over you and has overcome the issues in the world.

"For He Himself is our peace, who has made both one, and has broken down the middle wall of separation" (Eph. 2:14 NKJV).

Challenge of the day: Know Jesus as the one who gives you peace, even in the midst of the storms of life. His peace will calm you from the inside out.

To God be the glory! Many blessings to you and have a great day receiving God's peace for your life.

Day 133

I pray that all had a grand evening. Start your day off with God knowing you must gain understanding. Understand what we do and why we do it. Do not just do things out of habit or out of tradition. "For the Lord gives skillful and godly Wisdom; from His mouth come knowledge and understanding" (Prov. 2:6). Gaining and using understanding will allow us to operate even better in the gifts and the calling given to us by the Lord. We must understand that our destiny awaits us and is predicated upon our use of godly wisdom and knowledge. So be encouraged, sisters and brothers; act in the understanding that your destiny awaits you. Move forward and do not look back. Catch the vision that God has given you. No more hesitation and fear—move forward; God's plan is final.

"Give me understanding, that I may keep Your law; yes, I will observe it with my whole heart" (Ps. 119:34).

Challenge of the day: Put your heart into what you do for God and your dividends will be great.

To God be the glory! Many blessings and have a blessed day. Separate yourself for some special time with God and see what will happen with your worship experiences.

Day 134

I pray that all had a grand evening. Start your day off with God, knowing you must heed His words of wisdom and learning when to be quiet and sit still, instead of taking matters into your own hands. Being quiet and effective can make a positive and strong impact. "O, LORD I give my life to you. I trust in you, my God! Do not let me be disgraced, or let my enemies rejoice in my defeat. No one who trusts in you will ever be disgraced, but disgrace comes to those who try to deceive others. Show me the right path, O LORD; point out the road for me to follow" (Ps. 25:1-4 NLT). When we give our lives to God, we must follow the path He has set before us by using the wisdom He has given unto us. So be encouraged, brothers and sisters, and stay on the path that God has set before each of us.

"I waited patiently for the Lord to help me, and he turned to me and heard my cry" (Ps. 40:1 NLT).

Challenge of the day: Wait on God, use godly wisdom, and enjoy life.

To God be the glory, many blessings, and have a powerful worship experience this day. Expect great things to happen and they will.

Day 135

I pray that all is well with each of you this morning. Start your day off with God, knowing you must have confidence in God's ability to accomplish what He said He will accomplish in your life. Oftentimes we doubt God and lose faith when things don't always go our way or as we plan. Fret not, put doubt aside, rest easy, and trust God to be God. "Good comes to those who lend money generously and conduct their business fairly. Such people will not be overcome by evil. Those who are righteous will be long remembered. They do not fear bad news; they confidently trust the Lord to care for them" (Ps. 112:5-7 NLT). So be encouraged, sisters and brothers; God knows what's best for our lives. When we surrender to Him, we must trust and believe with confidence in our hearts that He will be Lord God over our lives.

"My heart is confident in you, O God; my heart is confident. No wonder I can sing your praises!" (Ps. 57:7 NLT).

Challenge of the day: Never doubt God! Put your heart at ease and sing His praises. God will take care of you.

To God be the glory, many blessings and have a powerful day. Do not doubt God.

Day 136

I pray that all had a grand evening. Start your day off with God knowing that God heals all of your diseases and sickness (Ps. 103). If you are sick or have any ailment, God can and will heal you. It is just a matter of your faith and God's time. Study the healing scriptures, fast, and pray. Believe and expect to be healed, because God is a Healer and Deliver. "But He was wounded for our transgressions, He was bruised for our guilt and iniquities; the chastisement [needful to obtain] peace and well-being for us was upon Him, and with the stripes [that wounded] Him we are healed and made whole" (Isa. 53:5). So this morning, sisters and brothers, I declare, "Let the healing process take place now. In the name of Jesus, be healed and whole by faith, and walk and live in victory. In Jesus' name. Amen." Be at peace; God has our best interests in His heart and His hand.

"And Jesus said to him, Receive you sight! Your faith (your trust and confidence that spring from your faith in God) has healed you" (Luke 18:42).

Challenge of the day: Walk by faith and be healed and whole. In Jesus' name, AMEN.

To God be the glory! Many blessings to you and have great day full of faith, never doubting, but only trusting and believing that all things are possible with God through Christ Jesus.

Day 137

I pray that all had a grand evening. Start your day off with God knowing that He is a friend that sticks closer than a brother. God is the one you can absolutely trust in die-hard moments. He is a friend like no other and He truly cares about your entire being. He desires that we know Him just as much as He knows and understands us. "The man of many friends [a friend of all the world] will prove himself a bad friend, but there is a friend who sticks closer than a brother" (Prov. 18:24). So be encouraged this morning, brothers and sisters, realizing that there is no friend like Jesus Christ—no not one. He'll cry when you cry and even sing when you sing; He'll rejoice when you rejoice. Jesus is indeed a friend of yours.

> "And [so] the Scripture was fulfilled that says, Abraham believed in (adhered to, trusted in and relied on) God, and this was accounted to him as righteousness (as conformity to God's will in thought and deed), and he was called God's friend" (James 2:23).

Challenge of the day: Knowing that God is our Friend, why should we concern ourselves with people who dislike us? Just trust Jesus as your Friend.

To God be the glory! Many blessings to you and have a blessed day, friend of God.

Day 138

I pray that you had a grand evening. Start your day off with God knowing you must never forget what God has done and is doing for you. God delivered us from things no one else could. God saved us from people who tried to destroy us and take us out. God delivered us even from ourselves. God can deliver like no one else. You shall never forget the awesome wonders of God. "THE LORD is my Shepherd [to feed, guide, and shield me], I shall not lack" (Ps. 23:1). The relationship becomes even more personal when we make a declaration of who the Lord is to us. If God is our Deliverer, then let Him be our Deliverer; if He is our Healer, then let Him be our Healer; and if He is our Savior, then let Him be our Savior. So be encouraged this morning, brothers and sisters, knowing that we must recognize God for who He is, Lord of all, love, almighty, and everlasting God. The Lord is much, much more.

"As for me, I will continue beholding Your face in righteousness (rightness, justice, and right standing with You): I shall be fully satisfied, when I awake [to find myself] beholding Your form [and having sweet communion with You]." (Ps. 17:15).

Challenge of the day: Chasing after the world will end in nothing, but running after the Lord will satisfy your soul forever.

To God be the glory! Many blessings to you and have a faith-packed week, trusting in the Lord.

Day 139

I pray that all had a grand evening. Start your day off with God knowing that you must truly rely on Him. He will give us the strength to survive the test of life and accomplish His will in our lives. Especially during our weakest moment, we are made strong in Him. God will always be on time to rescue us, even from ourselves. "Yet I am as strong today as I was the day Moses sent me; as my strength was then, so is my strength now for war and to go out and to come in" (Josh. 14:11). So be encouraged, sisters and brothers, this morning and know that we are strong in the Lord and we must rely on Him to guide us through this life. It does not matter our age, race, or creed; God's love is strong and He will use it as He deems. We must be ready like Joshua, who was ready to lead the children of Israel, even in his later years in life.

"Be strong and let your heart take courage, all you who wait for and hope for and expect the Lord!" (Ps. 31:24).

Challenge of the day: Be not afraid of the challenges ahead of you, but trust, rely, hope, and expect the Lord to be ever present in every situation you face.

To God be the glory! Many blessings to you and have a powerful day in the Lord.

Day 140

I pray that all had a grand evening. Start your day off with God, knowing that it is He who will supply you the peace and self-control during tough situations in life. There is no need for us to be hostile when others are hostile toward us. Exercise self control. "And in [exercising] knowledge [develop] self control and in [exercising] self control [develop [steadfastness (patience, endurance), and in [exercising] steadfastness [develop] godliness (piety)" (2 Pet. 1:6). So be encouraged, brothers and sisters; God understands what we need and when we need it and how we need it. We must receive and exercise godly character throughout our daily activities.

"He refreshes and restores my life (my self); He leads me in the paths of righteousness [uprightness and right standing with Him—not for my earning it, but] for His name's sake" (Ps. 23:3).

Challenge of the day: God restores us—not for our sake but for His name's sake—and we must exercise authority over those things that will or may hinder our walk and talk with God. Self-control is a must in our daily walk with God.

To God be the glory! Many blessings to you and have a blessed and powerful day in the Lord.

Day 141

I pray that all had a grand evening. Start your day off with God knowing that you must stay before Him. Getting before the Lord consistently will keep you grounded in your faith. Oftentimes the enemy will try to distract you from your walk and your assignment, but you must remain focused and walk uprightly before the Lord. "I have set the Lord continually before me: because He is at my right hand, I shall not be moved" (Ps. 16:8). Staying before God will allow us never to be moved by the circumstances of life, but to remain ever before the Lord. So be encouraged this morning, sisters and brothers; God awaits our communion with Him consistently. So be strong and stay the course of the Lord, as God will guide us all the way. He will complete the work in us that He started.

"Nevertheless I am continually with You, You do hold my right hand" (Ps. 73:23).

Challenge of the day: With God holding our right hand through this life, why be overly concerned with the trials and tribulations? Know that God will see us through them.

To God be the glory! Many blessings to you and have a glorious week in the Lord. Stay faithful and stay cool.

Day 142

I pray that all had a grand evening. Start your day off with God, knowing you must have faith, yes that of a mustard seed. You must believe in the impossible, not second guessing God, certainly not, but trusting in Him with your whole heart. Your faith in God must move the various mountains in your life, even those mountains that may hinder you from coming closer toward the living Lord Jesus Christ. "But without faith it is impossible to please and be satisfactory to Him. For whoever would come near to God must [necessarily] believe that God exists and that He is the rewarder of those who earnestly and diligently seek Him [out]" (Heb. 11:6).So be encouraged this morning; walk and live like the impossible can and will happen in our lives by our faith in Jesus Christ.

> "He said to them, Because of the littleness of your faith [that is, your lack of firmly relying trust]. For truly I say to you, if you have faith [that is living] like a grain of mustard seed, you can say to this mountain, move from here to yonder place, and it will move; and nothing will be impossible to you" (Matt. 17:20).

Challenge of the day: Will your faith cause the mountains in your life to rise up and move to where you need them to move? I challenge us all to look deep within and believe the impossible through faith in Jesus Christ. No matter how high our mountains may be in this life, they can move if we command them to by faith. Allow your faith in the impossible to live! Remember there is nothing too hard for our God.

To God be the glory! Many blessings to you and have a powerful day in the Lord and walk by faith.

Day 143

I hope and pray that all is well with each of you. Start your day off with God, knowing you must weather the storms of life . . . not being over whelmed with the many issues of life, but knowing and understanding how to handle them with God at the forefront. "And there will be a tabernacle for shade in the daytime from the heat, for a place of refuge, and for a shelter from storm and rain" (Isa. 4:6 NKJV). God desires to protect us and to be our refuge. Even when the storms of life get hard, hang in there and trust in the living Lord Jesus Christ. It is He who will deliver, heal, and release freedom during those storms. So be encouraged this morning, sisters and brothers; the storms of life will not destroy you, but strengthen you.

"He calms the storm, so that its waves are still" (Ps. 107:29 NKJV).

Challenge of the day: Be at peace: God can handle and calm any storm that comes His way.

To God be the glory, many blessings, and have a peaceful day full of God's favor upon each of you.

Day 144

I pray that all is well with each of you this morning. Start your day off with God knowing you must truly rely on the Holy Spirit to guide you in all your decision making. The Holy Spirit is indeed the Spirit of Truth, and He will not guide us wrong, His job is to make sure we know and understand the truth of all things. We sometimes may to want to hear or even receive what the Spirit is saying to us, so please be attentive to the Spirit of God. "For all who are led by the Spirit of God are sons of God. For [the Spirit which] you have now received [is] not a spirit of slavery to put you once more in bondage to fear, but you have received the Spirit of adoption [the Spirit producing sonship] in [the bliss of] which we cry, Abba (Father)! Father!" (Rom. 8:14-15). So be encouraged and know that being a child of God is an awesome experience, and we must operate as the Holy Spirit leads us.

"It is the Spirit Who gives life [He is the Life-giver]; the flesh conveys no benefits whatever [there is no profit in it]. The words (truths) that I have been speaking to you are spirit and life" (John 6:63).

Challenge of the day: Live by following the guidance of the Holy Spirit and understand the truth of God's living Word. His Word is alive and will cause you to live a better life.

To God be the glory! Many blessings to you and have a powerful worship experience. Go throughout your day expecting to receive what God would have you to receive. If you do not expect anything, then how can you receive anything?

Day 145

I pray that all had a grand evening. Start your day off with God knowing that you must honor God at all times. You must honor God in your speech. Speak pure things, things that will cause life and not death. Speak positively, rather than negatively. Positive speech will bring about life-changing action. "Let your speech at all times be gracious (pleasant and winsome), seasoned [as it were] with salt, [so that you may never be at a loss] to know how you ought to answer anyone [who puts a question to you]" (Col. 4:6). So be encouraged this morning, sisters and brothers, knowing that when we speak in a gracious manner, honor is brought unto the living Lord. Speak life and live!

"The mouth of the [uncompromisingly] righteous utters wisdom, and his tongue speak with justice" (Ps. 37:30).

Challenge of the day: Change your environment with words! Let your speech be clear and precise, having direction and power. In other words, give your words an assignment.

To God be the glory! Many blessings to you; speak life in your circumstances and watch your circumstances change.

Day 146

What a joy it is to greet each of you in the name of Jesus this morning! Start your day off with God, knowing you must be attentive to the voice of reason that belongs to the Lord. God's voice speaks volumes to and through our lives. Reason, without a doubt, is in the midst so that we may make sound decisions. "The watchman opens the door for this man, and the sheep listen to his voice and heed it: and he calls his own sheep by name and brings (leads) them out" (John 10:3). Salvation will come to those who are attentive to the voice that calls out their name. So be encouraged this morning, sisters and brothers; God's still calling our name, and we must be attentive to His voice and act accordingly.

"But know that the Lord has set a part for Himself [and given distinction to] him who is godly [the man of loving-kindness]. The Lord listens and heeds when I call to Him" (Ps. 4:3).

Challenge of the day: The Lord listens to our plea, and in turn we must be obedient to His response and be set apart from those things that are not pleasing unto Him.

To God be the glory! Many blessings to you and have a blessed and powerful day. Stay safe and enjoy the presence of the Lord.

Day 147

I pray that each and every one of you are doing extremely well. Start your day off with God knowing He is our Helper! God Himself is available at all times. You must call on Him, and He will answer the call. No matter what is going on in our lives, we must call on the Lord. He will guide us through every area of our lives, leaving no stone unturned. "Our inner selves wait [earnestly] for the Lord; He is our Help and our Shield" (Ps. 33:20). So be encouraged this morning, sisters and brothers; God's help is unmatched. We must ask Him for His assistance always and in all things.

"Be pleased, O Lord to deliver me; O Lord, make haste to help me!" (Ps. 40:13).

Challenge of the day: Good help is not hard to find, when the Help is He who created all things! Yes, the Help will never leave us helpless.

To God be the glory, many blessings, and have a blessed day. Always ask God for help.

171

Day 148

I pray that all had a grand day. Start your day off with God knowing that you must acknowledge God in all areas of your life. Your expectations must be God-centered and God-driven. You cannot move forward in life without the acknowledgment of the awesome power and love of the almighty and everlasting, living God. "In all your ways know, recognize, and acknowledge Him, and He will direct and make straight and plain your paths" (Prov. 3:6). So be encouraged this morning, sisters and brothers; acknowledge Him, and He will acknowledge all that we are doing for Him.

"Fine or arrogant speech does not befit [an empty-headed] fool-much less do lying lips befit a prince" (Prov. 17:7).

Challenge of the day: It's not how well we speak, but who we acknowledge and what we say that matters.

To God be the glory! Many blessings to you and have a blessed and powerful day. Speak life and use wisdom.

Day 149

I pray that you all had a grand evening. Start your day off with God knowing that you must appreciate God for who He is. Let the Lord know how much you adore Him and love Him. Oftentimes, we are asking God the Father, through Jesus Christ, to do this and do that for us. Let us show our adoration toward God this morning and, in fact, every morning. "I will extol You, my God, O King and I will bless Your name forever and ever [with grateful, affectionate praise] every day [with its new reasons] will I bless You [affectionately and gratefully praise You]: yes, I will praise Your name forever and ever" (Ps. 145:1-2). So be encouraged this morning, brothers and sisters, by blessing the Lord and letting Him know that you appreciate, adore, and extol Him.

"All Your works shall praise You, O Lord, and Your loving ones shall bless You [affectionately and gratefully shall Your saints confess and praise You]!" (Ps. 145:10).

Challenge of the day: Praise God anyhow. Every day is a new reason to shout unto the Lord our risen Savior. Shout the victory today!

To God be the glory! Many blessings to you and have a powerful day. Show the love of our risen Christ through love.

Day 150

I pray that all had a grand evening. Start your day off with God knowing that it is God who defends you. You do not have to defend yourself, so to speak, but allow God to defend what is rightfully His own. We belong to God — why should we fret over our accusers? "Who shall bring any charge against God's elect [when it is] God Who justifies [that is, Who puts us in right relation to Himself? Who shall come forward and accuse or impeach those whom God has chosen? Will God, Who acquits us?]" (Rom. 8:33). So be encouraged this morning, sisters and brothers; God is on our side, and we must be on His side. If God is for us, who will even dare to be against us?

"My defense and shield depend on God, Who saves the upright in heart" (Ps. 7:10).

Challenge of the day: Is your heart right enough toward God that He would defend your life? Right relationship with God through Jesus Christ is a must in order to complete our destiny.

To God be the glory, many blessings, and have a powerful and prosperous day.

Day 151

I pray that all is well each of you. Start your day off with God, knowing that it is He who sets the standards for you to follow. It is ingrained into your hearts, and you must be receptive of His Word. The Word of God is powerful and life-changing. We must use it wisely and live it out right. "For the Word of that God speaks is alive and full of power [making it active, operative, energizing, and effective]; it is sharper than any two-edged sword, penetrating to the dividing line of the breath of life (soul) and [the immortal] spirit, and of joints and marrow [of the deepest parts of our nature], exposing and sifting and analyzing and judging the very thoughts and purpose of the heart" (Heb. 4:12). So be encouraged, brothers and sisters; hear, receive, understand, and live the living and powerful Word of God. It is definitely food for your soul!

"For the word of the Lord is right; and all His work is done in faithfulness" (Ps. 33:4).

Challenge of the day: God is faithful to His Word, and we must remain faithful unto the Lord Jesus Christ. Because of Him we can breathe again.

To God be the glory, many blessings, and have a day full of opportunities to serve the living Lord.

Day 152

I pray that all had an enjoyable day. Start your day off with God, knowing that you must understand the whole matter of your duty and service toward God. "All has been heard; the end of the matter is: fear God [revere and worship Him, knowing that He is] and keep His commandments, for this is the whole of man [the full, original purpose of his creation, the object of God's providence, the root of character, the foundation of all happiness, the adjustment to all inharmonious circumstances and conditions under the sun] and the whole [duty] for every man" (Eccles. 12:13).So be encouraged this morning, knowing that duty calls us to fear and worship with a complete understanding of His commandments, a willing heart, and a mind to serve.

> "For the Lord knows and is fully acquainted with the way of the righteous, but the way of the ungodly [those living outside God's will] shall perish (end in ruin and come to nought)" (Ps. 1:6).

Challenge of the day: The way we travel speaks volumes of whom and how we serve.

To God be the glory! Many blessings to you and serve others better than we serve ourselves.

Day 153

I pray that you had a grand evening. Start your day off with God, knowing you must give honor, first to God and then to whom it is due. Show honor to all who serve in the armed forces, rending prayers for their safety and for wisdom to make sound decisions. "Render to all men their dues. [Pay] taxes to who taxes are due, revenue to whom revenue is due, respect to whom respect is due, and honored to whom honor is due" (Rom. 13:7). Serving at a greater capacity will cause one to make some hard decisions, and one must count the cost. So be encouraged and know that God desires and deserves all the glory and honor you can muster up to give Him.

"In whose eyes a vile person is despised, but he who honors those who fear the Lord (who revere and worship Him); who swears to his own hurt and does not change" (Ps. 15:4).

Challenge of the day: Heroes comes from all walks of life, but the honor of a person shall come from God.

To God be the glory, many blessings, and have a blessed and fruitful day.

Day 154

I pray that you had a great evening. Start your day off with God knowing you must recognize God as your help. You must look up and see Him and look around and know Him. We must walk and feel His very presence. "I WILL lift up my eyes to the hills [around Jerusalem, to sacred Mount Zion and Mount Moriah]—From whence shall my help come? My help comes from the Lord, Who made heaven and earth" (Ps. 121:1-2). So be encouraged and safe today; God is always on the scene. He will never leave us alone or comfortless. He will always be there, through the thick and the thin. God is ever-present.

"Remember all your offerings and accept your burnt sacrifice. Selah [pause and think of that]" (Ps. 20:3).

Challenge of the day: Never count God out! He is trustworthy and very mindful of what we do.

To God be the glory! Many blessings to you and have a blessed day. Give thanks to all who serve and have served in our armed forces.

Day 155

I pray that all had a grand evening. Start your day off with God, knowing that you should hope in all circumstances; no matter what the outcome may be, keep the faith! "Behold, the Lord's eye is upon those who fear Him [who revere and worship Him with awe], who wait for Him and hope in His mercy and loving-kindness" (Ps. 33:18). So this morning, brothers and sisters, be encouraged all the more; God understands what we go through—we just have to trust in Him and have faith and hope as we go through. Stay focused, God is not through with us yet!

"Wait for and expect the Lord and keep and heed His way, and He will exalt you to inherit the land; [in the end] when the wicked are cut off, you shall see it" (Ps. 37:34).

Challenge of the day: Wait and receive.

To God be the glory! Many blessings to you and have a blessed day and wait on the Lord.

Day 156

I pray that all had a grand evening. Start your day off with God knowing you must finish what you started. Finish the assignment God has given you and move to the next level. It will not always be easy, but the rewards are great. You will know when it is time to move on. It will be settled in your spirit. It's time to move on; it is just a matter of timing, and God's timing is perfect. "I will cry to God Most High, Who performs on my behalf and rewards me [Who brings to pass His purposes for me and surely completes them]!" (Ps. 57:2). So be encouraged this morning and hinder not what God has in store for you.

"To everything there is a season, and a time for every matter or purpose under heaven" (Eccles. 3:1).

Challenge of the day: Know the seasons and understand your assignments.

To God be the glory! Many blessings to you and have a blessed and powerful day, walking in the season for which you are meant.

Day 157

I pray that you all had a great evening. Start your day off with God, knowing that you must stay the course that is set before you. God desires that you remain on track with plans and visions and even purpose for your lives. It is so easy to get off track and get distracted by the things of life. Stay on course and follow the steps that God has ordered for you. "My steps have held closely to Your paths [to the tracks of the One Who has gone on before]: my feet have not slipped" (Ps. 17:5). So be encouraged this morning, sisters and brothers; God already has gone before us and has made the way plain for us to follow—through Jesus Christ the risen Savior.

"You have given plenty of room for my steps under me, that my feet would not slip" (Ps. 18:36).

Challenge of the day: Stay close to God and your feet will not slip or stray.

To God be the glory! Many blessings and have a powerful day. Stay close in Jesus' name.

Day 158

I pray that all of you are doing well. Start your day off with God, knowing that you must learn to be still sometimes, quiet your constant movement, and listen to the voice of God. "Be still and know that I am God; I will be exalted among the nations, I will be exalted in the earth" (Ps. 46:10 NKJV). When we submit to the voice of God, our directions from Him will be crystal clear. So be encouraged this day, sisters and brothers, knowing that it is okay to quiet down for a moment or two and listen to that still small voice of God.

"How precious also are Your thoughts to me, O God!
How great is the sum of them!" (Ps. 139:17 NKJV).

Challenge of the day: Silence is precious, particularly in the presence of God.

To God be the glory, many blessings, and have a powerful day. Know that the Lord is great.

Day 159

I greet you all in the wonderful name of Jesus, and I pray that each of you had a grand evening. Start your day off with God, knowing that you can and must laugh out loud sometimes. "He will yet fill your mouth with laughter [Job] and your lips with joyful shouting" (Job 8:21). Laughter is good, and we must learn to laugh—even when things are not always going our way. Laughter will cause us to forget about the pain and enjoy the spirit of rejoicing. So be encouraged this morning, sisters and brothers; no worries this morning. Laugh and enjoy what God has given us and will give us and what He will have us to do, knowing that we have another reason to shout in a victorious manner.

"O CLAP your hands, all you peoples! Shout to God with the voice of triumph and songs of joy!" (Ps. 47:1).

Challenge of the day: You cannot shout unless you know that you are victorious! Know that it is not over: God has the last say so, and we have the victory in Jesus Christ. Amen. Shout and rejoice as if you have already won the lottery of life.

To God be the glory! Many blessings to you and have a powerful day in God. Rejoice and enjoy life!

Day 160

I pray that all had a great evening. Start your day off with God knowing that you must focus on the things of God and not settle for anything. You must move out of your comfort zone and strive for excellence in all that you do. Don't settle; focus by seeking out God in everything that you do. "My soul yearns for You [O Lord] in the night, yes, my spirit within me seeks You earnestly; for [only] when Your judgments are in the earth will the inhabitants of the world learn righteousness (uprightness and right standing with God)" (Isa. 26:9). So be encouraged this morning, sisters and brothers. Seek God and focus on what He would have you to do.

"O GOD, You are my God, earnestly will I seek You; my inner self thirsts for You, my flesh longs and is faint for You, in a dry and weary land where no water is" (Ps. 63:1).

Challenge of the day: Seek God from the inside out first and watch how He will manifest Himself in our lives.

To God be the glory! Many blessings to you and have a blessed day and seek God's face.

Day 161

I pray that all is well with each of you. Start your day off with God knowing that you must come clean before Him. Clean hands and a pure heart. God desires that we present ourselves to Him in a pure manner. It is time—now more than ever—that we spend quality time in the presence of God, worshipping Him and getting direction and understanding from Him in His very presence. "Purge (clean out) the old leaven that you may be fresh (new) dough, still uncontaminated [as you are], for Christ, our Passover [Lamb], has been sacrificed" (1 Cor. 5:7). So be encouraged, sisters and brothers; God desires that we forget and leave the old stuff and come to Him anew.

"He who has clean hands and a pure heart, who has not lifted himself up to falsehood or to what is false, nor sworn deceitfully" (Ps. 24:4).

Challenge of the day: Come clean before God and be refreshed in all of your doings.

To God be the glory! Many blessings to you and have a powerful day in the Lord Jesus Christ, our Passover Lamb. Rejoice and be glad that we are alive and well in Christ Jesus! Rejoice and again I say rejoice.

Day 162

I pray that all is well with each of you. Start your day off with God knowing that you have a right to live victoriously. As a believer in Jesus Christ, why walk around like you are defeated? Don't you know that Christ Jesus defeated death and the evil one already? The trials and tribulations that you face do not mean that you are defeated; they are seasons for growth and strength. Realize who you are in the Lord: you have power, wisdom as you ask, and knowledge how to use the gifts within. Do not give up your authority when you do not have a right to give it up, because Jesus gave it to you to use for His glory and to keep the evil one in his place. You have the right to live as a victor. "Can anything separate us from Christ's love? Does it mean he no longer loves us if we have trouble or calamity, or are persecuted, or hungry, or destitute, or in danger, or threatened with death? (As the Scriptures say, 'For your sake we are killed every day; we are being slaughtered like sheep.') No, despite all these things, overwhelming victory is ours through Christ, who loved us" (Rom. 8:35-37 NLT). So be encouraged this morning and walk in the authority that God has given you; the victory is yours through Christ Jesus. Know that you are not a defeated believer because overwhelming victory is yours, so live like it!

> "For every child of God defeats this evil world, and we achieve this victory through our faith. And who can win this battle against the world? Only those who believe that Jesus is the Son of God" (1 John 5:4, 5 NLT).

Challenge of the day: The devil already is defeated, and you played a part in his defeat as a believer of Jesus Christ. No more pity parties, only victory dances. So dance your victory dance and glorify the Lord, because the battles that you face are already won. You just have to have faith, believe, and live as a victor in Christ Jesus. Give God glory!

To God be the glory! Many blessings to you and have a victorious day!

Day 163

I pray that all had an enjoyable evening. Start your day off with God knowing you must learn to give honor to God in all things. Show honor toward God in our daily actions. "So then, whether you eat or drink, or whatever you may do, do all for the honor and glory of God" (1 Cor. 10:31). So be encouraged, brothers and sisters, and honor God through everything that we do.

> "[What, what would have become of me] had I not believed that I would see the Lord's goodness in the land of the living!" (Ps. 27:13).

Challenge of the day: Live in such a manner that when God tells you something, you believe it and expect to see His goodness all around you.

To God be the glory! Many blessings to you and have a blessed day and show honor in all that you do.

Day 164

I pray that all had a grand evening. Start your day off with God, knowing that you must think on those things which are pure and wholesome. Your thought process easily can turn into action. It is imperative that you gain control of your thoughts and align them with the living Word of God. "For the rest, brethren, whatever is true, whatever is worthy of reverence and is honorable and seemly, whatever is just, whatever is pure, whatever is lovely and lovable, whatever is kind and winsome and gracious, if there is any virtue and excellence, if there is anything worthy of praise, think on and weigh and take account of these things [fix your minds on them]" (Phil. 4:8). So be encouraged this day, sisters and brothers, and think good and pure thoughts, watching your lives began to move in a closer direction toward God.

"You have put more joy and rejoicing in my heart than [they know] when their wheat and new wine have yielded abundantly" (Ps. 4:7).

Challenge of the day: The joy that God gives is unlimited, and we must experience His joy in all that we do! Let the joy of God move you into new levels, with new opportunities, in life.

To God be the glory! Many blessings to you and have a powerful worship service. Enjoy God and His presence through the risen Savior Jesus Christ! Rejoice and know that Christ is the Lord.

Day 165

I pray that all is well with each of you. Start your day off with God knowing that you must be kind toward one another. Looking out for one another is a sign of being a "brother's keeper"; sincerely showing that one cares will make a difference in others' lives. Many folk watch believers, who say they are Christians, wanting to see the real deal. They want to see Christ in us working, in order that they may believe as well. "Clothe yourselves therefore, as God's own chosen ones (His own picked representatives), [who are] purified and holy and well-beloved [by God Himself, by putting on behavior marked by] tenderhearted pity and mercy, kind feeling, a lowly opinion of yourselves, gentle ways, [and] patience [which is tireless and long-suffering, and has the power to endure whatever comes, with good temper]" (Col. 3:13). So be encouraged this morning and represent, through being kind—not only to those we know, but also to those who are estranged.

> "With the kind and merciful You will show Yourself kind and merciful, with an upright man You will show Yourself upright" (Ps. 18:25).

Challenge of the day: Find kindness within your heart and give it to others, and God will show Himself merciful and full of kindness toward you.

To God be the glory, many blessings, have an awesome day, and show kindness to all.

Day 166

I pray that all is well with each of you. Start your day off with God, knowing that you must trust God to be God while waiting on Him. Many times you may find yourselves waiting on God to do something, and you get over-zealous or anxious about it and may take things into your own hands. When God reveals to us that we must wait, then that is exactly what we must do—wait. Wait in the sense of continuing to fast and pray. Study and meditate on the Word of God. Waiting will allow the right door to open and God to set the right people in place. When you are tempted to "rush" God, do not do it. Allow God to be God! "My soul, wait only upon God and silently submit to Him; for my hope and expectation are from Him" (Ps. 62:5). So be encouraged this morning, brothers and sisters; rest easy and allow God to steer our lives. He has never lost a case, nor has He ever failed.

> "Let no one delude and deceive you with empty excuses and groundless arguments [for these sins], for through these things the wrath of God comes upon the sons of rebellion and disobedience" (Eph. 5:6).

Challenge of the day: Search and understand your surroundings and allow no one and no thing to hinder your walk of faith with God through Jesus Christ. Also understand that obedience leads to closeness, but disobedience leads one away from God.

To God be the glory, many blessings to you and have a blessed day getting understanding.

Day 167

I pray that all is well with each of you. Start your day off with God, knowing that you must believe, see, and expect the impossible! When things seem challenging and hard (at best), and there may not be a way around situations, expect the impossible to happen. You must allow your expectations to become greater than that which you see. You must visualize the impossible happening. "Now FAITH is the assurance (the confirmation, the title deed) of the things [we] hope for, being the proof of things [we] do not see and the conviction of their reality [faith perceiving as real fact what is not revealed to the senses]" (Heb. 11:1). So be encouraged this morning, brothers and sisters; expect God to reveal that which seems impossible to you in all areas of your lives. Believe, expect, and receive that which God has for you!

"He subdued peoples under us, and nations under our feet" (Ps. 47:3).

Challenge of the day: Rejoice, knowing that God protects us and listen as the enemies around us surrender to the power and the authority of God through Jesus Christ the risen Savior! Do not do anything to harm your enemies, but listen close to the voice of surrender.

To God be the glory! Many blessings and have a powerful day in God doing what is right.

Day 168

I pray that all is well with each of you. Start your day off with God knowing that you must understand the power of prayer. Prayer changes things, and God will change people, as they will to be changed. We cannot change folk; however, we can certainly pray for everyone. "Do not fret or have any anxiety about anything, but in every circumstance and in everything, by prayer and petition (definite requests), with thanksgiving, continue to make your wants known to God. And God's peace [shall be yours, that tranquil state of a soul assured of its salvation through Christ, and so fearing nothing from God and being content with its earthly lot of whatever sort that is, that peace] which transcends all understanding shall garrison and mount guard over your hearts and minds in Christ Jesus" (Phil. 4:6-7). So be encouraged this morning, brothers and sisters, and know that prayer is our key to communicating our thoughts and desires. We must ensure that we desire His will to be done in our lives.

"Pray for the peace of Jerusalem! May they prosper who love you [the Holy City]!" (Ps. 122:6).

Challenge of the day: Lift up God through prayer and know that our prayers will affect every nation in the world, yes, especially Jerusalem.

To God be the glory, many blessings, and enjoy communion with God through Jesus Christ!

Day 169

I pray that all had a grand evening. Start your day off with God, knowing that in tight and tough situations or circumstances, you must rely on God. You must trust God— no matter what the situations may look like at the beginning. Truly trust in the living God. "Therefore we will not fear, though the earth should change and though the mountains be shaken into the midst of the seas, though its waters roars and foam, though the mountains tremble at its swelling and tumult. Selah [pause, and calmly think of that]!" (Ps. 46:2-3). It may seem as if things are coming apart around us, but know that we must not be afraid of trouble or tough circumstances. We must know and think about who is actually in control. So be encouraged this morning, sisters and brothers; even though the rivers may be rough and the mountains around us may tremble, trust God and be not afraid. Amen.

"Trust (lean on, rely on, and be confident) in the Lord and do good; so shall you dwell in the land and feed surely on His faithfulness, and truly you shall be fed" (Ps. 37:3).

Challenge of the week: Trust God and live through the adversities of life. Be that conqueror that God has called you to be.

To God be the glory! Many blessings and have great day full of purpose.

Day 170

I pray that all had a good evening. Start your day off with God knowing that you must have a deep appreciation for the power of love. The power of love will cause us to withstand even the most difficult person. It will give us the power to love them beyond their difficult personality. Some folk know that they are difficult and will not do anything about it, yet we as believers must show them the power of true love in Jesus Christ. "Love bears up under anything and everything that comes, is ever ready to believe the best of every person, its hopes are fadeless under all circumstances, and it endures everything [without weakening]" (1 Cor. 13:7). So be encouraged this morning, sisters and brothers; walk in the power of love and allow others to see Christ in us.

"My heart is fixed, O God, my heart is steadfast and confident! I will sing and make melody" (Ps. 57:7).

Challenge of the day: Know that the power of the heart will cause the mind to react!

To God be the glory and many blessings and have confidence in the Lord.

Day 171

I pray that you all had a grand evening. Start your day off with God knowing that you must use the gifts He has given us wisely. Use the gifts to bring glory and honor unto the almighty and everlasting God. "In his grace, God has given us different gifts for doing certain things well. So if God has given you the ability to prophesy, speak out with as much faith as God has given you. If your gift is serving others, serve them well. If you are a teacher, teach well. If your gift is to encourage others, be encouraging. If it is giving, give generously. If God has given you leadership ability, take the responsibility seriously. And if you have the gift for showing kindness to others, do it gladly" (Rom. 12:6-8 NLT). So be encouraged this morning, brothers and sisters, and search for, know, and use the God-given gifts and talents given unto you, in order to bring glory and honor to God. Have a blessed day.

"My steps have stayed on your path; I have not wavered from following you" (Ps. 17:5 NLT).

Challenge of the day: Stay close to God and keep your feet planted where He assigns you.

To God be the glory, many blessings, and have a powerful day in the Lord. Keep the faith, be flexible, and remain focused.

Day 172

I pray that all had a safe evening yesterday. Start your day off with God knowing that we must praise God with and through singing unto Him. Sing with a glad heart and praise the Lord. Lift up your voices unto the Lord. Call on His matchless name. "Let the word [spoken by] Christ (the Messiah) have its home [in your hearts and minds] and dwell in you in [all its] richness, as you teach and admonish and train one another in all insight and intelligence and wisdom [in spiritual things, and as you sing] psalms and hymns and spiritual songs, making melody to God with [His] grace in your hearts" (Col. 3:16). So be encouraged this morning, brothers and sisters; sing and praise your way through the various issues of life. Keep the faith—God is not through with us yet! It shall not appear what we shall become. Hold on, God's grace will keep us through. Amen!

"I will sing a new song to You, O God; upon a harp, an instrument of ten strings, will I offer praises to You" (Ps. 144:9).

Challenge of the day: Praise God with your singing, no matter what you are going through in life. Offer God His just and due praise!

To God be the glory! Many blessings to you and a powerful day in the Lord Jesus Christ, the One who died for our sins and the sins of the world.

Day 173

I pray that all had a grand evening. Start your day off with God, knowing that the struggles you go through are temporary and they are for your growth. If you do not go through, how then do you expect to get to the next level of life? Struggling is not always easy; in fact, it is quite challenging, to say the least, but God's grace is more than enough to carry us through these trials of life. Not everyone will see these trials of life as a testament of growth; they will see them as failures and outright suffering, but the reality is that it is for our growth in Christ through His grace. "Moreover [let us also be full of joy now!] let us exult and triumph in our troubles and rejoice in our sufferings, knowing that pressure and affliction and hardship produce patient and unswerving endurance. And endurance (fortitude) develops maturity of character (approved faith and tried integrity). And character [of this sort] produces [the habit of] joyful and confident hope of eternal salvation. Such hope never disappoints or deludes or shames us, for God's love has been poured out in our hearts through the Holy Spirit Who has been given to us" (Rom. 5:3-5). Be of good cheer this morning, brothers and sisters; troubles do not last always!

> "Trust (lean on, rely on, and be confident) in the Lord and do good; so shall you dwell in the land and feed surely on His faithfulness, and truly you shall be fed" (Ps. 37:3).

Challenge of the day: Trust God in the midst of struggles, and you will eat the good of the harvest.

To God be the glory! Many blessings to you and have a blessed and powerful day, knowing that your struggles are over, given to God.

Day 174

I pray that all is well with each of you. Start your day off with God knowing that you must take the love of God to a greater capacity. You must love more in order to reach millions of souls. The love that has been provided to us must not go unused. Many have not tapped into the understanding of loving with cause. Jesus understands this type of love, which is why He went to the cross for us, so that we must be able to love in a greater way. Many souls are waiting and expecting us to show up and show them this type of love with cause. Certainly, there will be roadblocks and walls, but God's love will never fail and will prevail against any and everything. "For God so greatly loved and dearly prized the world that He [even] gave up His only begotten (unique) Son, so that whoever believes in (trusts in, cling to, relies on) Him shall not perish (come to destruction, be lost) but have eternal (everlasting) life" (John 3:16). We quote this verse often, and we must fully understand the plan of love and salvation in it. So be encouraged this morning, brothers and sisters; God's love is greater than any love. We must love with a cause and that cause, brothers and sisters, is for others to have a new life in Jesus Christ. Not only will others have a better, greater life, but we who are the practitioners of the faith will as well.

> "But as for me, I will enter Your house through the abundance of Your steadfast love and mercy; I will worship toward and at Your holy temple in reverent fear and awe of you" (Ps. 5:7).

Challenge of the day: Take God's love, multiply it to those in need, and watch in amazement God's response.

199

To God be the glory! Many blessings to you and have a blessed day full of the love of the living God.

Day 175

I pray that all is well with each of you. Start your day off with God knowing that you cannot survive this life without God. You cannot make it through each day without God. You must give Him praise and glory with thanksgiving in your hearts. You are never alone; it sometimes may seem like we are trailing along by ourselves, but God is right with us every step of the way. "No man shall be able to stand before you all the days of your life. As I was with Moses, so I will be with you; I will not fail you or forsake you" (Josh. 1:5). We are not alone, and we can survive everything that comes upon us, knowing that God is with us at all times. So be encouraged this morning, brothers and sisters; God is present, guiding us all the way through this journey we call life.

"I have been young and now am old, yet I have not seen the [uncompromisingly] righteous forsaken nor their seed begging bread" (Ps. 37:25).

Challenge of the day: The challenges we go through do not mean we are forsaken or that God has forgotten about us. The challenges we face simply mean growth!

To God be the glory! Many blessings to you and have a blessed day because God has not forsaken you.

Day 176

I pray that all is well with each of you. Start your day off with God, knowing that you must fight the good fight and run this race of life with endurance . . . never giving up, but moving forward in the strength and wisdom of God. This race of life will cause us to stand our ground and hold our peace (hold our mule) at times. You must know when and how to respond to every situation you come up against. Elijah the prophet understood this; he endured because the Lord was his God. King Ahab and his wife Jezebel wanted to destroy Elijah, but God delivered him and taught him endurance, even during the drought season of his life. "After a while the brook dried up because there was no rain in the land" (1 Kings 17:7). Sisters and brothers, when it seems like there is no rain and sunshine around you, it does not mean that God has forgotten about you. He always has a plan to brighten our dark and dry days; even when trouble is lurking around the corner, God has a plan for our protection. When the brook has dried up and there is no sign of the rain, look for the wheat and the oil. "For thus says the Lord, the God of Israel: The jar of meal shall not waste away or the bottle of oil fail until the day that the Lord sends rain on the earth" (1 Kings 17:14).

"My steps have held closely to Your paths [to the tracks of the One Who has gone on before]; my feet have not slipped" (Ps. 17:5).

Challenge of the day: Stay on course with God, endure the things of this life, and you will survive through Christ Jesus.

To God be the glory, many blessings! Have a blessed day, riding with the Lord.

Day 177

I pray that all is well with you. Start your day off with God knowing that happiness starts within Jesus Christ. One must truly desire to be happy with oneself. If there is no self-love or fulfillment, then how can you truly serve the needs and desires of others? No not being arrogant or overzealous, but truly taking care of our self-esteem . . . having confidence in Christ that all of our needs are met, yes even our emotional and spiritual needs. "Blessed and fortunate and happy and spiritually prosperous (in that state in which the born-again child of God enjoys His favor and salvation) are those who hunger and thirst for righteousness (uprightness and right standing with God), for they shall be completely satisfied!" (Matt. 5:6). So be encouraged this morning, sisters and brothers, and be hungry and thirsty to live well by knowing and loving who you are in Christ, with the confidence He has given to enjoy.

"As for me, I will continue beholding Your face in righteousness (rightness, justice, and right standing with You); I shall be fully satisfied, when I awake [to find myself] beholding Your form [and having sweet communion with You]" (Ps. 17:15).

Challenge of the day: Be who God has called you to be and love seeing the God in you.

To God be the glory! Many blessings and have a blessed and powerful day being who God called you to be.

Day 178

I pray that all is well with you. Start your day off with God knowing that His grace will keep you close to Him. You must strive to walk in the light and grace of God. No matter what may come upon us, God's grace is enough. Paul understood this best as he went through his many trials and tribulations of life. "And He said to me, 'My grace is sufficient for you, for My strength is made perfect in weakness.' Therefore most gladly I will rather boast in my infirmities, that the power of Christ may rest upon me" (2 Cor. 12:9 NKJV) So this morning, sisters and brothers, be encouraged knowing that God's grace is upon us and that is enough for us to survive any and all storms of life, through Jesus Christ.

> "For the LORD God is a sun and shield; the LORD will give grace and glory; no good thing will He withhold from those who walk uprightly" (Ps. 84:11 NKJV).

Challenge of the day: Fret not about the things and concerns of this world but rather live as if we know that the grace of God (the One who shields and protects us) is upon our lives.

To God be the glory, many blessings to you, and have a powerful day in the Lord. Do not look at the world for solutions, but trust in the Lord.

Day 179

I pray that all is well with you. Start your day off with God knowing that you must walk and live in forgiveness. You must forgive those who have trespassed against you, whether the occurrence happened when you were a child, in high school, college, or serving in the military. No matter where or when the offense happened, we can forgive the people (yes, even family members) who have offended us. "Brothers, listen! We are here to proclaim that through this man Jesus there is forgiveness for your sins" (Acts 13:38 NLT). Indeed, we are forgiven of our sins once we confess them before Christ; at the same time, we must be mindful to forgive those who have trespassed against us. Forgiveness is a powerful way of showing unconditional love, particularly to those who do not even know that they need forgiveness and love. So be encouraged this morning, brothers and sisters; forgive those who have transgressed you and be free to express unconditional love. Live now in the liberties of God and see how your life will change; remember forgiveness is one way of experiencing that liberty.

"The LORD of Heaven's Armies is here among us;
the God of Israel is our fortress" (Ps. 46:7 NLT).

Challenge of the day: The Lord will protect us against our enemies, but we must still operate in forgiveness.

To God be the glory! Many blessings to you and have a blessed day forgiving others.

Day 180

I stop by this morning to encourage your hearts and let you all know that everything will be okay. No matter how things may look, know that God has worked it out. Start your day off with God knowing that you must be strong and of good courage. When the giants of life come upon you and it seems like you cannot get over the mountain, know that God is for you. As changes come about in your lives, know that it is God who has equipped us to handle those changes. Stand tall, my sisters and brothers, and recognize God in the midst of our days. Even when the tears flow, do not worry, but trust God! "Be strong and courageous, for you are the one who will lead these people to possess all the land I swore to their ancestors I would give them. Be strong and very courageous. Be careful to obey all the instructions Moses gave you. Do not deviate from them, turning either to the right or to the left. Then you will be successful in everything you do" (Josh. 1:6-7 NLT). Stay strong and of good courage this morning, my sisters and brothers.

"Be still, and know that I am God! I will be honored by every nation. I will be honored throughout the world" (Ps. 46:10 NLT).

Challenge of the day: Stand still and listen to God.

To God be the glory, many blessings, and have a blessed day in the quietness of the Lord.

Day 181

I pray that all of you had a grand evening. Start your day off with God knowing that you must have effective communication with God. You must talk things over with God constantly, yes, the many issues of life. Pondering and studying the living and loving Word of God will move us even closer to the Lord our Savior. "In the morning You hear my voice, O Lord; in the morning I prepare [a prayer, a sacrifice] for You and watch and wait [for You to speak to my heart]" (Ps. 5:3). In any relationship, communication is vital to its survival. So be encouraged this morning, sisters and brothers, and open all lines of communication with the Lord Jesus Christ and others with whom we need to communicate in order to build an effective and life-changing relationship.

"But his delight and desire are in the law of the Lord, and on His law (the precepts, the instructions, the teachings of God) he habitually meditates (ponders and studies) by day and by night" (Ps. 1:2).

Challenge of the day: Make it a habit to communicate the things of God around the clock, in order to develop and improve your relationship with God and others.

To God be the glory! Many blessings to you and have a blessed day talking with the Lord.

Day 182

I pray that all is well with you. Start your day off with God, knowing you must have compassion toward others as God has toward you. Walking in compassion can be fulfilling through your daily communion with God, knowing that you are a part of the very compassionate family of God. "Indeed we count them blessed who endure. You have heard of the perseverance of Job and seen the end intended by the Lord — that the Lord is very compassionate and merciful" (James 5:11 NKJV). So be encouraged this day and have compassion toward those in need, even those who may frustrate you: love them and have compassion on them anyway.

"Though He causes grief, yet He will show compassion according to the multitude of His mercies" (Lam. 3:32 NJKV).

Challenge of the day: Have compassion toward others; even during your trials, have a compassionate heart.

To God be the glory! Many blessings to you and have a great day full of love, mercy, and compassion.

Day 183

I pray that you had a grand evening yesterday. Start your day off with God, knowing that you are all unique ... no finger-prints are the same. All of our personalities are different, and God did this on purpose. This gives us some understanding of how the knowledge of God is powerful enough to allow us to be ourselves in His image. Being unique and different is not a bad thing. In fact, it is welcomed to be your own unique self. "Thank you for making me so wonderfully complex! Your workmanship is marvelous—how well I know it" (Ps. 139:14 NLT). So be encouraged, sisters and brothers; God's love for us is great because He made us.

"Such knowledge is too wonderful for me, too great for me to understand!" (Ps. 139:6 NLT).

Challenge of the day: Go after the knowledge of God and understand your uniqueness.

To God be the glory, many blessings, and have a powerful day in the Lord seeking the knowledge of the Lord.

Day 184

I pray that all is well with you. Start your day off with God knowing that He will provide true friendship toward you. Friendship is important to God; He desires to be our friend, and at the same time wants us to have healthy friendships among one another. In fact, relationships are vital, symbolizing true connection with one another. "You are My friends if you keep on doing the things which I command you to do. I do not call you servants (slaves) any longer, for the servant does not know what his master is doing (working out). But I have called you My friends, because I have made known to you everything that I have heard from my Father. [I have revealed to you everything that I have learned from Him.]" (John 15:14, 15). So be encouraged this morning, sisters and brothers; true friendship starts with God through Jesus Christ. Always pray and ask God to surround you with the right people in your life.

"The man of many friends [a friend of all the world] will prove himself a bad friend, but there is a friend who sticks closer than a brother" (Prov. 18:24).

Challenge of the day: Choose our friends wisely and ensure we are true to our true Friend, Christ.

To God be the glory! Many blessings and have a blessed day being a friend of God.

Day 185

I pray that all is well with you. Start your day off with God knowing that you need to put your shield of faith up. You need to hold your shield of faith up high, hard, and strong. There are attacks against believers in all areas: marriages, finances, career, character, health, and the church in general. Why? Time is getting short, and we must be on our guard. Stand your ground and hold on to your faith. Indeed, we must walk in the entire armor of God; however, this morning, hold of the shield of faith. "In addition to all of these, hold up the shield of faith to stop the fiery arrows of the devil" (Eph. 6:16 NLT). So be encouraged this morning, brothers and sisters; keep you shield up and know that God's shield is already around us. He has us covered by the blood of the Lamb, Jesus Christ.

"The sacrifice you desire is a broken and repentant heart, O God" (Ps. 51:17 NLT).

Challenge of the day: Come clean before God and stand on your faith, no matter what is going on.

To God be the glory, many blessings, and have a blessed day being protected by God.

Day 186

I pray that all had a grand evening. Start your day off with God, knowing you can be restored and forgiven, no matter what has happened in your lives or what you have done. It is a matter of going to God and asking Him to restore you. God will restore you because He loves us unconditionally. "In just a short time he will restore us, so that we may live in His presence" (Hos. 6:2 NLT). So be encouraged this morning knowing we can live in the presence of God through restoration.

"He renews my strength. He guides me along right paths, bringing honor to his name" (Ps. 23:3 NLT).

Challenge of the day: Restoration comes when we decide to surrender to God.

To God be the glory and many blessings. Have a powerful day in the Lord being restored.

Day 187

I pray that all had a great day. Start your day off with God knowing that you must seek God's will above your own will at all times. This will require us also to search and ask for God's wisdom in all that we do. "Trust in the Lord with all your heart; do not depend on your own understanding. Seek his will in all you do, and he will show you which path to take" (Prov. 3:5, 6 NLT). So be encouraged this morning, sisters and brothers; seek the will of God for your lives and you will experience His wisdom.

> "Wisdom is a tree of life to those who embrace her; happy are those who hold her tightly" (Prov. 3:18 NLT).

Challenge of the day: The will of God will never take us where His grace cannot keep us, and we must embrace His wisdom in order to know His will.

To God be the glory, many blessings, and have a blessed day doing the will of God.

Day 188

I pray that all had a marvelous evening. Start your day off with God knowing that you must examine yourself. You must ensure you are doing all you can to line up with the Word of God. Our lifestyles must be in alignment with the Word, the way, and the will of God. "Let us test and examine our ways, and let us return to the Lord!" (Lam. 3:40). There will be many trials that will come about in our lives, and the test will be how we will respond to the crises and trials of life. Be encouraged this morning, sisters and brothers; our lives are at stake and we must be confident that our connections with Jesus Christ are sealed and secured through His love and our lifestyles.

"For the word of the Lord is right; and all His work is done in faithfulness" (Ps. 33:4).

Challenge of the day: Doing what is right is not always popular, but living up to the Word of God shows faithfulness.

To God be the glory, many blessings, and have a blessed day being faithful.

Day 189

I pray that all had a grand evening. Start your day off with God knowing that forgiveness is vital in your personal relationship with Christ. You must forgive those who have offended you and forgive yourself. "But there is a great difference between Adam's sin and God's gracious gift. For the sin of this one man, Adam, brought death to many. But even greater is God's wonderful grace and his gift of forgiveness to many through this other man, Jesus Christ" (Rom. 5:15 NLT). So be encouraged this morning, sisters and brothers, and move toward forgiving others and ourselves, because life is too precious and full of great expectations to hold on to small grudges.

"He forgives all my sins and heals all my diseases" (Ps. 103:3 NLT).

Challenge of the day: Jesus forgives all of our sins. Why can we not forgive also, be healed of the deep-rooted issues of life, and learn to live, love, and forgive each day through Jesus Christ?

To God be the glory, many blessings, and have a powerful day walking in your healing!

Day 190

I pray that all is well with you. Start your day off with God, knowing that He knew you from the very beginning of your existence and He knows how story will end. What will you do with the knowledge and gifts that are given to you by God? "Before I formed you in the womb I knew [and] approved of you [as My chosen instrument], and before you were born I separated and set you apart, consecrating you; [and] I appointed you as a prophet to the nations" (Jer. 1:5). As God Himself revealed His purpose to Jeremiah, He longs and desires to do the same for us today. So be encouraged this morning, sisters and brothers; God wants us to know our purpose and understand that we were set apart to do His will and not that of our own.

> "We are assured and know that [God being a partner in their labor] all things work together and are [fitting into a plan] for good to and for those who love God and are called according to [His] design and purpose. For those whom He foreknew [of who He was aware and loved beforehand], He also destined from the beginning [foreordaining them] to be molded into the image of His Son [and share inwardly His likeness], that He might become the firstborn among many brethren" (Rom. 8:28-29).

Challenge of the day: There are some things in life we cannot hide from . . . our destiny!

To God be the glory, many blessings, and have a blessed and powerful day in the Lord walking in your destiny.

Day 191

It is a great pleasure to greet you all this morning, and I pray that you all had a grand evening. Start your day off with God, knowing that you can take refuge in Him and you are protected by His unfailing love. When the enemy thinks we are down, he is sadly mistaken, because protection will never fail us. God's love is strong, and it is indeed a shield around us. "But let all who take refuge in you rejoice; let them sing joyful praises forever. Spread your protection over them, that all who love your name may be filled with joy. For you bless the godly, O LORD; you surround them with your shield of love" (Ps. 5:11-12 NLT). So be encouraged, sisters and brothers; no matter what things may seem like now, know that we are covered by God's shield of love. Amen.

"The Lord gives his people strength. The Lord blesses them with peace" (Ps. 29:11 NLT).

Challenge of the day: Know that God will give us strength through the trying times, and His peace is like none other.

To God be the glory, many blessings, and have a blessed and peaceful day!

Day 192

I pray that you all had a grand day. Start your day off with God, knowing you must not hold on to the past, but move forward in life with Christ. You must let the past be the past; let it go and grab hold of your future with Christ Jesus. In our lives, if we see no progress, it is because we are holding on to that which God is telling us to let go. Be not apprehensive about letting those things go which hinder your relationship with Christ Jesus. Let it go! "No, dear brothers and sisters, I have not achieved it, but I focus on this one thing: Forgetting the past and looking forward to what lies ahead, I press on to reach the end of the race and receive the heavenly prize for which God, through Christ Jesus, is calling us" (Phil. 3:13-14 NLT). So be encouraged this morning, brothers and sisters; God is not slack concerning His promises, and we must hold on to them and let go of our past. Let the past be the past the past and bury it.

"Only ask and I will give you the nations as your inheritance, the whole earth as your possession" (Ps. 2:8 NLT).

Challenge of the day: Why live in the past when our inheritance from God awaits us when we ask for it? Go for what God has ahead of you and leave the past behind.

To God be the glory, many blessings, and have an awesome day in God.

Day 193

I pray that all is well with you. Start your day off with God knowing that you must be mindful of what you think. You need to ensure that your thoughts line up with the Word of the living God. If your thoughts are not pure, then you need to rebuke those thoughts. Thoughts become action; everything that happens starts with a thought. "[Inasmuch as we] refute arguments and theories and reasonings and every proud and lofty thing that sets itself up against the [true] knowledge of God; and we lead every thought and purpose away captive into the obedience of Christ (the Messiah, the Anointed One)" (2 Cor. 10:5). So be encouraged this day, brothers and sisters, knowing that we must control our thoughts and not act out those that are not pure or in line with the Word of the living God.

"The Lord tests and proves the [unyieldingly] righteous, but His soul abhors the wicked and him who loves violence" (Ps. 11:5).

Challenge of the day: Do not let your thoughts cause you to miss God or allow you to be unruly, but allow them to cause you to live uprightly before God.

To God be the glory! Many blessings to you and have a powerful worship experience and think about what you do.

Day 194

I pray that all had a grand evening. Start your day off with God, knowing you must walk in unconditional love and not become judgmental. When you become more judgmental of others, you forget that they need love also. The power of love will change folk faster than being judged. "Judge not, that you be not judged. For with what judgment you judge, you will be judged; and with the measure you use, it will be measured back to you. And why do you look at the speck in your brother's eye, but do not consider the plank in your own eye?" (Matt. 7:1-3 NKJV). So be encouraged this morning, sisters and brothers; God's love and judgment are real, and as ambassadors of Christ, the accountability is greater on us to do that which is right. Knowingly, we must do that which is pleasing to God in all areas of our lives.

"The Lord shall preserve you from all evil; He shall preserve your soul. The Lord shall preserve your going out and your coming in from this time forth, and even forevermore" (Ps. 121:7-8 NKJV).

Challenge of the day: Live right and do well, knowing that God is our Keeper and Protector, who watches our every move.

To God be the glory, many blessings, and have a powerful day being kept in the Lord.

Day 195

I pray that all had a grand evening, starting your day off with God and knowing you must sing His praises. You must praise the Lord at all times. You must lift His name up on high. He is Lord and God, and you must sing with your whole heart unto Him. Yes, even if your voice may not sound like a famous singer, it should not stop you from singing unto the Lord. "I will thank the LORD because he is just; I will sing praise to the name of the LORD Most High" (Ps. 7:17 NLT). No matter what we are going through, we must shout and sing praises unto the Lord. Be encouraged this morning, brothers and sisters; God loves the praises of His people. So rejoice and be glad! God honors our praises unto Him.

"I will be filled with joy because of you. I will sing praises to your name, O Most High" (Ps. 9:2 NLT).

Challenge of the day: Sing praises toward God in spite of what is going on in your life. Know that He is God and can handle any and everything we are going through, so praise God anyhow!

To God to be the glory! Many blessings and have a blessed day, singing unto the Lord.

Day 196

I pray that all had a great evening. Start your day off with God, knowing that God's smile is upon your life as a way of showing you His favor and that He is pleased with your lifestyle. When God's smile is upon us, the people around us will know it and understand it. These people will begin to respect and cherish the God in us. The presence of God's smile upon our lives will determine the close relationship we have with the Lord. "May the LORD bless you and protect you. May the LORD smile on you and be gracious to you. May the LORD show you his favor and give you his peace" (Num. 6:24-26 NLT). The Lord told Moses to pass these blessings on to Aaron and his son, as a special blessing. This was a direct assurance that God would be with His people. So be encouraged, sisters and brothers; God's blessings are upon us and His smile is upon us as well. In addition, as God blesses us, we must pass His blessings on to others.

"May God be merciful and bless us. May His face smile with favor on us." (Ps. 67:1 NLT).

Challenge of the day: Walk in the favor of God, knowing His smile is upon us. We must allow His smile to be infectious to others all around us.

To God be the glory, many blessings, and have a powerful day smiling.

Day 197

I pray that you all had a grand evening. Start your day off with God, knowing that there is nothing that can surpass the power of God's love. If you as a believer would walk in the power of God's love, you would truly change and improve society. Love can move mountains and cover a multitude of sin. Love never fails. (Refer to 1 Cor. 13.) Jesus tells His disciples, "So now I am giving you a new commandment: Love each other. Just as I have loved you, you should love each other. Your love for one another will prove to the world that you are my disciples" (John 13:34-35 NLT). As we walk in the power of God's love, let us be mindful of who we are representing. So be encouraged this morning, brothers and sisters; God's love will prevail, and we must show His love in an unconditional manner—even to those who do not believe in the power of love.

"We know how much God loves us, and we have put our trust in his love. God is love, and all who live in love live in God, and God lives in them" (1 John 4:16 NLT).

Challenge of the day: Allow the power of God's love to reside in us, so we can live and love others as God commands.

To God be the glory, many blessings, and have a day full of giving unconditional love.

Day 198

I pray that all had a glorious evening. Start your day off with God knowing that it is He who will give you the strength to hold on. God will give you the strength when you think you can no longer handle things in your life. It is God who will lift us up; we must rejoice and be glad, knowing that God cares so much for us that He gave us the perfect gift His only son Jesus. We must know that it is through Him we can keep on living an upright life. "Don't be afraid, for I am with you. Don't be discouraged, for I am your God. I will strengthen you and help you. I will hold you up with my victorious right hand" (Isa. 41:10 NLT). So be encouraged this morning, sisters and brothers; God has our back and will carry us through each day! Hold on, Jesus is on the scene.

> "If I ride the wings of the morning, if I dwell by the farthest oceans, even there your hand will guide me, and your strength will support me" (Ps. 139:9, 10 NLT).

Challenge of the day: No matter where we are in life, we must understand that God is present. He is the Source we must know, because He is the source of our strength.

To God be the glory, many blessings, and have a blessed and victorious day!

Day 199

I pray that all is well with you. Start your day off with God, knowing that you must seek and ask for understanding. There is more information available to us today than ever before. Many traditions, both good and bad, but we must seek and ask God for understanding of all things. Many traditions are passed down that are not in alignment with the Word of God, and we are doing things without understanding. Please seek understanding, and we will have a greater appreciation of what Christ really did for us. "Your hands have made me and fashioned me; give me understanding, that I may learn Your commandments" (Ps. 119:73 NKJV). Be encouraged, brothers and sisters; God's love is unconditional and our sins are forgiven when we ask, because of Jesus Christ, who died on the cross.

"Jesus said to her, 'I am the resurrection and the life. He who believes in Me, though he may die, he shall live. And whoever lives and believes in Me shall never die. Do you believe this?'" (John 11:25-26 NKJV).

Challenge of the day: Believe and live. Gain understanding and know why and for whom you live.

To God be the glory! Many blessings to you and have a blessed, life-giving, and life-gaining day. Gain your life back through Jesus Christ.

Day 200

I pray that all had a great evening. Start your day off with God knowing that His mercies are new every day. You must learn to take advantage of every opportunity to serve God and others. Yes, even our spouses and children. Showing the love of God must first start at home and must be reflected each day. God's grace and mercy allows opportunities to make sure we make things right, by being honest with ourselves and others, doing that which pleases God. "Surely goodness and mercy shall follow me all the days of my life; and I will dwell in the hose of the LORD forever" (Ps. 23:6 NKJV). So be encouraged this morning, brothers and sisters; we have another opportunity to make things right with God and others because of God's mercy.

> "But the wisdom that is from above is first pure, then peaceable, gentle, willing to yield, full of mercy and good fruits, without partiality and without hypocrisy" (James 3:17 NKJV).

Challenge of the day: Honesty is the best answer, and wisdom will cause one to be honest.

To God be the glory, many blessings, and have a blessed and powerful day.

Day 201

I pray that all had a grand evening. Start your day off with God knowing that you must possess the right attitude toward life. You must be happy with who you are in God. Possessing the correct attitude means you must have great and godly thoughts. Our thought process must line up with the Word of God. "And now, dear brothers and sisters, one final thing. Fix your thoughts on what is true, and honorable, and right, and pure, and lovely, and admirable. Think about things that are excellent and worthy of praise" (Phil. 4:8 NLT). Having the right attitude toward life will cause your life to be even better, because your mind is focused on the things of God. So be encouraged this morning, brothers and sisters; God answers our prayers according to His will, but our attitude rests within us.

"For the despondent, every day brings trouble; for the happy heart, life is a continual feast" (Prov. 15:15 NLT).

Challenge of the day: You are what you eat has been said, but the reality is how you live displays who you are. (As an example, examine Jesus' life.)

To God be the glory! Many blessings to you and have a blessed and great week.

Day 202

I pray that all had a grand evening. Start your day off with God knowing that you must walk by faith and not by sight. Walk in the ways of God, not as man would have you to walk. Walk as we are called to walk: as the light of the world and the salt of the earth. Preserving and spreading the good news of Jesus Christ, the one who died on the cross for our sins and the sins of the entire world! "You are the light of the world—like a city on a hilltop that cannot be hidden. No one lights a lamp and then puts it under a basket. Instead, a lamp is placed on a stand, where it gives light to everyone in the house. In the same way, let your good deeds shine out for all to see, so that everyone will praise your heavenly Father" (Matt. 5:14-16 NLT). Walk into our assignments from God knowing that we were called, anointed, and chosen to do the things that God has placed in our hearts, which will bring Him glory and honor. Our walk must be a faith-based walk, based not on what we see but what we believe. Be encouraged this morning, sisters and brothers, knowing that God honors our walk with understanding that it is our faith in Him that will move His heart.

"If a person does not repent, God will sharpen his sword; he will bend and string his bow" (Ps. 7:12 NLT).

Challenge of the day: Repentance is necessary for a strong walk and life of faith.

To God be the glory! Many blessings and have a blessed day and walk close to the Lord.

Day 203

I pray that all had a grand evening. Start your day off with God, knowing that you need take off the masks you often wear. Unmask yourself and allow the real and true you stand up and out for God. Many wear masks to cover up things, but the reality is we cannot hide from God. He knows who we really are, although we often have identity crises when we are around certain people and pretend to be someone else. The Word of God gives many descriptions of who we are in God, and we must read and study the Word to know who we are in God and not try to pretend to be someone else. We must love ourselves as God Himself created us to be. "For He made Him who knew no sin to be sin for us, that we might become the righteousness of God in Him" (2 Cor. 5:21 NKJV). So be encouraged this morning, brothers and sisters; unmask yourself, recognize who you are in God, and maximize your potential to glorify God.

"But You, O Lord, are a shield for me, My glory and the One who lifts up my head" (Ps. 3:3 NKJV).

Challenge of the day: Why wear a mask, when God has us covered? Why be fearful of what others think about us, when God has revealed who He is to us and who we are to Him? Take the mask off and know who you really are in God.

To God be the glory, many blessings, and have a blessed day being who God made you to be.

Day 204

I pray that all is well with each of you. Start your day off with God knowing that you must live by faith. Our faith walk can and will determine great outcomes of all of your situations and circumstances. Our faith must be strong and solid . . . unmovable when things look bleak and dim. "And my righteous ones will live by faith. But I will take no pleasure in anyone who turns away" (Heb. 10:38 NLT). Be encouraged this morning, sisters and brothers, knowing that it is our faith that will cause God to move and act on our behalf. Have a blessed day and enjoy your worship experience with God through faith.

"Faith is the confidence that what we hope for will actually happen; it gives us assurance about things we cannot see" (Heb. 11:1 NLT).

Challenge of the day: Walk and live like things already are worked out in our lives.

To God be the glory! Many blessings to you and have a powerful day, having confidence in the Lord.

Day 205

I pray that you all had a grand evening. Start your day off with God knowing that you must live in the truth. Live in the truth of His Word, who God is and the truth about yourself. If we cannot live in the truth of all things, then how can we really worship God in spirit and truth? "And you will know the truth, and the truth will set you free" (John 8:32 NLT). Being free to live in truth is indeed liberating, to a point of yearning to always live in the truth of all things, particularly those that pertain to God. "So if the Son sets your free, you are truly free" (John 8:36 NLT). So be encouraged this morning, brothers and sisters; God is liberating us to move forward in His Word and His will. He does not want us to be bound by the things of this world. He deserves to be worshipped in spirit and in truth through our daily living.

"I will walk in freedom, for I have devoted myself to your commandments" (Ps. 119:45 NLT).

Challenge of the day: Live in freedom, and you will experience a lifetime of living in liberty with God.

To God be the glory! Many blessings and have a blessed day, experiencing the liberty of the Lord.

Day 206

I pray that all is well with each of you. Start your day off with God knowing that you must honor Him. Honor God in all that we do, say, act, and yes, even think. To honor God is to respect, reverence, and worship Him for who He is as God of all. To make it personal, who God is to you and what does it means to you to honor Him? When we say we honor God, we must show it. To honor is an action word: a sign or symbol of respect in high regard. "Honor the LORD, you heavenly beings; honor the LORD for his glory and strength. Honor the LORD for the glory of His name. Worship the LORD in the splendor of His holiness" (Ps. 29:1, 2 NLT). Be encouraged, brother and sisters, that God knows and understands your hearts. We must honor Him from the depths of our hearts. We must show honor unto Him in all that we do, and He will in turn honor us.

"Open up, ancient gates! Open up, ancient doors, and let the King of glory enter" (Ps. 24:7 NLT).

Challenge of the day: Open our hearts to receive and honor the King of glory. As David rendered honor and made way for the Lord to enter, let us make way for the Lord to enter every area of our lives. May God bless each of you.

To God be the glory! Many blessings to you and have a blessed day and receive the glory of the Lord.

Day 207

I pray that all is well with you. Start your day off with God knowing that you must give your best as a representative of God, giving your best in regard to all areas of your lives. Just as the Lord God gave us His best and continues to do so with everything that He gives us. We must strive daily to give our best. "For God loves the world so much that he gave his one and only Son, so that everyone who believes in him will not perish but have eternal life" (John 3:16 NLT). Be encouraged this morning, sisters and brothers, that God's gifts to us are unmatched. Because He gives us the best, we also must give our best, knowing that the best is always coming (neverending with God). Have a blessed and awesome day.

"The Lord is my shepherd; I have all that I need" (Ps. 23:1 NLT).

Challenge of the day: No need to worry about what we need; all of our needs have been met by the One who gives and offers us the best.

To God be the glory! Many blessings to you and have a powerful day in the Lord. Expect miracles, and they will happen.

Day 208

I pray that all had a grand evening. Start your day off with God knowing that you must thirst after righteousness. Having a true desire to live uprightly before the Lord is a must. Living right will cause others to see the light within us all. God earnestly desires to see the light and the righteousness in us all. Strive to live rightly and to live in love with all people. "God blesses those who hunger and thirst for justice, for they will be satisfied" (Matt. 5:6 NLT). Be encouraged this morning, brothers and sisters; allow your light to shine through living uprightly before the almighty God. Be encouraged that God's love is true and powerful enough to break all barriers of life.

"Be exalted, O God, above the highest heavens! May your glory shine over all the earth" (Ps. 57:5 NLT).

Challenge of the day: Exalt the Lord through your lifestyle and allow His glory to rest upon your life.

To God be the glory! Many blessings to you and have glorious day in God.

Day 209

I pray that all had a great and powerful day in the Lord. Start your day off with God knowing that You must honor His name. You must honor God's name in whatever you do . . . how you live, how you respond and react to the things and issues of life. You are His representatives, and His name must be glorified and His honor not tainted. "Then those who feared the LORD spoke with each other, and the LORD listened to what they said. In his presence, a scroll of remembrance was written to record the names of those who feared him and always thought about the honor of his name" (Mal. 3:16 NLT). Be encouraged this morning, brothers and sisters; God never forgets those who honor, respect, love, and fear Him.

"You keep track of all my sorrows. You have collected all my tears in your bottle. You have recorded each one in your book" (Ps. 56:8 NLT).

Challenge of the day: God knows and understands what we go through daily. He keeps track of what we do and go through, and His mercy has been given unto us.

To God be the glory! Many blessings to you and have a blessed day, walking in understanding and God's mercy.

Day 210

I pray that all is well with you. Start your day off with God, knowing that God's gift of life is eternal. Your sin is paid for through Jesus Christ, but you must be willing to repent and not die in it, BECAUSE the cost for you to bear is heaven. "For the wages which sin pays is death, but the [bountiful] free gift of God is eternal life through (in union with) Jesus Christ our Lord" (Rom. 6:23). So be encouraged this morning and know that you do not have the power or resources to pay your sins, Jesus did it for you. He gave His life for you. Receive His gift of life and let go of the sinful habits.

"To those who by patient persistence in well-doing [springing from piety] seek [unseen but sure] glory and honor and [the eternal blessedness of] immortality, He will give eternal life" (Rom. 2:7).

Challenge of the day: Be patient in living right for Christ, and you will receive eternal life.

To God be the glory, many blessings, and have a blessed day and be patient.

Day 211

I pray that all had a great and powerful evening in the Lord. Start your day off with God knowing that you must be a slave to righteousness and not to sin. Sin will lead to death, and you must surrender to doing that which is right and pleasing in the sight of God. "But thank God, though you were once slaves of sin, you have become obedient with all your heart to the standard of teaching in which you were instructed and to which you were committed. And having been set free from sin, you have become the servants of righteousness (of conformity to the divine will in thought, purpose, and action)" (Rom. 6:17-18). So be encouraged this morning and become a servant of righteousness.

"And you will know the Truth, and the Truth will set you free" (John 8:32).

Challenge of the day: Be truthful and do the right things and experience the freedom in the Lord.

To God be the glory! Many blessings to you and have a blessed day living righteously before the Lord.

Day 212

I pray that all is well with each of you. Start your day off with God knowing that you must seek Him first in all things. Seeking God for His answers is an honor and a privilege. God desires for us to commune with Him daily, in fact as often as possible. God wants to know about even the simplest thing in our lives. "Seek the Kingdom of God above all else, and live righteously, and he will give you everything you need" (Matt. 6:33 NLT). Many times we may forget about the small things and concentrate on asking God for the big things, but we must be mindful that God can turn the little things into big things. Be encouraged this morning, brothers and sisters; God's plan is perfect, and we must seek Him all the more. Have a blessed day.

> "Once I was young, and now I am old. Yet I have never seen the godly abandoned or their children begging for bread" (Ps. 37:25 NLT).

Challenge of the day: Focus on God and see how things will change for you and your environment of influence.

To God be the glory, many blessings, and have a great day focusing on the Lord.

Day 213

I pray that all had a great evening. Start your day off with God knowing that you must yearn to be in His presence. You must strive daily to get into the presence of God. It is in His presence that we will find peace, understanding, protection, guidance, love, joy, and a willingness to live a holy and upright life. Seek the Lord while He may be found. Search for Him and you will find Him. "The one thing I ask of the Lord—the thing I seek most—is to live in the house of the LORD all the days of my life, delighting in the LORD's perfections and meditating in his Temple" (Ps. 27:4 NLT). Be encouraged, brothers and sisters, this morning, for God is not far from us at all. We must seek His presence no matter where we are. Have blessed day.

> "And so, dear brothers and sisters, we can boldly enter heaven's Most Holy Place because of the blood of Jesus. By His death, Jesus opened a new and life-giving way through the curtain into the Most Holy Place. And since we have a great High Priest who rules over God's house, let us go right into the presence of God with sincere hearts fully trusting him. For our guilty consciences have been sprinkled with Christ's blood to make us clean, and our bodies have been washed with pure water" (Heb. 10:19-22 NLT).

Challenge of the day: We must go boldly with a sincere heart into the presence of God; He is waiting to commune with us.

To God be the glory, many blessings, and have a great day being sincere.

Day 214

I pray that all is well with you. Start your day off with God knowing that He reigns over everything. He reigns forever. "Tell all the nations, 'The Lord reigns!' The world stands firm and cannot be shaken. He will judge all peoples fairly" (Ps. 96:10 NLT). God's reign is a just reign, and His judgments are just across all barriers. Be encouraged this morning, brothers and sisters; God reigns in everything and His reign is from everlasting to everlasting, never ending. He has everything under control, yes, even the numbers of hair on our very heads. And as a nation, we must lift up the name of the Lord.

"The LORD is king! Let the nations tremble! He sits on his throne between the cherubim. Let the whole earth quake!" (Ps. 99:1 NLT).

Challenge of the day: Remember through the day that the Lord is King and is a just King, and the nations must praise and glorify Him. Pray for our nation, pray for our nation.

To God be the glory! Many blessings to you and have a blessed day and pray always.

Day 215

I pray that you had a grand evening. Start your day off with God knowing that He knows and understands your hearts and intentions. God is all understanding, and He knows the secret things in our hearts; there is nothing hidden from God, good or bad intentions. "Search me, O God, and know my heart; test me and know my anxious thoughts. Point out anything in me that offends you, and lead me along the path of everlasting life" (Ps. 139:23-24 NLT). Be encouraged, brothers and sisters, that God knows and understands the things we go through and the things we desire to do to please Him.

"Guard your heart above all else, for it determines the course of your life" (Prov. 4:23 NLT).

Challenge of the day: Protect your heart and the thoughts therein. No one needs to know every secret that God reveals to you; some may not understand like God understands. In other words, be careful how you share and with whom you share things. Not everyone has your best intentions in mind.

To God be the glory, many blessings, and have a blessed and powerful day.

Day 216

I pray that you all had a great evening. Start your day off with God knowing that you are an overcomer. You can overcome any situation or circumstance in Christ Jesus, no matter what it may be what obstacle is in our lives. "Guide my steps by your word, so I will not be overcome by evil" (Ps. 119:133 NLT). Be encouraged this morning, brothers and sisters, that we are guided by the One who will cause us to overcome situation in life and be victorious.

"I have told you all this so that you may have peace in me. Here on earth you will have many trials and sorrows. But take heart, because I have overcome the world" (John 16:33 NLT).

Challenge of the day: Fret not, for we belong to the great One, Jesus Christ, and in Him we are overcomers, because He has overcome the world through the death on the cross and His resurrection.

To God be the glory, many blessings, and have a great day (overcomers).

Day 217

I pray that you all are having a grand evening. Start your day off with God, knowing that God is for you and not against you. God is indeed willing and able to carry and protect us. "What then shall we then say to these things? If God is for us, who can be against us?" (Rom. 8:31 NKJV). The notion that God is for us makes things in this life a lot better. Who can fight against God? Who would want to fight against God in their right mind? No one! God is all-powerful and all-knowing, yet He has an understanding heart full of love. Be encouraged this day, brothers and sisters: God is on our side! What a joyous feeling, knowing that God looks out for us with our best interests in mind.

"If it had not been the LORD who was on our side, when men rose up against us" (Ps. 124:2 NKJV).

Challenge of the week: Fret not concerning evildoers, trust the Lord who is on our side.

To God be the glory, many blessings, and have an awesome day trusting in the Lord.

Day 218

I pray that you had a great evening. Start your day off with God knowing that you must live in a righteous and an uncompromising way. Our hearts must be aligned with the Word of God, staying focused on what God would have us all to do and accomplish for His glory and honor. We cannot compromise our character, because we represent Christ Jesus. "The eyes of the Lord are toward the [uncompromisingly] righteous and His ears are open to their cry" (Ps. 34:15). Be encouraged this morning, brothers and sisters, that God is watching us. See our goodness and righteousness in Him; in spite of what others are saying and doing, God knows His own.

> "The Lord judges the people; judge me, O Lord, and do me justice according to my righteousness [my rightness, justice, and right standing with You] and according to the integrity that is in me" (Ps. 7:8).

Challenge of the day: Live a righteous life for the honor and glory of God and do not let your integrity be at stake.

To God be the glory! Many blessings to you and have a powerful day in the Lord, giving Him glory and honor.

Day 219

I pray that you had a grand evening. Start your day off with God knowing that you must fear Him. You must fear God to the point of falling in loving with Him on a regular basis. Fear, as in reverence, Him. Respect Him, understand Him, appreciate Him, adore Him, honor Him, and love Him to the max. When we truly begin to reverence our heavenly Father, we will see the favor of God on our lives, and it will affect every area of our lives. "How joyful are those who fear the LORD—all who follow His ways! You will enjoy the fruit of your labor. How joyful and prosperous you will be! Your wife will be like a fruitful grapevine, flourishing within your home. Your children will be like vigorous young olive trees as they sit around your table. That is the LORD's blessing for those who fear him" (Ps. 128:1-4 NLT). So be encouraged this morning, brothers and sisters; fear the Lord and live a long and good life through trusting and resting on Jesus Christ.

"For the angel of the LORD is a guard; he surrounds and defends all who fear him" (Ps. 34:7 NLT).

Challenge of the day: Fear the Lord and live knowing that He sends His angels to guard and protect us.

To God be the glory, many blessings, and have an awesome day.

Day 220

I pray that you all had a grand evening. Start your day off with God, knowing that you must rejoice and give Him praise at all times, particularly when you are going through trials and tribulations. Be not faint-hearted, my brothers and sisters; only trust and believe that God will bring us out. Our trials are indeed blessings yet revealed. "You have given me greater joy than those who have abundant harvests of grain and new wine. In peace I will lie down and sleep, for you alone, O LORD, will keep me safe" (Ps. 4:7-8 NLT). Be encouraged, brothers and sisters, that God's joy is irremovable. We must display His joy in our lives, regardless of how things may seem.

"Come, everyone! Clap your hands! Shout to God with joyful praise!" (Ps. 47:1 NLT).

Challenge of the day: Praise God and lift up your hands with a joyful heart. Shout unto the Lord, knowing that He desires and deserves all the praise, glory, and honor. Serve the Lord with a glad heart in every assignment He has given to you.

To God be the glory, many blessings, and have a blessed and prosperous day!

Day 221

I pray that all is well with each of you. Start your day off with God knowing that He is committed to keeping His Word. God's Word is powerful, and it will accomplish that which it set out to do. No matter what happens, God's Word is true and we can rely on Him and His Words. We must, my brothers and sisters, be thirsty and hungry for the Word of God. "Beautiful girls and strong young men will grow faint in that day, thirsting for the LORD's word" (Amos 8:13 NLT). Is there a spiritual famine in the land, where folk are starving for the living Word of God? Are we as committed to keeping God's Word as He the Lord is true to keeping His Word? Fret not, my brothers and sisters, and be encouraged, knowing that we must not live by bread alone but by every word that comes from the mouth of God. (Refer to Matt. 4:4.) We do not have to starve spiritually; God's Word is available and ready for usage. If we do not know that Word, how then can we apply it?

"Heaven and earth will disappear, but my words will never disappear" (Matt. 24:35 NLT).

Challenge of the day: Stick to Word of God, it will never pass away. Cling to it, and it will sustain your life forever.

To God be the glory! Many blessings to you and have an awesome day and stay in the Word.

Day 222

I pray that all of you had a grand day. Start your day off with God knowing that He will not allow trouble to last always. We must keep the faith, believing that God will keep us and protect us at all costs. "I took my troubles to the LORD; I cried out to him, and he answered my prayer" (Ps. 120:1 NLT). My brothers and sisters, we must believe and have the will and strength to hope for a better tomorrow, in the midst of despair and trouble, knowing that God will keep us and be our guide. Be encouraged this morning, brothers and sisters, for help is on the scene and that Help is Jesus Christ. We must give Him all of our troubles; no matter what they are, give them to Jesus and everything will be alright. We must also keep in mind that trouble doesn't last always. AMEN!

"The LORD himself watches over you! The LORD stands beside you as your protective shade" (Ps. 121:5 NLT).

Challenge of the day: In the midst of trouble, know that the Lord is beside us guiding and watching over us.

To God be the glory, many blessings, and have a blessed day!

Day 223

I pray that you are had a grand evening. Start your day off with God, knowing that God will bring clarity to your purpose through His living Word and the leading of the Holy Spirit. On this journey of discovering our purpose, we must be attentive to the voice of God through the guidance of the Holy Spirit. "I will cry to God Most High, Who performs on my behalf and rewards me [Who brings to pass His purposes for me and surely completes them]!" (Ps. 57:2). Be encouraged, brothers and sisters, that God has not forgotten about us. He is waiting to complete the good work He started within us.

"And I am convinced and sure of this very thing, that He Who began a good work in you will continue until the day of Jesus Christ [right up to the time of His return], developing [that good work] and perfecting and bringing it to full completion in you" (Phil. 1:6).

Challenge of the day: Do not give up or stop working, because God's work in us will continue. Keep moving and living in your purpose through the direction of the Holy Spirit.

To God be the glory! Many blessings to you and have an awesome worship experience.

Day 224

I pray that you all had a great evening. Start your day off with God knowing that God desires you to be near Him. The closer we are to God, the clearer His directions will be for us to hear. "Come close to God and He will come close to you. [Recognize that you are] sinners, get your soiled hands clean; [realize that you have been disloyal] wavering individuals with divided interests, and purify your hearts [of your spiritual adultery]" (James 4:8). Be encouraged this morning, brothers and sisters, and come close to God and He will come close to you and allow your hearts to be pure.

> "Blessed (happy, enviably fortunate, and spiritually prosperous—possessing the happiness produced by the experience of God's favor and especially conditioned by the revelation of His grace, regardless of their outward conditions) are the pure in heart, for they shall see God!" (Matt. 5:8).

Challenge of the day: Examine your heart for purity.

To God be the glory, many blessings, and have a blessed and awesome day.

Day 225

I pray that all is well with you. Start your day off with God knowing that you must keep the faith. We must keep the faith, in spite of what things may look like or what our circumstances may be, because 2 Corinthians 5:7 declares, "For we walk by faith, not by sight" (NKJV). And our faith is increased daily as we hear and read the living Word of God. "So faith comes by hearing, that is, hearing the Good News about Christ" (Rom. 10:17 NLT). So be encouraged, brothers and sisters, by keeping the faith in Christ. Hold on just a little while longer; everything will be alright. Amen.

"But you, O LORD, are a shield around me; you are my glory, the one who holds my head high" (Ps. 3:3 NLT).

Challenge of the day: Keep your head up. God has got everything under control; He is indeed our shield of protection. If you have not had a hearty laugh in a while, learn to find time to laugh and enjoy the goodness of the Lord. :) Smile, God loves you more than you know.

To God be the glory, many blessings, and have an awesome day in Jesus.

Day 226

I pray that you had a grand evening. Start your day off with God, knowing that you cannot and must not give up when things are going south. Do not tend to worry about things you have no control over, only pray about those things and KEEP MOVING FORWARD. Keep moving forward in the direction that God has designed for you. If we slip back into old habits, it will take us that much longer to reach our destiny. Paul makes it very plain not to get caught up in the past or in the possessing of things, but press on in Christ Jesus. "I don't mean to say that I have already achieved these things or that I have already reached perfection. But I press on to possess that perfection for which Christ Jesus first possessed me" (Phil. 3:12 NLT). Paul ponders on the basics of survival in life, Jesus Christ. He thinks about his relationship, that it is Jesus Christ who first possessed him. So be encouraged this morning, brothers and sisters, and move forward in Jesus Christ. In fact, He had you covered from the very beginning.

> "Don't be impressed with your own wisdom. Instead, fear the LORD and turn away from evil" (Prov. 3:7 NLT).

Challenge of the day: Be mindful of who it is that provides wisdom to you, and humbly use wisdom wisely in all that you do.

To God be the glory, many blessings, and have an awesome day in the Lord.

Day 227

I pray that each of you had a great evening. Start your day off with God knowing that you are blessed. You are blessed, regardless of what is going on in your lives. God has spared us for such a time as this to recognize the blessings in and on our lives, so that you may indeed become a blessing to others, through the nation and worldwide. If we take a good look at Matthew 5:1-12, we see how blessed we can be when we are living with a blessed attitude . . . "God blesses you when people mock you and persecute you and lie about you and say all sorts of evil against you because you are my followers. Be happy about it! Be very glad! For a great reward awaits you in heaven. And remember, the ancient prophets were persecuted in the same way" (Matt. 5:11, 12 NLT). Be encouraged, brothers and sisters, knowing that you are blessed regardless of your situation. God's favor can and will rest upon your life, regardless of what others may say or do to you. Stand firm and strong on the living Word of God. Be blessed and know that you are blessed; wherever you go and in whatever you are doing, you are blessed and called to bring glory and honor in all areas of your life. God wants us know that we are complete in Him, whole in all areas of our lives.

"I take joy in doing your will, my God, for your instructions are written on my heart" (Ps. 40:8 NLT).

Challenge of the day: Find understanding in the Word of God and your heart will be filled with joy.

To God be the glory, many blessings, and have an awesome week in the Lord Jesus Christ, the risen Savior of the world.

Day 228

I pray that all is well with you. Start your day off with God, knowing that you must believe. Believe in God, even during the most difficult and challenging times in your life. Believe that God will deliver, heal, and set free our minds, bodies, and spirits as we go through the trials of life. Know that we are not alone, and believers across the globe are praying for us. The Holy Spirit will place our names and faces before fellow believers so that they can intercede on our behalf. Never doubt God or the power of prayer. A quick example or testimony, if you will: One Saturday morning, a child's face came before me, one I could not recognize. When I got up to take my daughter to the hairdresser, that child and her mother were there. I was moved to pray for healing for that child. By faith, I believe that child is healed. Be encouraged this morning, brothers and sisters. You are not alone; Jesus and other believers around the world are praying for you. "My prayer is not for the world, but for those you have given me, because they belong to you" (John 17:9 NLT).

"As I learn your righteous regulations, I will thank you by living as I should!" (Ps. 119:7 NLT).

Challenge of the day: Live like you believe that God is at work in your life; live by faith in Jesus Christ.

To God be the glory! Many blessings to you and have an awesome day and believe always.

Day 229

Start your day off with God knowing that He fights your battles. When trouble comes over the horizon, you must be ready to stand still and see the salvation of the Lord and know that God will give us peace within our inner being. Trouble may fall all around us, but we do not have to get caught in it. "Then all this assembly shall know that the LORD does not save with sword and spear; for the battle is the LORD's, and He will give you into our hands" (1 Sam. 17:47 NKJV). When we try to fight on our own accord, we can mess things up. Be encouraged this morning, brothers and sisters; let the Lord fight your battles, because the battles are the Lord's anyhow.

> "The LORD is my rock and my fortress and my deliverer; my God, my strength, in whom I will trust; my shield and the horn of my salvation, my stronghold. I will call upon the LORD, who is worthy to be praised; so shall I be saved from my enemies" (Ps. 18:2-3 NKJV).

Challenge of the day: Find understanding in the Word of God and your heart will be filled with joy.

To God be the glory! Many blessings and have a blessed day. Show love by expressing love always to everyone.

Day 230

Start your day off with God, knowing that you must see things before you see them and expect those things to manifest as God desires. God told Abraham that he would be a father of many nations, and even though he and his wife Sarah were old, he trusted God. "As for Me, behold, My covenant (solemn pledge) is with you, and you shall be the father of many nations. Nor shall your name any longer be Abram [high, exalted father]; but your name shall be Abraham [father of a multitude], for I have made you the father of many nations" (Gen. 17:4, 5). So be encouraged this morning and trust God to manifest those things which He has promised you.

> "So from one man, though he was physically as good as dead, there have sprung descendants whose number is as the stars of heaven and as countless as the innumerable sands on the seashore" (Heb. 11:12).

Challenge of the day: God is true to His Word; stay close and faithful to God, as Abraham did, and you will see His promises in your life.

To God be the glory and many blessings and have a great day in the Lord, remaining faithful.

Day 231

Start your day off with God by building on the foundation which is true, Jesus Christ. Constantly strive to grow in Christ Jesus. "Fear of the Lord is the foundation of wisdom. Knowledge of the Holy One results in good judgment" (Prov. 9:10 NLT). Be encouraged this morning, brothers and sisters, and build on that which is true, the living Word of God through Jesus Christ our risen Savior.

"For the word of God is alive and powerful. It is sharper than the sharpest two-edged sword, cutting between soul and spirit, between joint and marrow. It exposes our innermost thoughts and desires. Nothing in all creation is hidden from God. Everything is naked and exposed before his eyes, and he is one to who we are accountable" (Heb. 4:12, 13 NLT).

Challenge of the day: Build on the foundation of Christ, through understanding and living His basic principles and understanding the living Word of God.

To God be the glory, many blessings, and have a blessed and awesome day and keep building.

Day 232

I pray that you had a grand evening. Start your day off with God, knowing that you must carry the cross—not just on your day of worship, but every day of the week we must represent Christ. Godly character is needed and desired for such a time as this. Many are looking at believers to walk the talk that they talk. It is indeed a challenge to ensure that no one is offended or fall because they put their trust in one person versus putting their trust in Jesus Christ. "For once you were full of darkness, but now you have light from the Lord. So live as people of light! For this light within you produces only what is good and right and true. Carefully determine what pleases the Lord" (Eph. 5:8-10 NLT). Be encouraged this morning, brothers and sisters; let our light shine because of the light that is within us, through Jesus Christ who died on the cross for our sins. No matter who may get on your nerves, show Jesus Christ by doing that which is right.

"Live wisely among those who are not believers, and make the most of every opportunity" (Col. 4:5 NLT).

Challenge of the day: Live like Christ's ambassadors, representing Him in the highest esteem among all people.

To God be the glory, many blessings, and have a blessed and awesome day.

Day 233

I pray that you had a grand evening. Start your day off with God knowing that you are justified by faith in Christ Jesus. "This Good News tells us how God makes us right in his sight. This is accomplished from start to finish by faith. As the Scriptures say, 'It is through faith that a righteous person has life'" (Rom. 1:17 NLT). Brothers and sisters, it is nothing that we've done that causes us to be justified; it is through Jesus Christ. Our faith must hold true to who Christ is. Having faith in Christ means we absolutely trust in Him; without doubt and fear or dismay, we absolutely positively trust and believe in Christ. Be encouraged this morning, brothers and sisters, that Christ has made the pathway clear for us, as we have faith in Him and live a full and pleasing life.

"Look at the proud! They trust in themselves, and their lives area crooked. But the righteous will live by their faithfulness to God" (Hab. 2:4 NLT).

Challenge of the day: Don't let pride stop you from living a life that is pleasing toward God.

To God be the glory! Many blessings to you, have a blessed day, and do not be prideful.

Day 234

I pray that you had a great evening of rest. Start your day off with God knowing that you can recall His greatness and deliverance throughout your life. God has delivered us through many things, and at the same time, His wonders surround us. During the times of "going through," we must never forget to go to our own personal sanctuary. Our sanctuary must be a place of worship, meditation, prayer, and communion with God. It is there that we must learn to move forward, out of our situations. Most cannot move forward because they are stuck in the past . . . angry over things they had or have no control over. Let it go! Move into your sanctuary and discover that there is nothing too hard for God. "Jesus Looked at them intently and said, 'Humanly speaking, it is impossible. But with God everything is possible'" (Matt. 19:26 NLT). Be encouraged this morning, brothers and sisters; God is on His job as deliverer, protector. As always, just by His being God, everything will be alright. Let it go, whatever it is to you that may cause or bring hindrance to your relationship with God and others.

> "O God, your ways are holy. Is there any god as mighty as you? You are the God of great wonders! You demonstrate your awesome power among the nations. By your strong arm, you redeemed your people, the descendants of Jacob and Joseph. When the Red Sea saw you, O God, its waters looked and trembled! The sea quaked to its very depths" (Ps. 77:13-16 NLT).

Challenge of the day: God delivers! Trust Him to do so.

To God be the glory! Many blessings to you, have a blessed day, and expect deliverance.

Day 235

I pray that you all had a grand evening. Start your day off with God, knowing that you are forgiven of all of your sins and that you also must forgive those who have offended you. Forgiving someone who has brought offense upon you is not always easy. In fact, it is difficult. The human nature wants to see pain for pain, but I offer that we not seek pain for pain, but love and forgiveness instead. "In keeping with your magnificent, unfailing love, please pardon the sins of this people, just as you have forgiven them ever since they left Egypt" (Num. 14:19 NLT). Moses interceded for the people of Israel then, and now Jesus Christ intercedes on our behalf. We are forgiven of our sins through the birth, life, death, and resurrection of Jesus Christ. Be encouraged this morning, brothers and sisters; we are forgiven of our transgressions—not only when we ask for forgiveness, but also when we forgive those who transgressed against us.

"If you forgive those who sin against you, your heavenly Father will forgive you. But if you refuse to forgive others, your Father will not forgive your sins" (Matt. 6:14-15 NLT).

Challenge of the day: Forgiveness should not be an option; however, it is your choice. Choose to forgive and your life will be better.

To God be the glory, many blessings, and have a blessed day choosing to forgive.

Day 236

I pray that you all had a great day. Start your day off with God by knowing you have a great responsibility to walk in the authority to which you are called. Not being abusive or anything of that nature, but by setting things in order with a sound mind and strength. When God gives us an assignment, we must carry it out with the best of our ability. Being in positions of authority, we do not have to do things on our own; God is our help, and He has placed us all in our various positions. "Rulers lead with my help, and nobles make righteous judgments" (Prov. 8:16 NLT). Whether in the home, church, or at work, God will guide us through it all. We just have to call and connect with Him in order to get the job done right. Be encouraged this morning, brothers and sisters; God's mornings are great. Just enjoy His presence wherever you are, and lean and depend on Him to give you what you need to do what is needed.

> "My heart is confident in you, O God; my heart is confident. No wonder I can sing Your praises! Wake up, my heart! Wake up, O lyre and harp! I will wake the dawn with my song" (Ps. 57:7-8 NLT).

Challenge of the day: Be ready to praise God with confidence, regardless of what is going on or what day it is, even if you have the "Monday Morning" mentality.

To God be the glory! Many blessings to you and have a blessed day, praising the Lord.

Day 237

I pray that you all had a great evening. Start your day off with God, knowing that our steps are ordered by God and we must follow His leading through the direction of the Holy Ghost. "The steps of a good man are ordered by the LORD, and He delights in his way. Though he fall, he shall not be utterly cast down; for the LORD upholds him with His hand" (Ps. 37:23-24 NKJV). Be encouraged this morning, brothers and sisters, that God is holding us up with His own hands.

"The LORD knows the days of the upright, and their inheritance shall be forever" (Ps. 37:18 NKJV).

Challenge for the day: Know that God's hand is stronger than anyone, and no one can remove you from His hand.

To God be the glory, many blessings, and have an awesome worship experience.

Day 238

I pray that all is well you. Start your day off with God, knowing that He will respond to you in various ways when you call unto Him sincerely. It may not be the exact way you think it should be; however, God knows what's best for you. "Hear a just cause, O LORD, attend to my cry; give ear to my prayer which is not from deceitful lips. Let my vindication come from Your presence; let Your eyes look on the things that are upright" (Ps. 17:1-2 NKJV). Be encouraged this morning, brothers and sisters; God knows and understands our hearts and recognizes those who desire to do that which is right and pleasing in His sight.

"Let the words of my mouth and the meditation of my heart be acceptable in Your sight, O LORD, my strength and my Redeemer" (Ps. 19:14 NKJV).

Challenge of the day: Speak in a manner that God will hear you from your heart.

To God be the glory! Many blessings to you and have a blessed day, knowing that you are redeemed.

Day 239

I pray that you had a great evening. Start your day off with God by knowing how to be content. Learning how to move and operate in whatever state you find yourself will ease some of the stresses that life brings upon us (or the ones that we may cause ourselves). Paul understood contentment. "How I praise the Lord that you are concerned about me again. I know you have always been concerned for me, but you didn't have the chance to help me. Not that I was ever in need, for I have learned to be content with whatever I have. I know how to live on almost nothing or with everything. I have learned the secret of living in every situation, whether it is with a full stomach or empty, with plenty or little. For I can do everything through Christ, who gives me strength" (Phil. 4:10-13 NLT). Godliness with contentment is great gain. Be encouraged this morning, brothers and sisters, that God understands and teaches us through the Holy Spirit how to be content. This does not mean that we settle and accept any and everything, but that we have learned to be content with our circumstances and situations through Christ Jesus.

"Trust in the Lord with all your heart; do not depend on your own understanding. Seek his will in all you do, and he will show you which path to take" (Prov. 3:5-6 NLT).

Challenge of the day: Seek God and trust Him always.

To God be the glory, many blessings, and have a blessed day.

Day 240

I pray that you all had a great evening. Start your day off with God, knowing that everything is going to be alright as you give your cares to God. No matter the appearance of things, just have faith enough in God that all is well. "But let all who take refuge in you rejoice; let them sing joyful praises forever. Spread your protection over them, that all who love your name may be filled with joy. For you bless the godly, O LRD; you surround them with your shield of love" (Ps. 5:11-12 NLT). Be encouraged this morning, brothers and sisters, that God loves and cares for us all. There is no need to worry, just rejoice, knowing that we are loved by the best there is—God.

> "Those who know your name trust in you, for you,
> O LORD, do not abandon those who search for you"
> (Ps. 9:10 NLT).

Challenge of the day: Trust in God that everything will be okay. No need to worry, God has the helm.

To God be the glory, many blessings, and have a great day.

Day 241

I pray that you all had a joyous day. Start your day off with God knowing that He has us covered. We are covered in the precious blood of our risen Savior Jesus Christ. No matter what may come our way, we are protected and covered by the almighty and everlasting God. "He shall cover you with His feathers, and under His wings you shall take refuge; His truth shall be your shield and buckler" (Ps. 91:4 NKJV). Be encouraged this morning, my brothers and sisters, that God has us covered and He has covered and forgiven us through His dear Son Jesus Christ.

"Keep me as the apple of Your eye; hide me under the shadow of Your wings" (Ps. 17:8 NKJV).

Challenge of the day: Know that God's love is so great that He covers us, even when we do not think we deserve it. We are covered through the blood of Jesus Christ.

To God be the glory! Many blessings to you and have a great day, keeping your eye on the Lord.

Day 242

I pray that you all had a great day. Start your day off with God knowing that you must reflect the image in which you were created. You must carry the possibilities of knowing that some will notice that Christ dwells on the inside of us, by how we live and represent Christ. God the Creator knows all about us, even the number of hairs on our heads. Certainly, there are some things that God desires for us to share with Him in our personal relationship through Jesus Christ. "Then God said, 'Let Us make man in Our image, according to Our likeness; let them have dominion over the fish of the sea, over the birds of the air, and over the cattle, over all the earth and over every creeping thing that creeps on the earth" (Gen. 1:26 NKJV). Be encouraged this morning, brothers and sisters, that God did not make mistakes. We have to know and understand whose we are and who we are in Christ Jesus. When we find ourselves stuck or second guessing ourselves, reflect back on who we are and who created us and the purpose in which we were created.

"Create in me a clean heart, O God, and renew a steadfast spirit within me" (Ps. 51:10 NKJV).

Challenge of the day: Strive to live at peace within yourself, knowing that you are a reflection of God's great creation.

To God be the glory, many blessings, and have an awesome day.

Day 243

I pray that you had a great evening. Start your day off with God knowing that you must stand up for righteousness. Stand on your faith in God, no matter what the circumstances and situations may be. Stand on the Word of God and you cannot fail. Stand on the promises of God and live for His promises. Stand, my brothers and sisters, stand tall and see the salvation of the Lord all over our lives. "Stand your ground, putting on the belt of truth and the body armor of God's righteousness" (Eph. 6:14 NLT). Be encouraged this morning, brothers and sisters, by standing your ground and knowing that you are tied up in the truth of God. STAND.

"A final word: Be strong in the Lord and in his mighty power" (Eph. 6:10 NLT).

Challenge of the day: Know and understand what you are standing up for, particularly the things of God and that which concerns your life.

Challenge for worship service preparation: Pray ahead of time for what you are expecting when you enter into the house of God to worship Him.

To God be the glory! Many blessings to you and have a awesome worship experience in God, by the leading of the Holy Spirit.

Day 244

I pray that you had a great evening. Start your day off with God knowing that He has given us the necessary skills to do what we are called to do at home, work, and church. We must tap into the source of understanding and maximize our God-given talent and ability to glorify Him in all that we do. Sometimes we tend to say, "I am not capable of doing this or that." Certainly this can be considered a correct statement. We alone cannot do anything, but with Christ we can do all things. "For I can do everything through Christ who gives me strength" (Phil. 4:13 NLT). Be encouraged this morning, brothers and sisters; we do not have to do anything on our own strength, we can always count on Jesus.

"Wait patiently for the LORD, be brave and courageous. Yes, wait patiently for the LORD" (Ps. 27:14 NLT).

Challenge of the day: Preparation comes through testing and trials, yet we do not have to do or go through anything on our own accord. Christ will see us through; we must wait for His guidance.

To God be the glory! Many blessings to you and have a great day and work while it is day.

Day 245

I pray that you had an inspiring and great evening. Start your day off with God knowing that the favor of God rests on our lives. It may seems like trouble is pressing on every side, yet we are not harmed because God's favor rests well on our lives. Moses understood the importance of worshipping and fearing God. He knew that he needed God with him and the Children of Israel before they could go anywhere or live a proper life before God. "Moses immediately threw himself to the ground and worshiped. And he said, 'O, Lord, if it is true that I have found favor with you, then please travel with us. Yes, this is a stubborn and rebellious people, but please forgive our iniquity and our sins. Claim us as your own special possession.' The Lord replied, 'Listen, I am making a covenant with you in the presence of all your people. I will perform miracles that have never been performed anywhere in all the earth or in any nation. And all the people around you will see the power of the LORD—the awesome power I will display for you'" (Ex. 34:8-10 NLT). Be encouraged this morning, brothers and sisters, that no matter what things may look like, God's favor is ever present to those who trust and believe in Him.

> "What are mere mortals that you should think about them, human beings that you should care for them? Yet you made them only a little lower than God and crowned them with glory and honor" (Ps. 8:4-5 NLT).

Challenge of the day: Live like God has created us to live, in His image/likeness, in fear and worship of Him, and with glory and honor to His name. Then surely we will understand the favor of God and how valuable we are to Him.

To God be the glory, many blessings, and have a day filled with God's favor.

Day 246

I pray that you had a peaceful rest last night. Start your day off with God, knowing that He will provide guidance and direction. Evening when things seem dim and dreary, God will guide us through. He knows what we need, when we need it, and how we need it. When it rains, the sun never completely disappears; sometimes the sun is shining brightly on rainy days. As God provided guidance and direction to Moses from the burning bush, He will give us guidance and direction; we must be on the lookout for it. "There the angel of the LORD appeared to him in a blazing fire from the middle of a bush. Moses stared in amazement. Though the bush was engulfed in flames, it didn't burn up" (Ex. 3:2 NLT). Be encouraged this morning, brothers and sisters, that guidance and direction from God will come in unexpected packages. Just be ready and know that God will never leave us hanging.

"Show me the right path, O LORD; point out the road for me to follow. Lead me by your truth and teach me, for you are God who saves me. All day long I put my hope in you" (Ps. 25:4-5 NLT).

Challenge of the day: Hope is never lost, only given up on or given away. Keep hope and be guided by the Spirit of the living God, through Jesus Christ our Lord.

To God be the glory, many blessings, and have a great day full of hope and love.

Day 247

I pray that you had a peaceful evening. Start your day off with God knowing that He is sovereign. He knows all and understands all. Even when we may think that God does not understand, let me reassure you, He does. He understands what we are going through, the day-to-day operation of living a full and godly life. "Have you never heard? Have you never understood? The LORD is the everlasting God, the Creator of all the earth. He never grows weak or weary. No one can measure the depths of his understanding. He gives power to the weak and strength to the powerless. Even youths will become weak and tired, and young men will fall in exhaustion. But those who trust in the LORD will find new strength. They will soar high on wings like eagles. They will run and not grow weary. They will walk and not faint" (Isa. 40:28-31 NLT). Even when things get difficult at times, God understands and will give us all the strength we need to make it through. Be encouraged this morning, brothers and sisters, that God understands, knows, and cares about our day-to-day movements in this life.

"I cry out to God; yes I shout. Oh, that God would listen to me!" (Ps. 77:1 NLT).

Challenge of the day: God is not deaf, He hears and understands our tears and shouts! The question is—will we be still and know that He is God and that He is sovereign?

To God be the glory, many blessings, and have an awesome day and listen to God.

Day 248

Start your day off with God knowing that God is a forgiving and merciful Lord. He forgives us at the very moment we request it of Him. That's how loving God is. He does not question it or wait to second guess our motives. He forgives on the spot. "Oh, what joy for those whose disobedience is forgiven, whose sin is put out of sight!" (Ps. 32:1 NLT). God's forgiving power is so strong that even the thought of our hearts to ask God to forgive us is from God, and we can rejoice knowing that the love of God runs deeper than our sinful lives. His love is so deep that He gave us life (abundant and eternal) through His only Son Jesus Christ. Be encouraged this morning, brothers and sisters, that God's love is deep enough to forgive us our all of our unrighteousness.

"For God loved the world so much that he gave his one and only Son, so that everyone who believes in Him will not perish but have eternal life" (John 3:16 NLT).

Challenge of the day: Forgiveness is offered at a price, the cost of Christ dying on the cross, so that we may live again. Ask for forgiveness and forgive those who have wronged you.

To God be the glory, many blessings, and have a blessed and powerful day.

Day 249

I pray that you had a great evening. Start your day off with God knowing that God is just. He is faithful and loving. His righteousness exceeds all other righteousness. In our relationship with God, we must take to heart the measure of how trustworthy our God is and there is no God like our God. "Look to Me, and be saved, all the ends of the earth! For I am God, and there is no other" (Isa. 45:22 NKJV). God's dealing with us are faithful and true, His words will accomplish that which they are set out to do. As God is a just God, we must be a just people. "But the just shall live by faith [My righteous servant shall live by his conviction respecting man's relationship to God and divine things, and holy fervor born of faith and conjoined with it]; and if he draws back and shrinks in fear, My soul has no delight or pleasure in him" (Heb. 10:38). Be encouraged this day, brothers and sisters, knowing that God is just and there is no God like the God that we serve. We must hold true to His Word and live it out by being a just believer in Christ Jesus, trusting Him at His every Word.

> "Trust (lean on, rely on, and be confident) in the Lord and do good; so shall you dwell in the land and feed surely on His faithfulness, and truly you shall be fed" (Ps. 37:3).

Challenge of the day: Know that in our relationship with God, trust comes from both sides of the party.

To God be the glory, many blessings, and have a powerful worship experience.

Day 250

I pray that you all had a great night's rest. Start your day off with God knowing that it is He who judges. God judges all and knows all; we can only hope and pray that we are not in the direct lines of fire when God decides to pass judgment. "It is God alone who judges; he decides who will rise and who will fall" (Ps. 75:7 NLT). God knows all and will judge all; we as believers must trust and continue to believe, even when situations seem hopeless and without life. As God spoke to Ezekiel to prophesy to the dead dry bones in the valley, we also must speak to our dry bones, the hopeless situations in our lives. When we do speak life, we will soon see the situations turn around. Be encouraged this morning, brothers and sisters, that God knows all about what's going on. We must keep our eyes on Him and be not faint-hearted.

> "And we know that God causes everything to work together for the good of those who love God and are called according to his purpose for them. For God knew his people in advance, and he chose them to become like his Son, so that his Son would be the firstborn among many brothers and sisters" (Rom. 8:28-29 NLT).

Challenge of the day: Know that God is the Judge: He controls who wins and loses in life, who lives or dies. And no matter what the situation we face may be, just know that it is good!

To God be the glory, many blessings, and have an awesome day.

Day 251

I pray that you had a great evening. Start your day off with God knowing that you must understand the power of prayer. When you gain knowledge of the power of prayer, you will than know how to pray effectively, praying the Word of God with understanding and, yes, with power. Prayer changes things and situations and, indeed, circumstances. We as believers must know when and how to pray and for whom we are praying. "I urge you, first of all, to pray for all people. Ask God to help them; intercede on their behalf, and give thanks for them. Pray this way for kings and all who are in authority so that we can live a peaceful and quiet lives marked by godliness and dignity. This is good and pleases God our Savior, who wants everyone to be saved and to understand the truth" (1 Tim. 2:1-4 NLT). My brothers and sisters, be encouraged this morning and know that God already has given us the power to pray. We must pray with power in order to see and recognize the change that God has brought.

"Listen to my prayer for mercy as I cry out to you for help, as I lift my hands toward your holy sanctuary" (Ps. 28:2 NLT).

Challenge of the day: Pray and worry not.

To God be the glory, many blessings, and have an awesome and powerful day in God.

Day 252

I pray that you had a great evening. Start your day off with God knowing that you must praise Him with a joyful spirit. Praise God in the morning, in the midday, the evening, and even in the midnight hour. In spite of what we are going through, let the praises of God resound throughout our being. "Come, everyone! Clap your hands! Shout to God with joyful praise" (Ps. 47:1 NLT). God yearns for us to praise Him. We as His people must acknowledge that He is indeed our God. Searching for victory in your life? Shout that you have the victory in God through praise! Make a joyful sound unto the Lord, let your praises be heard from your heart to heaven, and watch how things will begin to turn around for you in your life. So be encouraged this morning, brothers and sisters, that God is not dead. He is alive, our risen Savior Jesus Christ is at His right hand. We can rejoice and be exceedingly glad, because we have a shout down on the inside waiting to come forth.

"Sing a new song to the LORD, for he has done wonderful deeds. His right hand has won a mighty victory; his holy arm has shown his saving power!" (Ps. 98:1 NLT).

Challenge of the day: Shout with a triumphant voice, knowing that you have the victory in God.

To God be the glory! Many blessings to you and have an awesome day in the Lord.

Day 253

I pray that you had a great evening. Start your day off with God, knowing that He has already provided everything that you need to do what is required of you. You must tap into Him as the source of your strength. "The LORD is my light and my salvation; whom shall I fear? The LORD is the strength of my life; of whom shall I be afraid?" (Ps. 27:1 NKJV). As we learn to tap into our Source of strength, we will begin to realize that we can endure every circumstance and situation that we face or that may come upon us. As Abraham told Isaac that God Himself would provide the lamb for the burnt offering, this promise is true today that God will provide (Gen. 22:8). "And Abraham called the name of the place, The-LORD-Will-Provide; as it is said to this day, 'In the Mount of the LORD it shall be provided'" (Gen. 22:14 NKJV). Be encouraged this morning, brothers and sisters, for provision already has been made and we have the strength to endure through our risen Savior Jesus Christ. So whatever you need or may be going through, God is aware of it and we must tap into Him first for the answers and guidance we are seeking.

"But seek first the kingdom of God and His righteousness, and all these things shall be added to you" (Matt. 6:33 NKJV).

Challenge of the day: Seek God and know that everything is provided for you and you already posses the strength and endurance to run this race of life.

To God be the glory, many blessings, and have a blessed day.

Day 254

Start your day off with God knowing that we can have our minds renewed in Him. The more and more we strive to have our minds renewed in Christ, the less we see of ourselves and more of Christ. "Let this mind be in you which was also in Christ Jesus, who, being in the form of God, did not consider it robbery to be equal with God, but made Himself of no reputation, taking the form of a bondservant, and coming in the likeness of men" (Phil. 2:5-7 NKJV). The mind is where the thoughts begin; whether good or bad, they all start within the mind. "And do not be conformed to this world, but be transformed by the renewing of your mind, that you may prove what is that good and acceptable and perfect will of God" (Rom. 12:2 NKJV). Be encouraged this morning, brothers and sisters, and know that we must keep our minds on Christ and the things thereof. We must understand that we must constantly renew our minds in the living Word of God, through Jesus Christ. Keep your mind on Christ and your mind will be transformed, as well as your life. "For as he thinks in his heart, so is he . . ." (Prov. 23:7 NKJV).

> "Blessed is the man who walks not in the counsel of the ungodly, nor stands in the path of sinners, nor sits in the seat of the scornful; but his delight is in the law of the LORD, and in His law he meditates day and night. He shall be like a tree planted by the rivers of water, that brings forth its fruit in its season, whose leaf also shall not wither; and whatever he does shall prosper" (Ps.1:1-3 NKJV).

Challenge of the day: "Mind over matter" does matter, and it is up to us to put the right things in our minds.

To God be the glory! Many blessings to you and have a blessed day, walking close in the sight of the Lord.

Day 255

I pray that you had a great evening. Start your day off with God knowing that God yearns for you to reflect His character. In all that we do, we who believe must show that God is alive in our lives. What better time than now to display God's love through how we live in the now, hoping and praying for a better tomorrow. "Since everything will be destroyed in this way, what kind of people ought you to be? You ought to live holy and godly lives as you look forward to the day of God and speed its coming. That day will bring about the destruction of the heavens by fire, and the elements will melt in the heat. But in keeping with his promise we are looking forward to a new heaven and a new earth, the home of the righteousness" (2 Pet. 3:11-13 NIV). Indeed, we have something grand to look forward to, but in the meantime we must live a godly life displaying God's characteristics. Be encouraged this morning, brothers and sisters; God's plan has not changed. He holds our future in His hands; we just have to live out His will in our lives.

"As for me, I will continue beholding Your face in righteousness (rightness, justice, and right standing with You); I shall be fully satisfied, when I awake [to find myself] beholding Your form [and having sweet communion with You]" (Ps. 17:15).

Challenge of the day: Know that God is watching to see His reflection in us.

To God be the glory and much blessing. Have a blessed worship experience.

Day 256

I pray that you had a great evening. Start your day off with God knowing that He desires all of you to be a part of His family. Family is vital to the Lord, and we need to understand the value of family. Family is not limited to just your bloodline, but through relationships we can build up our family. So look around you and see who is actually a part of your family (those who are living out the will of God), and you will be surprised at the outcome. "For whoever does the will of God is My brother and My sister and mother" (Mark 3:35 NKJV). Be encouraged this morning, brothers and sisters, that you are not alone in your walk with Christ. Help is always available, sometimes through the forgotten members of the family. As believers we cannot walk this walk by ourselves, so it is important to understand the value of our spiritual family.

> "But let all those rejoice who put their trust in You; let them shout for joy, because You defend them; let those also who love Your name be joyful in You. For You, O LORD, will bless the righteous; with favor You will surround him as with a shield" (Ps. 5:11-12 NKJV).

Challenge of the day: Finding comfort from those within the "family" will give peace to the soul and mind that need rest.

To God be the glory! Many blessings to you and have a blessed day; be comforted in the Lord.

Day 257

I pray that you had a great evening yesterday. Start your day off with God knowing that God is consistent. He changes not. "Jesus Christ is the same yesterday, today, and forever" (Heb. 13:8 NLT). We must keep this in the forefront of our minds. God never changes, He is very consistent in His Word and always (and I do mean always) displays love. As we pursue our journey with Christ, let us be consistent in all that we do, knowing that we live for Christ. Be encouraged this morning, brothers and sisters, that God is not through with us yet. Let's remain attentive to and in His living Word, because as God is consistent so is His Word!

"Come, let us tell of the LORD's greatness; let us exalt his name together" (Ps. 34:3 NLT).

Challenge of the day: Be consistent with service, love, and faithfulness, even as God has demonstrated His love, faithfulness, and service toward us.

To God be the glory, many blessings, and have a great day being consistent in the Lord.

Day 258

I pray that you had a peaceful rest last night. Start your day off with God knowing that God rewards those who diligently seek Him. Seeking God out is a true sign of your desire to know Him better through having faith in Him. "And it is impossible to please God without faith. Anyone who wants to come to him must believe that God exists and that he rewards those who sincerely seek him" (Heb. 11:6 NLT). Seeking God is a must, especially in this day and age. We must be aware of what is going on, and our prayer life must be effective. Seek the Lord while He may be found. Our time is valuable, and the more we spend it seeking God on the issues of our lives, the closer we come toward God. Be encouraged this morning, my brothers and sisters, that God is near, particularly when we seek Him.

> "Therefore, let all the godly pray to you while there is still time, that they may not drown in the floodwaters of judgment. For you are my hiding place; you protect me from trouble. You surround me with songs of victory. The Lord says, 'I will guide you along the best pathway for your life. I will advise you and watch over you'" (Ps. 32:6-8 NLT).

Challenge of the day: Seeking God will improve your life, so start today and watch your life unfold into what God desires it to be.

To God be the glory, many blessings, and have a powerful day seeking the Lord.

Day 259

Start your day off with God knowing that He is real. God is real and true. "God is faithful, by whom you were called into the fellowship of His Son, Jesus Christ our Lord" (1 Cor. 1:9 NKJV). At the very thought of His name, we must praise God for who He is and how He brought us through. So this morning, my brothers and sisters, be encouraged and praise God for being God, the real deal, because there is none like the Lord God we serve. I ask that you all pray for our nation and keep our service members in prayer.

> "Oh, sing to the LORD a new song! For He has done marvelous things. His right hand and His holy arm have gained Him the victory. The LORD has made known His salvation; His righteousness He has revealed in the sight of the nations. He has remembered His mercy and His faithfulness to the house of Israel; all the ends of the earth have seen the salvation of our God" (Ps. 98:1-3 NKJV).

Challenge of the day: Know that God has given us something to shout about—life—and He is faithful and just to preserve our life. So shout about your life this morning, in spite of the circumstances you may be facing, shout anyhow, because we have the victory in God.

To God be the glory! Many blessings to you and please be safe tonight. I pray for God's peace and protection on each of you all.

Day 260

Start your day off with God knowing that God's grace will keep you close to Him. It is His grace that will keep us during the winter months of our lives. When the seasons of our lives change, we can rest assured that God's grace will not fade away. As Paul urges Timothy to ". . . Be strong through grace that God gives you in Christ Jesus" (2 Tim. 2:1 NLT). We also must be strong and rely upon God to bring us through and keep us safe while we are on this journey we call life. I have often heard, "The will of God will never lead you where the grace of God cannot keep you." God's grace will keep us throughout life, no matter where we are or what season we are going through. So this morning, be encouraged, brothers and sisters, because God is able to handle everything for you and to keep you at the same time, through His unlimited grace (unmerited favor).

"You can be sure of this: The LORD set apart the godly for himself. The LORD will answer when I call to him" (Ps. 4:3 NLT).

Challenge of the day: Stay close to God and know that you are covered and kept by the almighty and living God.

To God be the glory, many blessings, and seek the Lord daily.

Day 261

I pray that you all had a great evening. Start your day off with God knowing that He understands you like no one else. He even knows the secrets within our hearts. One cannot run or hide—not even their thoughts—from God. "Would not God discover this? For He knows the secrets of the heart" (Ps. 44:21). So it is very important that we be very mindful of what we think and even what we say. You must try our best not to lash out in anger or display temper tantrums. You must be quite mindful that God is ever present, and displaying self-control is vital in our daily walk and relationship with Jesus Christ. So be encouraged this morning, my brothers and sisters; stop and meditate on the Word of God, even in the midst of a heated discussion or a compelling situation. Listen to the inner voice from within as God speaks to us through His Word.

"I have better understanding and deeper insight than all my teachers, because Your testimonies are my meditation" (Ps. 119:99).

Challenge of the day: Allow the secrets things within us to be the Word of God, on which we must meditate day and night.

To God be the glory! Many blessings to you and have a blessed day in the Lord.

Day 262

I pray that you all had a great evening. Start your day off with God knowing that He is our safe haven. He is indeed our strong tower. When trouble embarks upon us, we can run and be safe in His arms. "The name of the LORD is a strong fortress; the godly run to him and are safe" (Prov. 18:10 NLT). God is there for us. He never misses a beat, always willing and able to guide and protect His sheep. Just like the shepherd that He is, God cares and knows with understanding all about our troubles and woes. So in order that our minds may be taken off of our troubles, be a giver. Give. Give love, laughter, and life to those around us. This morning, my brothers and sisters, be encouraged for you and I are safe in the arms of God. We can rejoice, knowing that we can give in spite of our woes and fears. This morning, I personally pray for the gift of joy and love, with a great deal of laughter, in each and every one of your lives.

"The Lord is my rock, my fortress, and my savior; my God is my rock, in whom I find protection. He is my shield, the power that saves me, and my place of safety" (Ps. 18:2 NLT).

Challenge of the day: Fear not, for we are safe in the arms of the One who loves us most. The One who teaches us to give, in spite of all that may trouble us.

To God be the glory! Many blessings to you and have an awesome day in the Lord and only fear the Lord.

Day 263

I pray that you had a great day. Start your day off with God knowing that you must have faith in the impossible. Believe that even the impossible can happen with God. Not knowing when it will happen, but that it will happen. "Faith is the confidence that what we hope for will actually happen; it gives us assurance about things we cannot see" (Heb. 11:1 NLT). Be encouraged this morning, brothers and sisters, knowing that God has our best interest at heart. We must believe in the impossible; whether you are believing for a healing or for a miracle, God stands by awaiting our petitions.

"But as for me, I almost lost my footing. My feet were slipping, and I was almost gone" (Ps. 73:2 NLT).

Challenge of the day: Do not give up on anything, have faith in God. He will catch you when you are about to slip away.

To God be the glory! Many blessings to you, have a great day, and do not give up on life.

Day 264

I pray that you all had an awesome evening. Start your day off with God, knowing that it is in Him that you can have that perfect peace . . . the peace that only He gives. When things may seem restless around you, be at peace in God. When turmoil is erupting around you, be at peace. "Therefore, having been justified by faith, we have peace with God through Jesus Christ" (Rom. 5:1 NKJV). Our faith in God will cause us to be at peace, no matter what is going on in our lives. I often quote this scripture: "And the peace of God, which surpasses all understanding, will guard your hearts and minds through Christ Jesus" (Phil. 4:7 NKJV). When we have the peace of God within our lives, we can move through the trials of life. Particularly during the special days (often the happiest and saddest moments of the year for those who have lost loved ones and no longer can share this special time of year, or have financial burdens, or whatever the case may be), I pray for God's peace for each and every one of us and that our minds and hearts will be at rest on the Lord God. So this morning, I would like to personally say thanks to each of you for allowing me to share God's Word, and I want to encourage you all to enjoy God at every opportunity that you get. Enjoy the family and loved ones that you all have, and for those who are no longer in your life, be at peace and trust God anyhow.

"You will keep him in perfect peace, whose mind is stayed on You, because he trusts in You" (Isa. 26:3 NKJV).

Challenge of the day: Be at peace and trust God always to be available to provide His comfort and love.

To God be the glory! Many blessings to you and have a blessed and safe day.

Day 265

I pray that you had a great evening. Start your day off with God, knowing that you must be obedient unto Him, to walk worthy and uprightly before the great God almighty. A choice we are all given is to listen to the voice and the living Word of God. Daily we must listen closely unto Him. Spend time searching and responding to His Word through our daily actions, either physically, emotionally, vocally, and spiritually. God calls us all to obedience. Searching with our minds and hearts to know the truth and live it will require us to do a great deal of self checkups . . . a constant view in the mirror and upfront honesty with ourselves. As Paul often completed his personal self-checks, we also must do the same. "O wretched man that I am! Who will deliver me from this body of death? I thank God—through Jesus Christ our Lord!" (Rom. 7:24-25a NKJV). Be encouraged this morning, brothers and sisters; in spite of what has happened or what we have done, God is not through with us yet. We shall behold what we shall become through Jesus Christ.

"For He is our God, and we are the people of His pasture, and the sheep of His hand. Today, if you will hear His voice: Do not harden your hearts, as in the rebellion, as in the day of trial in the wilderness" (Ps. 95:7-8 NKJV).

Challenge of the day: Hear and obey, live and correct what you know is not right.

To God be the glory! Many blessings to you and have an awesome day obeying the voice of God.

Day 266

I pray that all is well with you. Start your day off with God knowing that you must surrender total praise unto Him. Regardless of what is going on in your life, when we decide to surrender total praise out of our total being (mind, body and spirit), we shall behold the greatness of God. We always must find ourselves giving God glory and praise through the day. Just at the thought of His name, we ought to praise Him. At the remembrance of what He has done and is doing, we shall praise Him. Total praise toward God must come from within our very being. Give Him glory at all times and watch how things will turn out. "Let them praise Your great and awesome name—He is holy" (Ps. 99:3 NKJV). Be encouraged this morning, my brothers and sisters, knowing that in the midst of our total praise toward God, His delays are not His denials. God keeps His promises; it is just a matter of timing. (Remember, Sarah was promised Isaac, but decided to birth Ishmael. However, I declare unto you this morning that your promise is coming; do not go out and birth Ishmael. Keep the praises going out! [Gen. 15-21]).

"Praise the Lord! For it is good to sing praises to our God; for it is pleasant, and praise is beautiful!" (Ps. 147:1 NKJV).

Challenge of the day: Praise God with total surrender; even through trials praise the Most High, living God, through Jesus Christ.

To God be the glory! Many blessings to you and have an awesome day in the Lord, giving Him praise.

Day 267

I pray that you have grand evening. Start your day off with God knowing that you must never doubt God's ability to do what He said He would do. When you doubt, it's like you are crippling your faith. When you believe, your faith is strengthened all the more. In Luke chapter 7, John the Baptist sends out two of his disciples to ask Jesus, "Are you the Messiah we've been expecting, or should we keep looking for someone else?" (Luke 7:20 NLT). At that moment, Jesus cured many of their diseases, and He told John's disciples, "Go back to John and tell him what you have seen and heard—the blind see, the lame walk, the lepers are cured, the deaf hear, the dead are raised to life, and the Good News is being preached to the poor. And tell him, 'God blesses those who do not turn away because of me'" (Luke 7:22-23 NLT). So this morning, my brothers and sisters, be encouraged and believe that miracles are still occurring today, just like in Jesus' day. The question is: do we have enough faith to believe?

"O God, you have taught me from my earliest childhood, and I constantly tell others about the wonderful things you do" (Ps. 71:17 NLT).

Challenge of the day: Never doubt, only believe and take God at His Word.

To God be the glory! Many blessings to you and please keep believing; no matter what it looks like, keep believing.

Day 268

I pray that you had a great evening. Start your day off with God, knowing that His purpose in your life will bring out some defining moments. You may not always know the exact time, but you will recall His glory and direction. The Lord called upon Abram to leave his country and kinfolk to go to a land that God would show him (Gen. 12). Then God proceeded to give him his assignment, and his assignment was to be a great nation, to be blessed, and to be a blessing. God even told him that for those who would bless him, He Himself would bless, and those who cursed him, He Himself would curse. God provided many defining moments for Abram's life. Like today, He is always giving us assignments that are often defining moments, which will draw us closer to Him. Some of our assignments will cause us to move out of our comfort zone. So, this morning as you go through your day, ponder the defining moments that God has given you, which will continue to define your purpose in life. "Now the LORD said to Abram: 'Get out of your country, from your family and from your father's house, to a land that I will show you'" (Gen. 12:1 NKJV). Be encouraged this morning and know that God's purpose for our lives will never cease, it will only increase as we grow in Him. We may not always understand the assignment at that moment, or the folk that come along with it, but rest assured that God is defining and refining us through every experience.

> "Nevertheless I am continually with You; You hold me by my right hand. You will guide me with Your counsel, and afterward receive me to glory" (Ps. 73:23, 24 NKJV).

Challenge of the day: Be still and know that God is defining His purpose in our lives through the assignments He has given us.

To God be the glory! Many blessings to you and have a blessed day listening to the defining moments in your life.

Day 269

I pray that you have a great evening. Start your day off with God knowing that you are secured in Him. He gives us the required rest needed and the peace to go along with it. He also is the One who will carry our burdens. With love as the Source, you must recognize the strength that is within His love and know that you are secured and cared for deeply. Why? Because God is love. "He who does not love does not know God, for God is love" (1 John 4:8 NKJV). He is indeed the Source of our strength, and we can rest assured that He will protect us like no one else can, because He is GOD! When you realize that you are secured in God, and your feet are planted on His sure foundation, you cannot be moved by the circumstances of today. We must trust in, rely on, and abide in God and in His Word, through Jesus Christ our risen Savior. We must walk by faith and not by sight (2 Cor. 5:7). Be encouraged and enlightened this morning, my brothers and sisters, for God has not forgotten about you, me, or the promises that He has made us. Rest easy within your spirit, for God has everything under control and we are safe in His arms of love.

"Cast your burden on the LORD, and He shall sustain you; He shall never permit the righteous to be moved" (Ps. 55:22 NKJV).

Challenge of the day: Do not hold on to your burdens; give them to the Lord and He will take care of them and keep you in peace.

To God be the glory! Many blessings to you and have a powerful day releasing your burdens and experiencing freedom in Christ.

Day 270

I pray that you had a peaceful evening. Start your day off with God knowing that your joy in the Lord cannot be removed. "These things I have spoken to you, that My joy may remain in you, and that your joy may be full" (John 15:11 NKJV). You can allow folk to interrupt your joy by responding to things in negative ways or even by being disobedient. You must keep in mind that Jesus desires for us to have joy and that it be full, meaning in spite of what may come our way, the joy we have in Christ will stand within our being. The joy of knowing that all is well with you in Christ is astounding! We must feed on this, whether we are feeling good or not so good. I have often heard the saints of old say, "This joy that I have, the world did not give it to me and the world cannot take it away." Be encouraged, my brothers and sisters, this morning by James 1:2-4 (NKJV): "My brethren, count it all joy when you fall into various trials, knowing that the testing of your faith produces patience. But let patience have its perfect work, that you may be perfect and complete, lacking nothing."

> "For His anger is but for a moment, His favor is for life, weeping may endure for a night, but joy comes in the morning" (Ps. 30:5 NKJV).

Challenge of the day: Speak and live joyously, knowing that joy resides within you.

To God be the glory, many blessings, and have a blessed and spiritually prosperous worship experience.

Day 271

I pray that you had a great rest last night. Start your day off with God knowing that His grace is sufficient for you. His grace will carry you beyond where you think you cannot go. His grace is unlimited and has an insurmountable level that only He can maintain. God's grace through Jesus Christ is new every day, and His grace will lead us closer to Him, as we meditate on how awesome He is. He protects and shields us from all harm and danger; He keeps us humble and meets all of our needs. He knows how to respond to our prayers on time and with exactly what we need. The response to our prayer may not be exactly what we expected, but it will cover more than enough. "And He said to me, 'My grace is sufficient for you, for My strength is made perfect in weakness . . .'" (2 Cor. 12:9 NKJV). Paul prayed that the thorn in his flesh would depart; in fact, he prayed three times, but God said His grace was enough. We must learn to receive God's answers to our prayers, knowing that His grace is enough. Be encouraged this morning, my brothers and sisters, for God's grace through His Son Jesus Christ has us all covered.

"For the LORD God is a sun and shield; the LORD will give grace and glory; no good thing will He withhold from those who walk uprightly" (Ps. 84:11 NKJV).

Challenge of the day: Live like you know that God's grace is all you need.

To God be the glory, many blessing, and have an awesome day in God.

Day 272

I pray that you all had a peaceful rest last night. Start your day off with God knowing that we have the victory! No matter what our circumstances made be or what others are doing or saying about us, we are more than conquerors and we are victorious in Jesus Christ. If we are told that we can't do this and we can't do that, that's okay, my brothers and sisters. We have the victory. When it comes to promotion, we who believe know and understand that our promotion comes from God. When it comes to being elevated, we know that it comes from God. No matter what the enemy comes up with, he already is defeated. "Can anything ever separate us from Christ's love? Does it mean he no longer loves us if we have trouble or calamity, or are persecuted, or hungry, or destitute, or in danger, or threatened with death? (As the scriptures say, 'For your sake we are killed every day; we are being slaughtered like sheep.') No, despite all these things, overwhelming victory is ours through Christ, who loved us" (Rom. 8:35-37 NLT). Be encouraged this morning, my brothers and sisters, for we have the victory in Christ Jesus!

"Victory comes from you, O LORD. May you bless your people" (Ps. 3:8 NLT).

Challenge of the day: The victory is yours; you must walk and live like you know you are victorious.

To God be the glory, many blessings, and have a victoriously blessed day!

Day 273

I pray that you had a peaceful evening. Start your day with God, knowing that it is He who renews, regenerates, and causes us to keep on going, even when we do not think we have the strength to do so ourselves. "He gives power to the weak, and to those who have no might He increases strength. Even the youths shall faint and be weary, and the young men shall utterly fall, but those who wait on the LORD shall renew their strength; they shall mount up with wings like eagles, they shall run and not be weary, they shall walk and not faint" (Isa. 40:29-31 NKJV). The twenty-eighth verse sets the tone for us to search within and know where our strength and renewal will come from: "Have you not known? Have you not heard? The everlasting God, the LORD, the Creator of the ends of the earth, neither faints nor is weary. His understanding is unsearchable" (Isa. 40:28 NKJV). This morning, my brothers and sisters, be encouraged and renewed in the presence of God; know that God is our help in the time of trouble and He is always available. But are we available to receive the renewed strength? Stay close to God in Christ Jesus, my brothers and sisters.

"He renews my strength. He guides me along right paths, bringing honor to his name" (Ps. 23:3 NLT).

Challenge of the day: Draw close to God and feel and know that our strength will be renewed in Him.

To God be the glory, many blessings, and have an awesome day in God.

Day 274

I pray that all is well and that you all had a great evening yesterday. Start your day off with God knowing that He is our Redeemer. Knowing that we have been redeemed and bought with a price is a great feeling. We can rejoice at the very thought of this. We have been redeemed from the troubled waters of life, from the hands of the enemy, from imprisonment, from the storms of the sea, and even from our very own wilderness and valley experience. "Let the redeemed of the LORD say so, whom He has redeemed from the hand of the enemy" (Ps. 107:2 NKJV). We must declare that we have been redeemed through the blood of Jesus Christ. "Now all things are of God, who has reconciled us to Himself through Jesus Christ, and has given us the ministry of reconciliation, that is, that God was in Christ reconciling the world to Himself, not imputing their trespasses to them, and has committed to us the word of reconciliation" (2 Cor. 5:18-19 NKJV). Come back to God and run and tell that we have been redeemed like the Samaritan woman, who ran into the city to tell all who would hear her about Jesus (John 4). Rejoice and be exceedingly glad this morning, brothers and sisters, that we are redeemed through Jesus Christ, the One who has demonstrated the greatest love of all.

> "Who redeems your life from destruction, who crowns you with lovingkindness and tender mercies, who satisfies your mouth with good things, so that your youth is renewed like the eagle's" (Ps. 103:4, 5 NKJV).

Challenge of the day: Run and tell of the goodness of God and all that He has done for us. Run and speak out that we are redeemed.

To God be the glory, many blessings, and have an awesome and blessed day!

Day 275

I pray that you had a peaceful rest yesterday. Start your day off with God, knowing that He is our heavenly Father and His care for us is like none other. His arms of love are from everlasting to everlasting, His love for us cannot and will not be broken, no matter what happens in our lives or what decisions we make, God's love will never fail. His timing is perfect and His understanding of us is better than our parents, friends, and close relatives. His love stretches beyond our imagination. "Even if my father and mother abandon me, the LORD will hold me close" (Ps. 27:10 NLT). God our Father will make sure every void is completely filled in our lives; no matter what our age or our circumstances, God our Father holds us near and dear to His heart. Be encouraged this morning, my brothers and sisters. God our Father, through His loving Son Jesus Christ, loves us beyond what we can see.

> "I will thank the Lord because he is just; I will sing praise to the name of the LORD Most High" (Ps. 7:17 NLT).

Challenge of the day: Understand the power of the love from our Father in heaven and walk close to Him, because He desires to be close to you and me.

To God be the glory, many blessings, and have a blessed day. No matter what happens, have a blessed day!

Day 276

I pray that you all had a great evening. Start your morning off with God knowing that He is available to you. God is always available, no matter what time or place. "Behold, He who keeps Israel shall neither slumber nor sleep" (Ps. 121:4 NKJV). This is one of the many things I love about the God that we serve, we can call on Him anytime of the day. We can be driving down I-95, on Delta flight 17, or walking in the mall; He is indeed available to us at all times. He gives us that comfort, that peace, and understanding that we need. We must recognize His strength; even in the midst of our weakest moments, we must know that God is available through His Son Jesus Christ, the One who made it possible for all of us to be redeemed through His blood on the cross.

"Save me, O God, by Your name, and vindicate me by Your strength" (Ps. 54:1 NKJV).

Challenge of the day: Rest easy, knowing that you have Someone greater than yourself available to you so that your mind may be at ease and you can stop worrying about things over which you have no control.

Preparation for worship service: Have a constant mindset of total worship of God before entering your worship service. This may mean turning everything off so you have no distractions and can completely focus on God. Be very mindful that it is about giving God praise, glory, and honor. This not only will draw you closer to God, but will strengthen your own heart and faith.

To God be the glory, many blessings, and have a blessed worship experience.

Day 277

I pray that you had a great evening yesterday. Start your day off with God knowing that He is your Shepherd. He protects, cares, feeds, guides, and directs your paths. He leads us as we submit to Him daily in a one-on-one personal relationship. When David said, "The Lord is my shepherd," he made a personal proclamation concerning his personal relationship with God. There are a great deal of personal things that may be going on in our lives, which others may not understand or know about or may even disagree with, but the Shepherd gives guidance on how to live and deal with each and every situation we face through His living Word. Let's break Psalm 23:1 down: "The Lord is . . ." To me this is saying the Lord is everything I need, desire, and want. Because He Is, I shall not want anything or go lacking in any area of my life. David understood the comfort of the Lord and His concern for his personal well-being. Even today this is true! God our heavenly Father, through His dear Son Jesus Christ, ultimately is concerned about our personal well-being, and He desires to know about every detail in our lives. "I am the good shepherd; and I know My sheep and am known by My own" (John 10:14 NKJV). Be encouraged this morning, my brothers and sisters, that everything is already taken care of by our "Good Shepherd" Jesus Christ.

"THE LORD is my Shepherd [to feed, guide, and shield me], I shall not lack" (Ps. 23:1).

Challenge of the day: When we are hungry, we must look to Him who will feed us, both physically and spiritually, because His supplies are unlimited.

To God be the glory! Many blessings to you and have an awesome day and make a personal choice to feed on the Word of God.

Day 278

I pray that you all had a great night's rest, full of replenishment for today. Start your day off knowing that God is your Father and He cares deeply for you. His care for you is so great that He is oh-so-willing to hear and respond to your requests, especially when you ask Him to teach us how to live Holy and uprightly before Him and in the sight of humankind. It may not be often we may ask God the Father to teach us through the Holy Spirit how to live holy lives; but when a request like this is made, stand by and be prepared to go through an experience that you will never forget. A call to be holy has been mandated for years. "But as the One Who called you is holy, you yourselves also be holy in all your conduct and manner of living. For it is written, You shall be holy, for I am holy" (1 Pet. 1:15-16, refer also to Lev. 11:44, 45). Being holy is not just an outward appearance; it is from within, first understanding that to be holy is a great reflection of God. His characteristics are all over us as we are set apart and totally committed and dedicated toward Jesus Christ. To be holy requires action, even in the midst of being persecuted. Our holiness must stand out in the midst of all the horrific things that may be going on around us, and we must stand up for that which is right and pleasing in the sight of God. Our lifestyle must reflect the character of God, the place of dwelling for the Spirit of God is within us.

"Blessed is the man who walks not in the counsel of the ungodly, nor stands in the path of sinners, nor sits in the seat of the scornful; but his delight is in the law of the LORD, and in His law he meditates day and night" (Ps. 1:1, 2 NKJV).

Challenge of the day: Know where you stand with God and understand that God's care for us is greater than our fears.

To God be the glory, many blessings, and have a great day.

Day 279

I pray that you all had an awesome evening with family and friends yesterday. Start your day off with God knowing that He is your Protector. God protects us like a hen protects her chicks. He also is guarding over us with His heavenly angels. Even when the least amount of trouble appears, He is there ready and willing to protect what is rightfully His possession. "For You, Lord, will bless the [uncompromisingly] righteous [him who is upright and in right standing with You]; as with a shield You will surround him with goodwill (pleasure and favor)" (Ps. 5:12). Also know that when God places His favor upon you, people who you least expect will begin to bless you and even show you favor, even though they do not know why they are doing what they are doing. What an awesome God that we serve, One who is willing to protect us and provide us with His personal favor! Be encouraged this morning, my brothers and sisters, that God is not done with us yet. He has our best interests at heart and He holds in His hands the keys to open doors of opportunity. Stand fast and watch what God will do in our lives.

"But You, O Lord, are a shield for me, my glory, and the lifter of my head" (Ps. 3:3).

Challenge of the day: Be not concerned about those who come against you, know that God is your Shield and He will give you His favor.

To God be the glory, many blessings, and have a blessed and awesome day in God.

Day 280

I pray that you had a great evening yesterday. Start your day off with God knowing that He is a God of order. Everything has an order to it, in some shape or form. With God, everything must be done in decency and order. There must be order in our lives, both at home, work, and certainly at church. Establishing the presence of God in all of our dwelling places must first start with a true commitment toward God, particularly in view of how we go about conducting our day-to-day operations. There must be a sense of obedience and understanding of our purpose; no matter where we go or what we are doing, we are indeed a reflection of God, simply because we say we are Christians. This holds true to everything that we do; we must do it as to the Lord. "Whatever may be your task, work at it heartily (from the soul), as [something done] for the Lord and not for men, knowing [with all certainty] that it is from the Lord [and not from men] that you will receive the inheritance which is your [real] reward. [The One Whom] you are actually serving [is] the Lord Christ (the Messiah)" (Col. 3:23-24).

> "Oh come, let us worship and bow down; let us kneel before the LORD our Maker. For He is our God, and we are the people of His pasture, and the sheep of His hand" (Ps. 95:6, 7 NKJV).

Challenge of the day: Establish yourself as God has already established the foundation in which you dwell. Understanding that you are not placed in positions (at home, work, or where your serve) for your sake, but for the sake of glorifying God's holy name. (Always keep this before your mind and in your spirit.)

To God be the glory, many blessings, and have a blessed day following the order of the Lord.

Day 281

I pray that you had a peaceful rest last night. Start your day off with God, knowing that He keeps His promises and He is not slack concerning His promises. Oftentimes you may walk away from the promises of God because the principles may be hard to follow, like when the rich young ruler asked what he had to do to have eternal life and Jesus told him he must keep the commandments. The young rule asked which ones, and "Jesus said, '"You shall not murder," "You shall not commit adultery," "You shall not steal," "You shall not bear false witness," "Honor your father and mother," and, "You shall love your neighbor as yourself."' The young man said to Him, 'All these things I have kept from my youth. What do I still lack?' Jesus said to him, 'If you want to be perfect, go, sell what you have and give it to the poor, and you will have treasure in heaven; and come, follow Me.' But when the young man heard that saying, he went away sorrowful, for he had great possessions" (Matt. 19:18b-22 NKJV). Keeping the Word of God is vital to our relationship with God as believers; although things get hard sometimes, we must remember that God honors and keeps His Word. If God has told you something, do not give up or walk away from His promises, because He has your back. "He refreshes and restores my life (my self); He leads me in the paths of righteousness [uprightness and right standing with Him— not for my earning it, but] for His name's sake" (Ps. 23:3). He will neither leave you nor forsake you. Return to your rightful place in God and know that He still loves you.

"He is [earnestly] mindful of His covenant and forever it is imprinted on His heart, the word which He commanded and established to a thousand generations" (Ps. 105:8).

Challenge of the day: Know that God is mindful of what He said and He is mindful of our well-being; it is up to us to follow and keep what was told to us.

To God be the glory! Many blessings to you and have a blessed day and follow close to the Lord.

Day 282

I pray that yesterday was full of thanks, giving and the love of God for each and every one of you. Start your day off with God by blessing and praising His name at all times. "I WILL bless the Lord at all times; His praise shall continually be in my mouth" (Ps. 34:1). We must continue to lift up the name of the Lord Jesus Christ at all times, regardless of what is going on in our lives. Call on the Lord and He will hear us and will respond to our cry, as we have a sacrifice of praise on our lips. No matter what happened yesterday or what you are expecting to happen today, God knows about it already and He is watching and waiting on how you and I will respond to our situations. Will we praise and bless His name or will we say "I don't know what to do or who to turn to"? I am glad that God's love is boundless enough to respond to us; regardless of how we may be feeling or what happened in our past, He will respond to our cry in His time. "The eyes of the Lord are toward the [uncompromisingly] righteous and His ears are open to their cry" (Ps. 34:15).

"Behold, the Lord's eye is upon those who fear Him [who revere and worship Him with awe], who wait for Him and hope in His mercy and loving-kindness" (Ps. 33:18).

Challenge of the day: The Lord is watching us closely with a loving heart. How will we bless His name if we are running from Him?

To God be the glory, many blessings, and have a blessed day!

Day 283

Start your day off with God, knowing that at the remembrance of God's holy name we must give thanks. Thank Him for everything, yes, for even the small things in life we must be thankful. "In everything give thanks; for this is the will of God in Christ Jesus for you" (1 Thess. 5:18 NKJV). One having a thankful heart would really appreciate people and those things around them. No matter what is going on in your life, every day ought to be a day full of thanks, especially unto God, who has created us in His likeness and has given us authority and dominion over the things of the earth. We must appreciate and love God for who He is and respect the things with which He has blessed us, in order that we may enjoy this life. Be thankful always, realizing that every day we wake up is a day of thanksgiving. "That I may proclaim with the voice of thanksgiving, and tell of all Your wondrous works" (Ps. 26:7 NKJV). So be encouraged and always give thanks unto the Lord.

> "Let the words of my mouth and the meditation of my heart be acceptable in Your sight, O Lord, my [firm, impenetrable] Rock and my Redeemer" (Ps. 19:14).

Challenge of the day: Be thankful always and be mindful of that upon which you meditate.

To God be the glory, many blessings, and be thankful always.

Day 284

I pray that you had a great day and peaceful sleep last night. Start your day off with God knowing that God is AWESOME. There is no God like the One we serve, there is no God who will love us unconditionally. There is no God anywhere that can cause the rain to cease and to commence, like the God that we serve. There is no God like the one God we serve; there is no God who can love us unconditionally. There is no God anywhere that can cause the rain to cease and to commence, like the God that we serve. In God, we can find so many spectacular yet simple things in life at which to be amazed. It is in His attitude of creation that we can find inexpressible words. "Sing out the honor of His name; make His praise glorious. Say to God, 'How awesome are Your works! Through the greatness of Your power Your enemies shall submit themselves to You" (Ps. 66:2-3 NKJV). As believers, it is our duty to sing praises unto God, for who He is and for what He has done through His dear Son Jesus Christ! We must read and tell our own story of how awesome God is to us.

"Come and see the works of God; He is awesome in His doing toward the sons of men" (Ps. 66:5 NKJV).

Challenge for the day: Reflect on the greatness of God, knowing that it is because of Him we can do all things.

Challenge for worship service: Be ready to let your light shine before men, so they may see your good works and glorify you heavenly Father. Be ready to tell your story and sing with your heart and see how things will continue to change in your life.

To God be the glory, many blessings, and have a blessed day.

Day 285

I greet you with great joy and I pray that you had a good night's rest. Start your day off with God knowing that it is indeed a new day. A fresh start in the morning is our opportunity to praise and be thankful unto God, first for His being God and second for it being a new day. A new start is available, in spite of what happened yesterday. The truth is yesterday is gone and we can do nothing about it; we certainly cannot change it, just either accept it or forget about it. "Great is his faithfulness; his mercies begin afresh each morning" (Lam. 3:23 NLT). God is faithful and He gives us a fresh start every morning, with new mercies through Jesus Christ (who displayed great love toward all humankind by going to the cross and the grave and not staying there, but rising and sitting on the right hand of God the Father). We must indeed be grateful and glad about it. This morning, my brothers and sisters, be encouraged; it is a new day, yet with the same God, who is not slack concerning His promises. "No eye has seen, no ear has heard, and no mind has imagined what God has prepared for those who love him" (1 Cor. 2:9b NLT).

"Surely your goodness and unfailing love will pursue me all the days of my life, and I will live in the house of the LORD forever" (Ps. 23:6 NLT).

Challenge of the day: Rejoice knowing that God is ready to give us a new start every morning with His new mercies. Rejoice and be exceedingly glad about it!

To God be the glory, many blessings, and have a blessed day, rejoicing in the Lord.

Day 286

I pray that you had a grand evening. Start your day off with God, knowing how to rejoice in His creation and your daily surroundings. You must take some time to smell the roses every now and then and rejoice, knowing that all is well with our soul first and all of our situations. Paul let us know in Philippians 4:4: "Rejoice in the Lord always. Again I will say, rejoice!" (NKJV). Rejoicing in all matters should bring about a constant reminder that we are victorious, as we believe in Jesus Christ and in spite of what we may be facing at the moment. This morning, my brothers and sisters, rejoice knowing that God has everything under control as we maintain a prayerful heart. "Rejoicing in hope, patient in tribulation, continuing steadfastly in prayer" (Rom. 12:12 NKJV). "And we know that all things work together for good to those who love God, to those who are the called according to His purpose" (Rom. 8:28 NKJV).

"Rejoice in the Lord, O you righteous! For praise from the upright is beautiful" (Ps. 33:1 NKJV).

Challenge of the day: In the midst of trials and even changes, rejoice anyhow, knowing that God is in control!

To God be the glory, many blessings, and have a blessed day knowing that God is in control.

Day 287

I pray that you had a joyful evening. Start your day off with God, knowing that He is a Keeper. God will keep you in perfect peace, and He will protect you in the midst of storms and trials. God will keep you when the rain is pouring down and when the sun is shining bright; even when the clouds are hanging low, I declare to you this morning that God will keep you and will be your Guide this morning. "For this is God, our God forever and ever; He will be our guide even to death" (Ps. 48:14 NKJV). Keep your eyes focused on God this morning, and He will keep you and your heart and mind in perfect peace.

"The Lord is your keeper; the Lord is your shade on your right hand [the side not carrying a shield]" (Ps. 121:5).

Challenge of the day: Keep your eyes on God and be aware of His presence, especially during hard times. At all times, look toward the hills, "from whence comes [your] help" (Ps. 121:1b NKJV). Your help comes from God!

To God be the glory, many blessings, and have a great day!

Day 288

I pray that you had a peaceful night. Start your day with God, knowing that you must serve and please Him with a constant praise on your lips and in your heart. Praise Him when things are right and when things are going wrong. Praise Him in the morning, the noon day, evening, and at midnight. The beautiful thing about praising the Lord is that we can praise anywhere, anytime, and in any form, but we must praise God. "Serve the Lord with gladness; come before His presence with singing" (Ps. 100:2 NKJV). We should have a song of praise on our hearts regularly. How do we please God? By having faith in Him. "But without faith it is impossible to please and be satisfactory to Him. For whoever would come near to God must [necessarily] believe that God exists and that He is the rewarder of those who earnestly and diligently seek Him [out]" (Heb. 11:6).

> "PRAISE THE Lord! For it is good to sing praises to our God, for He is gracious and lovely; praise is becoming and appropriate" (Ps. 147:1).

Challenge of the day: Praise God every moment you get and serve Him with a glad heart, through faith in Jesus Christ, knowing this will build and strengthen your faith in God daily!

To God be the glory! Many blessings to you and have a blessed day and praise the Lord.

Day 289

I pray that you all had an awesome worship experience like I did. It is truly something when you prepare to enter into the house of God. Start your day off knowing that God is the Healer; He will heal you and make you whole. This will come about through your faith in God's ability to do what His Word declares in Exodus 15:26: "Saying, if you will diligently hearken to the voice of the Lord your God and will do what is right in His sight, and will listen to and obey His commandments and keep all His statues, I will put none of the diseases upon you which I brought upon the Egyptians, for I am the Lord Who heals you." God will heal you, you just have to believe. He is the same God today, yesterday, and forever; He changes not. "Is anyone among you sick? He should call in the church elders (the spiritual guides). And they should pray over him, anointing him with oil in the Lord's name. And the prayer [that is] of faith will save him who is sick, and the Lord will restore him; and if he has committed sins, he will be forgiven" (James 5:14-15).

"Who forgives [every one of] all your iniquities, Who heals [each one of] all your diseases" (Ps. 103:3).

Challenge of the day: Know that God will heal you. Just allow Him in and watch Him work the miracles that you need in your life, through faith in Jesus Christ! I believe that He can, do you?

To God be the glory, many blessings, and have a blessed day. God still heals.

Day 290

I pray that your day is starting off well knowing that God is love. God loves us more than we could ever imagine. Even in the darkest times in our lives, God's love is ever present. God's love will never fail you or hinder you, but will encourage and strengthen you during challenging times in your life. God's love never fails. "Love suffers long and is kind; love does not envy; love does not parade itself, is not puffed up; does not behave rudely, does not seek its own, is not provoked, thinks no evil; does not rejoice in iniquity, but rejoices in the truth; bears all things, believes all things, hopes all things, endures all things. Love never fails . . ." (1 Cor. 13:4-8 NKJV). The love that God has displayed toward us will keep us in line with His will and way. The love of God is unconditional, and likewise we must return the same love toward ourselves and others. Often we can be too hard on ourselves, even forgetting to love ourselves and others according to the will of God.

"For I know the thoughts I think toward you, says the LORD, thoughts of peace and not of evil, to give you a future and a hope" (Jer. 29:11 NKJV).

Challenge of the day: It matters what God thinks of you, so why fret the small things in life? Think and see yourself like God thinks and sees you (like only a loving Father can).

A challenge for worship service: Prepare to enter your worship service before going there. Start a prayer and meditation service within your preparation time, prior to getting to church. Once you arrive, you will notice a complete difference and you will be truly ready to worship God in spirit and truth.

To God be the glory, many blessings, and have a blessed day. God is love.

Day 291

I pray that you had a blessed evening, one full of peace and joy. Start your day with God, knowing that there is nothing too hard for God and all things are possible to them that believe. If you have faith enough to believe it will happen, then it will happen. Whatever your "it" is, just believe and understand what this verse means to you personally "Jesus said to him, 'If you can believe, all things are possible to him who believes'" (Mark 9:23 NKJV). Believe that you are destined for greatness, beloved, and know that Him who created you is not done with you yet! Be encouraged this morning, my brothers and sisters, that God has completed the work. We just have to believe and know that Jesus is Lord over our lives.

> "Oh, clap your hands, all you peoples! Shout to God with the voice of triumph! For the LORD Most High is awesome; He is a great King over all the earth" (Ps. 47:1-2 NKJV).

Challenge of the day: Take the limits off of God, let Him be Lord of your life, and watch how your life will change!

To God be the glory! Many blessings to each of you and have a blessed and AWESOME day!

Day 292

I greet you this morning with the love of Christ in my heart, and I pray that you all had an awesome and blessed evening. Start your day with God knowing that He is your comfort and joy. The Holy Spirit the Comforter will guide us into all truth, because He is the Spirit of truth. Knowing that in our lifetime, things will happen and we may not understand it then, but the Spirit of God will comfort us during that period in our lives and His joy will be upon us. "I still have many things to say to you, but you cannot bear them now. However, when He, the Spirit of truth, has come, He will guide you into all truth; for He will not speak on His own authority, but whatever He hears He will speak; and He will tell you things to come" (John 16:12-13 NKJV). Be encouraged—all is not lost. Trust God by knowing and understanding His truth.

> "Yea, though I walk through the valley of the shadow of death, I will fear no evil; for You are with me; Your rod and Your staff, they comfort me" (Ps. 23:4 NKJV).

Challenge of the day: Look for the truth in all things, knowing that God has your back, front, and both sides. In other words, know that you are comforted and covered by God, through His loving Son Jesus Christ.

To God be the glory! Many blessings to you and have a blessed day loving the Word of God.

Day 293

I pray that you all had a great evening. Start your day with God, knowing that He will guide you on the right path. No matter what may come your way, trust God to set your pathway straight. On this pathway you will find peace that only God can give. "And the peace of God, which surpasses all understanding, will guard your hearts and minds through Christ Jesus" (Phil. 4:7 NKJV). Walking in the pathway of God's counsel will cause you to triumph over many of the trials that you may encounter throughout your life, but His peace will keep your mind and heart clear from turmoil.

> "Blessed is the man who walks not in the counsel of the ungodly, nor stands in the path of sinners, nor sits in the seat of the scornful; but his delight is in the law of the LORD, and in His law he meditates day and night" (Ps. 1:1-2 NKJV).

Challenge of the day: Walk uprightly before God and notice how your life will begin to turn around for the better.

To God be the glory! Many blessings and have a blessed day, living uprightly before God and humankind.

Day 294

I pray that you had a safe and enjoyable evening. When starting your day off with God, you must reflect on how AWESOME God is! Also reflect on how much He loves and delights in us—so much that He sent His only begotten Son Jesus Christ. Understanding that God is AWESOME enough to set apart those who are godly for Himself: His personal worship, pleasure, and enjoyment! What an AWESOME God we serve. "Shall not His majesty make afraid, and should not your awe for Him restrain you?" (Job 13:11). So be encouraged this morning and step back and ponder the awesome power and love of God.

"But know that the LORD has set apart for Himself him who is godly; the LORD will hear when I call to Him" (Ps. 4:3 NKJV).

Challenge of the day: Know that you are truly special in the sight of God, no matter what others may say or think about you, or even how you may feel about yourself, you are indeed set apart for God by God.

To God be the glory and many blessings. Have a blessed day thinking about the wonders of the Lord.

Day 295

I pray that you all had a peaceful night. Start your day off with God, knowing that He is a Keeper and Protector, who truly adores us, His creation. He is a Shield and Buckler for all who trust in Him. Dealing with change is not always easy; however, the certainty of God's love and protections should comfort us during the time of change. We must understand that God will never leave us or forsake us; He always will be there for us at all times.

"Show Your marvelous lovingkindness by Your right hand, O You who save those who trust in You from those who rise up against them. Keep me as the apple of Your eye; hide me under the shadow of Your wings" (Ps. 17:7, 8 NKJV).

Challenge of the day: Whatever your surroundings or situations may be, understand that you are kept by God.

To God be the glory and many blessings and have a blessed day

Day 296

I pray that you all had a blessed evening. Starting your day off with God can be like having a conversation with your best friend. God indeed desires to be our friend. John 15:14-16 says, "You are my friends if you do whatever I command you. No longer do I call you servants, for a servant does not know what his master is doing; but I have called you friends, for all things that I heard from My Father I have made known to you. You did not choose Me, but I chose you and appointed you that you should go and bear fruit, and that your fruit should remain, that whatever you ask the Father in My name He may give you" (NKJV). Know that all that we do must be for the love of Jesus Christ, as He commands us in John 15:17 to love one another. Starting your morning with a conversation with God is essential to your personal walk with Christ.

"My voice You shall hear in the morning, O LORD;
in the morning I will direct it to You, and I will look
up" (Ps. 5:3 NKJV).

Challenge of the day: Look up in the morning and speak to your best friend; God is waiting to hear from you.

To God be the glory and many blessings. Speak to the Lord and He will speak back to you.

Day 297

I pray that all of you had a blessed day and also will have a blessed week ahead. Rising early this morning, start your day with God. Meditate on seeking the face of God. "One thing I have desired of the LORD, that will I seek: that I may dwell in the house of the LORD all the days of my life, to behold the beauty of the LORD, and to inquire in His temple" (Ps. 27:4 NKJV). Everything about God is awesome, and we must seek constantly to be with Him, from the rising of the sun until the going down of the same, knowing and understanding this to be our desire . . . to be with Him all the days of our lives. Seek God, and live according to His will for your life!

"But seek first the kingdom of God and His righteousness, and all these things shall be added to you (Matt. 6:33 NKJV).

Challenge of the day: Enjoy the beauty of being in the presence of God. In spite of what the day may hold for you, seek the Lord always, and you shall live through the blood of Jesus Christ the risen Savior as you confess Him as your Lord and Savior.

To God be the glory, many blessings, and enjoy the presence of God.

Day 298

I pray that all is well with each of you and your family. Start your day off with God knowing that we must walk in the light of the Lord. We must rely on the Holy Spirit to guide and direct our steps. The Spirit of the Lord will reveal unto us the things that we need to do. Recognizing the Holy Spirit is vital to our walk in the light and our relationship with Christ. "But if we [really] are living and walking in the Light, as He [Himself] is in the Light, we have [true, unbroken] fellowship with one another, and the blood of Jesus Christ His Son cleanses (removes) us from all sin and guilt [keeps us cleansed from sin in all its forms and manifestations]" (1 John 1:7). So be encouraged this morning and praise God for the ability to walk and live under His guidance and direction. Certainly know without a doubt that we are forgiven because of the blood of Christ Jesus.

"And such some of you were [once]. But you were washed clean (purified by a complete atonement for sin and made free from the guilt of sin), and you were consecrated (set apart, hallowed), and you were justified [pronounced righteous, by trusting] in the name of the Lord Jesus Christ and in the [Holy] Spirit of our God" (1 Cor. 6:11).

Challenge of the day: Don't live in what you used to be, live in who God declares that you are now, through the blood of Christ. Live in the light and walk uprightly before God. Know that you are consecrated and set apart for the work of the kingdom of God.

To God be the glory! Many blessings to you and have a powerful day living a consecrated life in Christ.

Day 299

I pray that all is well with you. Start your day off with God knowing that you must walk through the open doors that God provides for us. Sometimes it may seem that the blessings coming our way are not real or are hard to believe; well, believe it, my brothers and sisters. God is not slack concerning His promises for you and your life. God will provide opportunities for us to represent Him on all levels, but we must be available and hearken to His voice. "Now when I arrived at Troas [to preach] the good news (the Gospel) of Christ, a door of opportunity was opened for me in the Lord" (2 Cor. 2:12). So be encouraged this morning and walk through the doors of opportunity and allow God to do the rest. He has provided you with His favor, so why fret?

> "Be earnest and unwearied and steadfast in your prayer [life], being [both] alert and intent in [your praying] with thanksgiving. And at the same time pray for us also, that God may open a door to us for the Word (the Gospel), to proclaim the mystery concerning Christ (the Messiah) on account of which I am in prison" (Col 4:2, 3).

Challenge of the day: Pray and step out on faith. Walk through the open doors and do not be moved by what you see, just believe God to lead you.

To God be the glory! Many blessings and have a powerful day observing God opening doors that no one can open.

Day 300

I pray that all is well with you. Start your day off with God, knowing that we were created in the image and likeness of God, uniquely made by the hand of the almighty and everlasting God. We should not fear what others say about us or how one may categorize us. We must be grateful that the hand of God is resting upon our lives. "God said, Let Us [Father, Son, and Holy Spirit] make mankind in Our image, after Our likeness, and let them have complete authority over the fish of the sea, the birds of the air, the [tame] beasts, and over all of the earth, and over everything that creeps upon the earth" (Gen. 1:26). So be encouraged this morning and know that we are in the likeness of God the Father, Son, and Holy Spirit. Do not be afraid to express that which is in us, the living Word of God, or allow others to see Christ within us, because we may be the only sermon they will ever see or hear. Speak Jesus daily through your actions and likeness of Him.

"And have clothed yourselves with the new [spiritual self], which is [ever in the process of being] renewed and remolded into [fuller and more perfect knowledge upon] knowledge after the image (the likeness) of Him Who created it" (Col. 3:10).

Challenge of the day: Be like Christ.

To God be the glory! Many blessings to you and have a powerful day being Christlike, serving others with humility, love, and compassion.

Day 301

I pray that all is well with you. Start your day off with God knowing that you must come to God with clean hands and a pure heart. You must not try to hide from God; the truth is we cannot hide from God, because He is present. Lift your hearts unto the Lord and listen close to His guidance and act upon His request. "Who shall go up into the mountain of the Lord? Or who shall stand in His Holy Place? He who has clean hands and a pure heart, who has not lifted himself up to falsehood or to what is false, nor sworn deceitfully. He shall receive blessing from the Lord and righteousness from the God of his salvation" (Ps. 24:3-5). So be encouraged this morning and lift up your hands and heart to the Lord; live uprightly before Him and walk in His blessings and salvation.

> "Blessed (happy, enviably fortunate, and spiritually prosperous—possessing the happiness produced by the experience of God's favor and especially conditioned by the revelation of His grace, regardless of their outward conditions) are the pure in heart, for they shall see God!" (Matt. 5:8).

Challenge of the day: Prepare yourself in such a manner to live uprightly before God daily, so that your heart will be pure before Him and you will receive your just reward and favor.

To God be the glory! Many blessings and have a powerful day surrendering your hands and heart to the Lord Jesus Christ.

Day 302

I pray that you had a great rest and that your family is in order and at peace. Start your day off with God knowing that you must possess a sense of accountability to one another. We as believers must look out for one another, care for one another, and always pray for one another. Not just for the folk in our small circle, but for believers all over. The power of prayer can mean life for someone on the mission field in Africa or in Russia. We are to be our "brother's keeper." (Refer to Gen. 4:9.) We are not designed to walk in this faith walk alone, and we are never lonely, because God is ever-present. "So that there should be no division or discord or lack of adaptation [of the parts of the body to each other], but the members all alike should have a mutual interest in and care for one another" (1 Cor. 12:25). So be encouraged this morning and care for and take a sincere interest in one another; it is good for the entire body of Christ. Caring and praying for one another will increase the effectiveness of ministering and sharing the gospel of Jesus Christ globally. Reach out and touch the hearts of others through loving them and being accountable as a believer in Jesus Christ.

"For I have no one like him [no one of so kindred a spirit] who will be so genuinely interested in your welfare and devoted to you interests" (Phil. 2:20).

Challenge of the day: Be devoted and sincere about the interests of others. Care enough about them to love them.

To God be the glory! Many blessings and have a powerful day helping others!

Day 303

I pray that all is well with each of you and your family. Start your day off with God knowing that we must eat the good of the land. Feed on the Word of God and rejoice, knowing that life is available to us through Jesus Christ. He has made every opportunity available to us to serve Him, love Him, know Him, and especially to love others. "And out of the ground the Lord God made to grow every tree that is pleasant to the sight or to be desired—good (suitable, pleasant) for food; the tree of life also in the center of the garden, and the tree of the knowledge of [the difference between] good and evil and blessing and calamity" (Gen. 2:9). So be encouraged this morning, brothers and sisters, and let the Word of God fill your soul, mind, and heart. Feast on it because it is food for the soul.

> "He who is able to hear, let him listen to and give heed to what the Spirit says to the assemblies (churches). To him who overcomes (is victorious), I will grant to eat [of the fruit] of the tree of life, which is in the paradise of God" (Rev. 2:7).

Challenge of the day: Listen, overcome, and be victorious through the Word of God and eat for life, now and forever!

To God be the glory! Many blessings and have a blessed day feeding on and living out the Word of the living God through Jesus Christ our risen Savior, with the guidance and direction of the Holy Spirit.

Day 304

I pray that all is well with each of you and your family. Start your day off with God knowing that you must understand and receive the joy of the Lord. You cannot afford to walk around being sad or disappointed when things do not go your way. We must lift our heads up high, sing the songs of Zion, and shout with a joyful heart unto the Lord. Because He still loves us in spite of our situations and circumstances in life, we still must have joy in Jesus Christ. He died on the cross for us, so what do we really have to be sad and downhearted about? It is He who will provide and give us what we need. "If you keep My commandments [if you continue to obey My instructions], you will abide in My love and live on in it, just as I have obeyed My Father's commandments and live on in His love. I have told you these things, that My joy and delight may be in you, and that your joy and gladness may be of full measure and complete and overflowing" (John 15:10-11). So be encouraged this morning and receive the Lord's joy. Be steadfast in living out His Word and do not follow the mood swings of this world, but have faith and live in the joy of the Lord.

> "May the God of your hope so fill you with all joy and peace in believing [through the experience of your faith] that by the power of the Holy Spirit you may abound and be overflowing (bubbling over) with hope" (Rom. 15:13).

Challenge of the day: Believe that the Holy Spirit will cause your hope, joy, and peace to overflow during the storms of life. Hold on; God is not done with you yet! Do not give up, face the things (issues) of life with faith in God.

To God be the glory! Many blessings to you, have a peaceful day in the Lord, and experience God's joy like never before.

Day 305

I pray that all is well with each of you and your family. Start your day off with God knowing that you must live by faith. Our faith will move the heart of God. You must find yourselves in the Word of God and allow the Word to abide deep within your hearts, and the Word will manifest itself through your daily actions by faith. "Now it is evident that no person is justified (declared righteous and brought into right standing with God) through the Law, for the Scripture says, The man in right standing with God [the just, the righteous] shall live by and out of faith and he who through and by faith is declared righteous and in right standing with God shall live" (Gal. 3:11). So be encouraged this morning and move the heart of God by your faith walk. Let not the troubles of this world get you down or hold you back. Trust God and live by faith, knowing that faith comes by hearing and hearing by the Word of God. (Refer to Rom. 10:17.)

"For in the Gospel a righteousness which God ascribes is revealed, both springing from faith and leading to faith [disclosed through the way of faith that arouses to more faith]. As it is written, The man who through faith is just and upright shall live and shall live by faith" (Rom. 1:17).

Challenge of the day: When challenges come your way, allow your faith in God to provide the comfort and understanding of how to handle those challenges of life. Move by faith and not by your circumstances, because your faith in God will change the circumstances of life.

To God be the glory! Many blessings to you and have a powerful day serving the Lord and living by faith.

Day 306

I pray that all is well with each of you and that you and your family are living in good health. Start your day off with God, knowing that we must strive to live in peace with one another, not being quarrelsome or envious, but in love and peace. Many walk around holding on to old grudges and will not offer a smile, a handshake, or even a word to the person that upset them. As believers of Christ and in Christ, we must be at peace with one another, because the reality is we do not know when it will be our last day on earth. So smile, love, have joy, and be at peace with everyone. "Now also we beseech you, brethren, get to know those who labor among you [recognize them for what they are, acknowledge and appreciate and respect them all]—your leaders who are over you in the Lord and those who warn and kindly reprove and exhort you. And hold them in very high and most affectionate esteem in [intelligent and sympathetic] appreciation of their work. Be at peace among yourselves" (1 Thess. 5:12-13). So be encouraged this morning and walk in peace among everyone, from your home to your office or job site, showing the love of Jesus Christ.

> "Strive to live in peace with everybody and pursue that consecration and holiness without which no one will [ever] see the Lord" (Heb. 12:14).

Challenge of the day: Do not be particular with whom you choose to live in peace, pursue it with everyone as you are striving to live a holy and consecrated life before the Lord Jesus Christ.

To God be the glory! Many blessings to you and have a powerful day living in peace with all who walk across your life.

Day 307

I pray that all is well with each of you and your family. Start your day off with God knowing that we are a chosen people. We are special to God. He chose us to do His will and to be obedient unto Him. God's love for us is deeper than we can ever imagine. He cares for us, and every opportunity that He gets He wants to bless us; in fact, He wants His blessings to overtake us. So why fret or be concerned about what others may say about you? They may say that we cannot do this, or that we will never amount to anything, but hold up a second, we belong to God, the Creator of the universe! And we are His chosen people; He created us in His image and with authority and power, so we are not weak nor should we be fearful. We are royal priests, a peculiar nation, so why accept anything less than what God has in store for . . . the best? "You whom I [the Lord] have taken from the ends of the earth and have called from the corners of it, and said to you, You are My servant—I have chosen you and not cast you off [even though you are exiled]" (Isa. 41:9). So be encouraged this morning and do not let your past hinder your future. You are chosen by God, and there is nothing anyone or thing can do about it. Rest well and serve the Lord.

> "Who gave Himself on our behalf that He might redeem us (purchase our freedom) from all iniquity and purify for Himself a people [to be peculiarly His own, people who are] eager and enthusiastic about [living a life that is food and filled with] beneficial deeds" (Titus 2:14).

Challenge of the day: Live like you are chosen and a peculiar child of the Most High God. Jesus paid the cost, so do not spend your life wasting time; do the business of the Father and love those whom you are to serve.

To God be the glory! Many blessings to you and have a powerful day in the Lord walking and speaking as a chosen generation.

Day 308

I pray that all is well with each of you and your family. Start your day off with God, knowing that you must be clear about what it is God desires for you to be doing in your life. He will not have us lost and without direction. The Holy Spirit will guide and direct you, but you must be obedient to the Spirit of God and follow His leading. Do not be confused about what it is you are supposed to be doing; seek and ask God to reveal your gifts and purpose for life. Have that certainty with God through constantly developing your relationship with Jesus Christ. "Making your ear attentive to skillful and godly Wisdom and inclining and directing your heart and mind to understanding [applying all your powers to the quest for it]" (Prov. 2:2). So be encouraged this morning and set your mind on the things of God. Be attentive to godly wisdom, in order that your path of life will be straight on doing the will of God, and that there will be no confusion or misguiding about what it is you must do for the Lord.

"A man's mind plans his way, but the Lord directs his steps and make them sure" (Prov. 16:9).

Challenge of the day: When God direct your steps, expect to follow His guidance and know for certain that everything will work out for His glory and your good.

To God be the glory! Many blessings and have a powerful day following the plans that God has laid before you.

Day 309

I pray that all is well with each of you and your family. Start your day off with God, knowing that we must be willing to know God better. He knows all about us and what we are in need of; in fact He knows what we like and dislike, and we in turn must know the likes and dislikes of God. Esteeming God as the most important factor and person in our lives will cause us to know God better each and every day. "And He replied to him, You shall love the Lord your God with all your heart and with all your soul and with all your mind (intellect). This is the great (most important, principal) and first commandment" (Matt. 22:37-38). So be encouraged this morning, desire and be willing to get to know God better by loving Him more than yourself. Spend time communicating with God and discovering what it is He desires from you on a daily basis. Seek Him out and at the same time find out more about the abilities that are within you that you have not yet tapped into.

"I have come in My Father's name and with His power, and you do not receive Me [your hearts are not open to Me, you give Me no welcome]; but if another comes in his own name and his own power and with no other authority but himself, you will receive him and give him your approval. How is it possible for you to believe [how can you learn to believe], you who [are content to seek and] receive praise and honor and glory from one another, and yet do not seek the praise and honor and glory which come from Him Who alone is God?" (John 5:43-44).

Challenge of the day: Put nothing or no one before God; develop your personal relationship, seek the Lord, and you will find Him and find out who you really are in the Lord. Be willing to receive the Lord and know Him better.

To God be the glory! Many blessings and have a blessed day spending time knowing the Lord like never before.

Day 310

I pray that all is well with you and your family this morning. Start your day off with God knowing that there is life in the spoken word. If you speak something, then it will manifest itself sooner or later. The power of words came from the beginning of creation. God spoke and things happened. We, being created in the image and likeness of the Lord God, possess the same authority. So take authority over the words that you speak and carefully and wisely choose your words. "For by your words you will be justified and acquitted, and by your words you will be condemned and sentenced" (Matt. 12:37). So be encouraged this morning and listen to the words around you and to those you speak. Take note how words can change your life and when you speak, ponder on the living Word of God and the nature of its power.

> "Death and life are in the power of the tongue, and they who indulge in it shall eat the fruit of it [for death or life]" (Prov. 18:21).

Challenge of the day: What words are you speaking to your situation: are they life or death, positive or negative? Whatever words you are speaking, they are what your situation will become. It will be evident by the fruit that the words bear. So speak life, the Word (Jesus), and live through your situation. How can you speak Jesus? You must know the Word of God and the power thereof.

To God be the glory! Many blessings to you and have a powerful day, letting the rivers of living water flow in your life.

Day 311

I pray that all is well with you and your family. Start your day off with God, knowing that we must be loyal and committed unto the Lord, because you were bought with a price—the love, death, and resurrection of Christ Jesus. We must display our loyalty unto the Lord, because He is faithful and just unto us; in spite of what we've done or even are doing in our lives, the Lord remains faithful. "You were bought with a price [purchased with a preciousness and paid for by Christ]; then do not yield yourselves up to become [in your own estimation] slaves to men [but consider yourselves slaves to Christ]" (1 Cor. 7:23). So be encouraged this morning and consider who you are loyal and committed to. Christ has already made His determination; what about you?

"For we [Christians] are the true circumcision, who worship God in spirit and by the Spirit of God and exult and glory and pride ourselves in Jesus Christ, and put no confidence or dependence [on what we are] in the flesh and on outward privileges and physical advantages and external appearances" (Phil. 3:3).

Challenge of the day: Let the Christ in you be glorified and not be overzealous with the things of the world.

To God be the glory! Many blessings to you and have a powerful day being loyal to the Lord Jesus Christ.

Day 312

I pray that all is well with you and your family. Start your day off with God knowing that we must live holy lives. You must be willing to separate yourselves from the things of the world and lay hold of the things of God. Holiness is not just a word that stands out, but one that requires action on our part. We must bear the characteristics of Jesus Christ. It is not only about how we dress or speak, but also about our lifestyle for Christ. "And put on the new nature (the regenerate self) created in God's image, [Godlike] in true righteousness and holiness" (Eph. 4:24). So be encouraged this morning and wear your holy lifestyle like it is near and dear to you. Grow into it and develop it daily.

> "For in the time being no discipline brings joy, but seems grievous and painful; but afterwards it yields a peaceable fruit of righteousness to those who have been trained by it [a harvest of fruit which consists in righteousness—in conformity to God's will in purpose, thought, and action, resulting in right living and right standing with God]" (Heb. 12:11).

Challenge of the day: Accept discipline; in fact, learn to discipline your life and watch how holiness and right living will become a habit.

To God be the glory! Many blessings and have a powerful day living a holy and upright life before the Lord Jesus Christ.

Day 313

I pray that all is well with you and that your family is soaring like an eagle in the Lord. Start your day off with God knowing that you must know the Lord as your protector and stronghold. He is our refuge and shelter; even in times of trouble and hard times, God will be there to encourage us to move on and walk under His protective arms. The Lord will make His presence known in our situations; we just have to be attentive to His voice and presence. "The Lord will thunder and roar from Zion and utter His voice from Jerusalem, and the heavens and the earth shall shake; but the Lord will be a refuge for His people and a stronghold to the children of Israel" (Joel 3:16). So be encouraged this morning and fall under the Lord's shield and stronghold. Know and feel His presence; regardless of what is going on in your life, stay close to the Lord and know Him as your refuge, protector, and stronghold. Relax, God's got everything under control; breathe again.

"THE LORD is my Light and my Salvation—whom shall I fear or dread? The Lord is the Refuge and Stronghold of my life—of whom shall I be afraid?" (Ps. 27:1).

Challenge of the day: Know the Lord as your Light, your Guide, and your Salvation—in whom you have spiritual (life) and freedom. Fear not; only believe God to be Lord of all.

To God be the glory! Many blessings and have a powerful day, walking as one who is protected by the Lord and without fear.

Day 314

I pray that all is well with you and your family. Start your day off with God, knowing that we must hear God clearly, listen attentively to the voice of God, and reason well. In the midst of excitement or uncertainty, you must know the voice of God and make your move with peace of heart and mind. Do not jump to conclusions, know the heart of the matter and hear God's voice. "Come now, and let us reason together, says the Lord. Though your sins are like scarlet, they shall be as white as snow; though they are red like crimson, they shall be like wool. If you are willing and obedient, you shall eat the good of the land; but if you refuse and rebel, you will be devoured by the sword. For the mouth of the Lord has spoken it" (Isa. 1:18-20). So be encouraged this morning and hear God's voice concerning your life. Move responsively and with a clear mind and heart. May God's peace rest upon your life, and there will be no fear amongst you.

"Behold, You desire truth in the inner being; make me therefore to know wisdom in my inmost heart. Purify me with hyssop, and I shall be clean [ceremonially]; wash me, and I shall [in reality] be whiter than snow" (Ps. 51:6-7).

Challenge of the day: Stand clean before the Lord, seek wisdom for your life, listen to the voice of God with your heart, and make that change that He is calling you to make in your life.

To God be the glory! Many blessings to you and have a powerful day and listen for the voice of the Lord Jesus Christ.

Day 315

I pray that all is well with you and your family. Start your day off with God, knowing that we must not be caught up in gossip or backbiting, but we must always show love toward one another. Gossip and backbiting only cause pain and misery; nothing good ever comes out of it. As believers, we must be cautious not to fall in these traps, but be watchful and prayerful all the time. "For I am fearful that somehow or other I may come and find you not as I desire to find you, and that you may find me too not as you want to find me—that perhaps there may be factions (quarreling), jealousy, temper (wrath, intrigues, rivalry, divided, loyalties), selfishness, whispering, gossip, arrogance (self-assertion), and disorder among you. [I am fearful] that when I come again, my God may humiliate and humble me in your regard, and that I may have to sorrow over many of those who sinned before and have not repented of the impurity, sexual vice, and sensuality which they formerly practiced" (2 Cor. 12:20-21). So be encouraged this morning and release your heart from those practices that will hinder you in your relationship with Christ. Do not get caught up in them again, but repent and be released.

"Now which do you prefer? Shall I come to you with a rod of correction, or with love and in a spirit of gentleness?" (1 Cor. 4:21).

Challenge of the day: The choice is yours; receive a rod of correction or receive love with a spirit of gentleness. The determination will be based on how you are living your life.

To God be the glory! Many blessings and have a powerful day. Be encouraged to live right before the Lord and be in good company.

Day 316

I pray that all is well with you and your family. Start your day off with God knowing that we are strengthened and guided by the Holy Spirit. We cannot walk in our own strength, but we must rely on the strength of the Lord. "May He grant you out of the rich treasury of His glory to be strengthened and reinforced with mighty power in the inner man by the [Holy] Spirit [Himself indwelling your innermost being and personality]. May Christ through your faith [actually] dwell (settle down, abide, make His permanent home) in your hearts! May you be rooted deep in love and founded securely on love" (Eph. 3:16-17). So be encouraged this morning and stand strong in the Lord and the power of His might; follow the guidance of the Holy Spirit from the inside out and receive and acknowledge the glory of the Lord upon your life. Also allow Christ to reside permanently within your heart, and your life must reflect such dwelling thereof.

> "That you may walk (live and conduct yourselves) in a manner worthy of the Lord, fully pleasing to Him and desiring to please Him in all things, bearing fruit in every good work and steadily growing and increasing in and by the knowledge of God [with fuller, deeper, and clearer insight, acquaintance, and recognition]. [We pray] that you may be invigorated and strengthened with all power according to the might of His glory, [to exercise] every kind of endurance and patience (perseverance and forbearance) with joy, giving thanks to the Father, Who has qualified and made us fit to share the portion which is the inheritance of the saints (God's holy people) in the Light" (Col. 1:10-12).

Challenge of the day: Walk in the strength that the Lord has given you, producing good fruit in all that you do. Desire to please the Lord and share in the inheritance that belongs to us, His holy children, through Christ Jesus.

To God be the glory! Many blessings to you and have a powerful day.

Day 317

I pray that all is well with you and your family and may God's peace be within your households. Start your day off with God knowing that you have the measure of faith. You have faith; you just have to operate in it and not be afraid of what can be accomplished in God. We must be willing to examine yourselves and your faith walk with God, not being prideful or puffed up. Know where you stand with God and seek His guidance daily, as you walk this walk as a believer of Christ in faith. "For by the grace (unmerited favor of God) given to me I warn everyone among you not to estimate and think of himself more highly than he ought [not to have an exaggerated opinion of his own importance], but to rate his ability with sober judgment, each according to the degree of faith apportioned by God to him" (Rom. 12:3). So be encouraged this morning and use the faith that God has given you; tap into it and be not afraid of what God can do in you and through you for His glory.

> "Yet grace (God's unmerited favor) was given to each of us individually [not indiscriminately, but in different ways] in proportion to the measure of Christ's [rich and bounteous] gift. Therefore it is said, when He ascended on high, He led captivity captive [He led a train of vanquished foes] and He bestowed gifts on men" (Eph. 4:7, 8).

Challenge of the day: You have God-given gifts (and His grace); find out what they are and use them in the faith that God has already given to you. Use them according to your ability, with the mindset of God will get the glory. The path is already cleared for you, just walk with faith and in grace.

To God be the glory! Many blessings and have a powerful day walking in faith and using the gifts within.

Day 318

I pray that all is well with you. Start your day off with God knowing you must rely on Him. Relying on and trusting in God means the self factor is out of the window. Self can be self-destructive spiritually if we are not careful. God must be at the forefront of our lives in order to truly live a life that is pleasing unto the Lord. Oftentimes it is easy to put the cart before the horse, but in this day and age, God needs to be driving and directing us in the cart on the path of righteousness. "Who among you fears the LORD? Who obeys the voice of His Servant? Who walks in darkness and has no light? Let him trust in the name of the LORD and rely upon his God" (Isa. 50:10 NKJV). So be encouraged this morning; trust, rely, and lean on the living God, the Lord Jesus Christ who is the Lord of life, the Lord of Lords, and the King of Kings. Trust God to bring us out of our comfort zones and live a life that is pleasing unto Him.

"Yea though I walk through the valley of the shadow of death, I will fear no evil; for You are with me; Your rod and staff, they comfort me" (Ps. 23:4 NKJV).

Challenge of the day: Although darkness and trials may be around you, it does not mean you have to give up on life. Trouble comes and trouble goes, but God always will be with you. So trust and rely on God for deliverance.

To God be the glory! Many blessings to you and trust in the living God during this time and for always. He will never leave you or forsake you. Have a powerful day and week in the Lord, leaning on the promises of Jesus Christ.

Day 319

This is the day the Lord has made; let us rejoice and be glad in it. I pray that all is well with you. Start your day off with God knowing we must recognize the fire and passion within to serve the living God. Jeremiah the prophet proclaimed God's Word of judgment and destruction until it came to pass. He was at a point of giving up and throwing in the towel, but the Word was too consuming for him and he could not hinder the Word from going forth. "Then I said, 'I will not make mention of Him, nor speak anymore in His name.' But His word was in my heart like a burning fire shut up in my bones; I was weary of holding it back and I could not" (Jer. 20:9 NKJV). So be encouraged this morning and let the fire of God's Word and the Holy Spirit rest within and move you to serve the living God. Declare and share in the Word of God, in order that people will have hope and know the power and love of Jesus Christ the risen Savior, who died on the cross for the sins of the entire world. Do not lose the fire, but desire to serve the living God.

"My heart was hot within me; while I was musing, the fire burned. Then I spoke with my tongue" (Ps. 39:3 NKJV).

Challenge of the day: Speak the Word of the Lord with passion, power, authority, and love. Do not let the fire die out or allow anything or anyone to subdue your passion to speak about the Lord or serve Him, through your living for Jesus Christ.

To God be the glory! Many blessings and have a powerful day serving the Lord with passion and fire.

Day 320

I pray that all is well with you. Start your day off with God, knowing that you must recognize the power of the living and breathing Word of God. God's Word is life changing. Any and everything in our lives can be affected and changed through the living Word of God. God's Word will not change; nor does God change. We as believers must rely on the power thereof to change, heal, deliver, set free, and liberate us, according to our faith and the power of God's written and spoken Word. We ought to be wise and careful of the things we say and even what we think constantly; daily ponder what will come out of your mouth. "Death and life are in the power of the tongue, and those who love it will eat its fruit" (Prov. 18:21 NKJV). "Every word of God is pure; He is a shield to those who put their trust in Him. Do not add to His words, lest He rebuke you, and you be found a liar" (Prov. 30:5, 6 NKJV). So be encouraged this morning and watch the words that are coming out of your mouth, because there is power to change the course of our lives in the words that we speak and even think.

> "The words of the LORD are pure words, like silver tried in a furnace of earth, purified seven times" (Ps. 12:6 NKJV).

Challenge of the day: The Word of God will purify us and change us daily into His likeness, as we sit, study, meditate, and live out the pureness of His living Word.

To God be the glory! Many blessings to you and have a powerful day being captivated in and through the pureness and power of God's living Word.

Day 321

I pray that all is well with you. Start your day off with God, knowing you must get the required rest in God in order to stay spiritually alert. Going like the Energizer bunny all the time will cause one's body and system to shut down. We must use wisdom when operating in the things of God. Rest when you can get the opportunity or, better yet, create the opportunity and time. We need the rest to be refreshed in Christ. "Come to Me, all you who labor and are heavy laden, and I will give you rest. Take My yoke upon you and learn from Me, for I am gentle and lowly in heart, and you will find rest for your souls. For My yoke is easy and My burden light" (Matt. 6:28-30 NKJV). So be encouraged this morning and find time to rest in Jesus Christ, learn from Him, and be at ease within your mind, body, and spirit. Do not worry or fret about things; just trust God.

"Rest in the LORD, and wait patiently for Him; do not fret because of him who prospers in his way, because of the man who brings wicked schemes to pass" (Ps. 37:7 NKJV).

Challenge of the day: Be at ease and rest in the Lord, trust Him for guidance, and do not move on your own accord; trust the timing of God.

To God be the glory! Many blessings and have a powerful day in the Lord, trusting and relying on God to put you at ease and in peace, so you may get the proper rest needed.

Day 322

I pray that all is well with you. Start your day off with God knowing that you must understand the power of giving. When we give, it opens up doors to share the love of Jesus Christ. During certain times of the year, giving is a "big to-do," but what about the rest of the year? If we were to give and share in the love of Jesus Christ consistently, the doors of opportunity to share the gospel would remain adjured. Giving, mind you, does not always have to be in the form of a gift. Sharing or giving—just a hug or a little time or conversation—can change a person's life, because one may not always know what the other person is facing. Jesus' ministry was powerful and effective because He understood how to give of Himself to help others in need. "Command those who are rich in this present age not to be haughty, nor to trust in uncertain riches but in the living God, who gives us richly all things to enjoy. Let them do good, that they be rich in good works, ready to give, willing to share, storing up for themselves a good foundation for the time to come, that they may lay hold on eternal life" (1 Tim. 6:17-19 NKJV). So be encouraged this morning, brothers and sisters, and give not because it is the "season" to give, but make it a daily habit to share the love of Jesus Christ and give accordingly, as the Spirit of God moves upon your heart to do.

> "So let each one give as he purposes in his heart, not grudgingly or of necessity; for God loves a cheerful giver" (2 Cor. 9:7 NKJV).

Challenge of the day: If you are not giving out of the kindness of your heart, then keep it to yourself. God loves a cheerful giver, not a complainer about life or about giving. Jesus did not complain when He went to the cross for our sins, so why should we complain about giving?

To God be the glory! Many blessings and have a powerful day giving of yourself to others in need sharing in the love of Jesus Christ.

Day 323

I pray that all is well with you. Start your day off with God knowing you must worship the Lord Jesus Christ, the King of Kings and Lord of Lords. It is He who we celebrate: the birth, life, and resurrection of the true and living Christ Jesus, who was born to save the entire world from sin. It was and is His living legacy, which we must never forget but pass on from generation to generation until the end of time. "Lift up your heads, O you gates! And be lifted up, you everlasting doors! And the King of glory shall come in. Who is the King of Glory? The LORD strong and mighty, The LORD mighty in battle. Lift up your heads, O you gates! Lift up, you everlasting doors! And the King of glory shall come in. Who is this King of glory? The LORD of hosts, He is the King of glory" (Ps. 24:7-10 NKJV). So be encouraged this morning and celebrate the Lord of Hosts, the King of Glory. Give Jesus praise for life; celebrate and lift Jesus Christ this morning.

"Open the gates, that the righteous nation which keeps the truth may enter in. You will keep him in perfect peace, whose mind is stayed on You, because he trusts in You" (Isa. 26:2, 3 NKJV).

Challenge of the day: Live right and stay in perfect peace because of Jesus Christ the Prince of Peace keep you on course as you surrender until Him. Live well and know Christ.

To God be the glory! Many blessings to you and have a powerful day in Christ as we give of ourselves to one another.

Day 324

I pray that all is well with you. Start your day off with God knowing that you must adhere to the voice of God. You must listen attentively and carefully to the Word and the guidance of the Holy Spirit. The Holy Spirit is a gentleman; He will not force Himself on us, but He is ready and waiting patiently to assist and guide us through our day-to-day living. "Behold, I stand at the door and knock; if anyone hears and listens to and heeds My voice and opens the door, I will come in to him and will eat with him, and he [will eat] with Me" (Rev. 3:20). So be encouraged this morning, listen to the voice of God, and be guided the right way through Jesus Christ and by following the leading of the Holy Spirit. Surely you will find life more pleasant and enjoyable with God and experience what it means to be guided by the Lord. Listen and be ready to respond.

"Therefore, as the Holy Spirit says; Today, if you will hear His voice, do not harden your hearts, as [happened] in the rebellion [of Israel] and their provocation and embitterment [of Me] in the day of testing in the wilderness, where you fathers tried [My patience] and tested [My forbearance] and found I stood their test, and they saw My works for forty years. And so I was provoked (displeased and sorely grieved) with that generation, and said, They always err and are led astray in their hearts, and they have not perceived or recognized My ways and become progressively better and more experimentally and intimately acquainted with them. Accordingly, I swore in My wrath and indignation, They shall not enter into My rest" (Heb. 3:7-11).

Challenge of the day: Listen and hear the voice of the Lord today, receive life, and remember what He has done for you all year. Reflect on the greatness of the Lord and look continuously on Him as your salvation for life.

To God be the glory! Many blessings to you and have a powerful worship experience with the Lord.

Day 325

I pray that all is well with you. Start your day off with God knowing you must rely on His Word to carry you through life. The Word of God will sustain you through any and everything. It is our reference book and guide to a successful life, now and forever. Being guided by the Spirit of the Lord and His Word will keep us on track for life. Nowadays it is easy to fall readily off the path because of the many distractions, but I declare unto you to hold on and to have discipline. We must possess discipline and constantly look at ourselves in the mirror to review and capture the changes that God is making in and around our lives. "When I was a child, I talked like a child, I thought like a child, I reasoned like a child; now that I have become a man, I am done with childish ways and have put them aside. For now we are looking in a mirror that gives only a dim (blurred) reflection [of reality as in a riddle or enigma], but then [when perfection comes] we shall see in reality and face to face! Now I know in part (imperfectly), but then I shall know and understand fully and clearly, even in the same manner as I have been fully and clearly known and understood [by God]" (1 Cor. 13:11-12). So be encouraged this morning and reflect upon your life through the living Word of God and know where you stand with God always. He is indeed a forgiving and loving God, who cares enough about us to give us an understanding of His Word and our lives.

"I will worship toward Your holy temple and praise Your name for Your loving-kindness and for Your truth and faithfulness; for You have exalted above all else Your name and Your word and You have magnified Your word above all Your name!" (Ps. 138:2).

Challenge of the day: Spend time in the Word and see what God sees in you. You are destined to live out God's Word, so know and practice what you are living.

To God be the glory! Many blessings to you and have a powerful day living out the Word of God in your life.

Day 326

I pray that all is well with you. Start your day off with God knowing you must trust God to be God in your life. As this year comes to a close, you must rejoice, knowing that God, being who He is, brought us through the many storms of life that came this past year. We must trust God more with great expectation and faith to carry us through another year. We must know for certain that God is great and He means us no harm; if God is for us, then who will dare be against us? Trust God to bring us through, by faith and grace, to His unmerited favor. "So trust in the Lord (commit yourself to Him, lean on Him, hope confidently in Him) forever; for the Lord God is an everlasting Rock [the Rock of Ages]" (Isa. 26:4). So be encouraged this morning and walk in the confidence that God has shown you and given unto you through this year and move forward with great expectation of what will be a glorious year to come for you. To God be glory always and rejoice in the Lord.

"The steps of a [good] man are directed and established by the Lord when He delights in his way [and He busies Himself with his every step]. Though he falls, he shall not be utterly cast down, for the Lord grasps his hand in support and upholds him" (Ps. 37:23-24).

Challenge of the day: Stay close to the Lord and follow His direction. Walk as the Lord directs, be obedient to His voice, and He will keep you close and steady your ways. He will also keep you out of harm's way.

To God be the glory! Many blessings to you and have a powerful day serving the Lord.

Day 327

I pray that you had a great evening. Start your day off with God by being grateful. We must give thanks unto the Lord for He is good. We must be grateful unto Him for allowing us to start the year off right, by submitting unto the Lord as our living Savior Jesus Christ, who died on the cross for our sins. Praise His holy name. "In Him we also were made [God's] heritage (portion) and we obtained an inheritance; for we had been foreordained (chosen and appointed beforehand) in accordance with His purpose, Who works out everything in agreement with the counsel and design of His [own] will, so that we who first hoped in Christ [who first put our confidence in Him have been destined and appointed to] live for the praise of His glory! In Him you also who have heard the Word of Truth, the glad tidings (Gospel) of your salvation, and have believed in and adhered to and relied on Him, were stamped with the seal of the long-promised Holy Spirit. That [Spirit] is the guarantee of our inheritance [the firstfruits, the pledge and foretaste, the down payment on our heritage], in anticipation of its full redemption and our acquiring [complete] possession of it—to the praise of His glory" (Eph. 1:11-14). So be encouraged and grateful this year, because you have a great inheritance waiting through Jesus Christ, and the Holy Spirit will guarantee it. Celebrate life with Jesus and live abundantly in Him.

> "For while the Law was given through Moses, grace (unearned, undeserved favor and spiritual blessing) and truth came through Jesus Christ" (John 1:17).

Challenge of the year: Know Jesus more than you know your church doctrine and live out the Word of the one and only true and living God and understand what it means to receive grace and truth in Christ.

To God be the glory! Many blessings to you and have a great and powerful day bearing fruit for Jesus Christ in love, so that others may come to know Him as their personal Lord and Savior.

Day 328

I pray that all is well with you. Start your day off with God knowing you must trust God to protect you. When harm may seem imminent, we must rely on God to keep His hand of protection on us and commence to give Him glory and praise during the storms of life. If we trust God to protect us, surely we will must not concern ourselves with who will be against us. "HE WHO dwells in the secret place of the Most High, shall remain stable and fixed under the shadow of the Almighty [Whose power no foe can withstand]" (Ps. 91:1). "Who shall bring any charge against God's elect [when it is] God Who justifies [that is, Who puts us in right relation to Himself? Who shall come forward and accuse or impeach those whom God has chosen? Will God, Who acquits us?]" (Rom 8:33). We must be encouraged and fret not this morning, because God's hedge of protection cannot be easily broken. It is God Himself who puts us in right relation with Him, and we have nothing to fear because of God's love and protection for His very own elect.

"Who shall ever separate us from Christ's love? Shall suffering and affliction and tribulation? Or calamity and distress? Or persecution or hunger and destitution or peril or sword? Even as it is written, For Thy sake we are put to death all the day long; we are regarded and counted as sheep for the slaughter. Yet amid all these things we are more than conquerors and gain a surpassing victory through Him Who loved us. For I am persuaded beyond doubt (am sure) that neither death nor life, nor angels nor principalities, nor things impending and threatening nor things to come, nor powers, nor height nor depth, nor anything else in all creation will be able to separate us from the love of God which is in Christ Jesus our Lord" (Rom. 8:35-39).

Challenge of the day: Do not allow anyone or anything to separate you from the love of God. No matter what or who it is, God's love and His relationship with you must be priority!

To God be the glory! Many blessings to you and a glorious day in the Lord, trusting Him for His great hedge of protection around you and your loved one's lives.

Day 329

I pray that all is well with you and your family. Start your day off with God knowing that you must rely on God to be there for us. We are never alone nor are we forsaken. He is ever-present and mindful about what is going on within our lives. "And they rose early in the morning and went out into the Wilderness of Tekoa: and as they went out, Jehoshaphat stood and said, Hear me, O Judah, and you inhabitants of Jerusalem! Believe in the Lord your God and you shall be established; believe and remain steadfast to His prophets and you shall prosper" (2 Chron. 20:20). So be encouraged this morning and remain steadfast in the Lord Jesus Christ, for He is indeed reliable. Believe in Him and keep the faith. Do not be moved by your circumstances, but trust God to see you through.

> "Yes through I walk through the [deep, sunless] valley of the shadow of death, I will fear or dread no evil, for You are with me; Your rod [to protect] and Your staff [to guide], they comfort me" (Ps. 23:4).

Challenge of the day: Fear God, not your situations.

To God be the glory! Many blessings to you and have a powerful day. Expect to bask in the presence of the Lord as you surrender to Him, not giving in to the circumstances of life.

Day 330

I pray that all is well with you and that your family is doing well. Start your day off with God knowing that you must resist temptation. When temptation is staring you in the face, run; do not try to handle it on our own and get into deeper things than what you expect. Such arrogance God does not like or approve of. "For no temptation (no trial regarded as enticing to sin), [no matter how it comes or where it leads) has overtaken you and laid hold on you that is not common to man [that is, no temptation or trial has come to you that is beyond human resistance and that is not adjusted and adapted and belonging to human experience, and such as man can bear]. But God is faithful [to His Word and to His compassionate nature], and He [can be trusted] not to let you be tempted and tried and assayed beyond your ability and strength of resistance and power to endure, but with the temptation He will [always] also provide the way out (the means of escape to a landing place), that you may be capable and strong and powerful to bear up under it patiently" (1 Cor. 10:13). So be encouraged this morning and hold your head up high and rest easy. God has made the way of escape for you to flee and resist temptation; give Him glory for providing you the strength to stand and be bold during the times of trial and temptation.

> "God is faithful (reliable, trustworthy, and therefore ever true to His promise, and He can be depended on); by Him you were called into companionship and participation with His Son, Jesus Christ our Lord" (1 Cor. 1:9).

Challenge of the day: Know that you can depend on God to deliver you in the face of adversity, trials, and temptations. Stand easy in the company of the Lord and fret not; only trust

Him for deliverance as you resist and flee temptation. Know also that God called you into companionship with Christ, so why would He leave you stranded?

To God be the glory! Many blessings and have a powerful day staying close to Jesus and recognizing the power of God to deliver you and provide a way of escape from temptation.

Day 331

I pray that all is well with you and your family and that the miracles of God are all around you. Search for them and expect them by faith. Start your day off with God knowing that no weapon shall hurt you; nothing that is against a child of the Most High God will prosper. God has designed it so that our walk of faith will be successful, regardless of how it may appear. We will accomplish the mission that God has set before us and we must walk according to the will of God. "But no weapon that is formed against you shall prosper, and every tongue that shall rise against you in judgment you shall show to be in the wrong. This [peace, righteousness, security, triumph over opposition] is the heritage of the servants of the Lord [those in whom the ideal Servant of the Lord is reproduced]; this is the righteousness or the vindication which they obtain from Me [this is that which I impart to them as their justification], says the Lord" (Isa. 54:17). So be encouraged this morning and walk uprightly before the Lord and acknowledge your inheritance in the Lord. Because you are guarded by God, no weapon or tongue shall hurt you, and you must walk in connection to your relationship with the Servant of the Lord, His Son Jesus Christ, in which you are reproduced.

"You shall establish yourself in righteousness (rightness, in conformity with God's will and order): you shall be far from even the thought of oppression or destruction, for you shall not fear, and from terror, for it shall not come near you" (Isa. 54:14).

Challenge of the day: Walk like you are being established by God and be far away from those things that may harm you. Conform to the Word and will of God; it is in your best interest, because nothing will harm you.

To God be the glory! Many blessings to you and have a powerful day walking in your inheritance and knowing that nothing will prosper that attempts to harm you or your family.

Day 332

I pray that all is well with each of you and your family. Start your day off with God knowing that we must recognize the healing power of God. God can and will heal all diseases; it is just a matter of asking, believing with faith in God to do it in our lives. God still heals; He changes not and He is able to do all things. Speak healing: confess that which you want God to do in your life. "Then shall your light break forth like the morning, and your healing (your restoration and the power of a new life) shall spring forth speedily; your righteousness (your rightness, your justice, and your relationship with God) shall go before you [conducting you to peace and prosperity], and the glory of the Lord shall be your rear guard" (Isa. 58:8). So be encouraged this morning and confess your healing as your recognize it in your personal relationship with Jesus Christ. Live out your healing, believe it, expect it, and receive it in Jesus' name.

"And the Angel of God Who went before the host of Israel moved and went behind them; and the pillar of the cloud went from before them and stood behind them" (Ex. 14:19).

Challenge of the day: God is present. In every situation He is there, even during our healing process, so confess the healing and watch God move.

To God be the glory! Many blessings to you and have a powerful day expecting the healing power of God to flow in and around our lives as a sphere of influence.

Day 333

I pray that all is with each of you and your family. Start your day off with God knowing that we must live holy and uprightly before God. You must live with a heart of love and compassion, quick to forgive, having deep understanding and appreciation for others. A life of holiness and righteousness is not about you, but about what you do for others and how you represent Christ. "And put on the new nature (the regenerate self) created in God's image, [Godlike] in true righteousness and holiness. Therefore, rejecting all falsity and being done now with it, let everyone express the truth with his neighbor, for we are all parts of one body and members one of another" (Eph. 4:24, 25). So be encouraged this morning and live for God, caring for and appreciating others. We come from the same root—the image and likeness of God. Be in harmony with one another, live in peace, and walk in holiness and righteousness. Do something nice for someone today. Smile, God loves you, and you must show that love to someone else.

"These are the things that you shall do: speak every man the truth with his neighbor; render the trust and pronounce the judgment or verdict that makes for peace in [the courts at] your gates" (Zech. 8:16).

Challenge of the day: Speak the truth and live in peace with everyone as you live with an attitude of holiness and righteousness.

To God be the glory! Many blessings to you and have a powerful day looking out for one another in Christ Jesus.

Day 334

I pray that all is well with you and your family. Start your day off with God, knowing that we must recognize the power of the blood of Jesus Christ. It is because of His blood and death on the cross that we are redeemed and justified. Because of His blood we are healed. It is because of His blood we can live again in the newness of life. The shedding of the blood of Jesus was the greatest sacrifice of all times. There is power in the blood of Jesus, power to love well, live well, and to do well; as we commune with Christ, we can do His bidding. "He who feeds on My flesh and drinks My blood dwell continually in Me, and [in like manner dwell continually] in him. Just as the living Father sent Me and I live by (through, because of) the Father, even so whoever continues to feed on Me [whoever takes Me for his food and is nourished by Me] shall [in his turn] live through and because of Me" (John 6:56-57). So be encouraged this morning and feast with Christ Jesus, partake of His blood covenant, abide in Him, and live a full and complete life.

"In this [union and communion with Him] love is brought to completion and attains perfection with us, that we may have confidence for the day of judgment [with assurance and boldness to face Him], because as He is, so are we in this world" (1 John 4:17).

Challenge of the day: Know the One with whom you commune and walk in the confidence, love, and power thereof.

To God be the glory! Many blessings and have a powerful day recognizing the power of the blood on and in your life.

Day 335

I pray that all is well with you and your family. Start your day off with God knowing that you can withstand the fire. When situations arise that may seem hard to handle, trust God in the midst of the fire. He will bring deliverance like none other. Remain calm and have your thoughts collected, because God will be right there with you in the midst of the fire. "Then King Nebuchadnezzar was astonished; and he rose in haste and spoke, saying to his counselors, 'Did we not cast three men bound into the midst of the fire?' They answered and said to the king, 'True, O king.' 'Look!' he answered, 'I see four men loose, walking in the midst of the fire; and they are not hurt, and the form of the fourth is like the Son of God'" (Dan. 3:24, 25 NKJV). So be encouraged this morning, knowing you are not in the fire alone; Jesus will be there with you. Do not hesitate to call on Him and He will deliver you; He can handle all things.

> "When you pass through the waters, I will be with you; and through the rivers, they shall not overflow you. When you walk through the fire, you shall not be burned, nor shall the flame scorch you. For I am the LORD your God, the Holy One of Israel, your Savior; I gave Egypt for your ransom, Ethiopia and Seba in your place. Since you were precious in My sight, You have been honored, and I have loved you; therefore I will give men for you, and people for your life" (Isa. 43:2-4 NKJV).

Challenge of the day: Stand tall in the midst of trials and tribulations, they will not harm or hurt you. There will not even be the smell of smoke amongst you. Walk with the Lord and know and receive His salvation.

To God be the glory! Many blessings to you and have a soaring day. Know the Lord as Savior and Lord of your life.

Day 336

I pray that all is well with you and your family. Start your day off with God knowing that you will never thirst again in Christ Jesus. Come and partake of the living water of Christ; He will restore you and give you a divine drink of the living water, and you will never thirst again. Come and allow your inner self thirst for Him to be satisfied one last time, and you will be filled. "Jesus replied, I am the Bread of Life. He who comes to Me will never be hungry, and he who believes in and cleaves to and trusts in and relies on Me will never thirst any more (at any time)" (John 6:35). So be encouraged this morning and thirst after Christ; know Him and drink from the fountain of the living water and feast on the Bread Life. Make Him to be the Lord over your life and your Savior daily.

"My inner self thirsts for God, for the living God. When shall I come and behold the face of God?" (Ps. 42:2).

Challenge of the day: Come clean from the inside out. Know God and you will behold His glory. Ask for a revelation of what you need to do and commence doing it.

To God be the glory! Many blessings to you and live your day for Christ, beholding His glory.

Day 337

I pray that all is well with you and your family. Start your day off with God knowing that Jesus is your Intercessor. Jesus is praying to the Father on your behalf, so neither worry nor fret. When Jesus is for us, who would dare be against us? "Who shall bring any charge against God's elect [when it is] God Who justifies [that is, Who puts us in right relation to Himself? Who shall come forward and accuse or impeach those whom God has chosen? Will God, Who acquits us?] Who is there to condemn [us]? Will Christ Jesus (the Messiah), Who died, or rather Who was raised from the dead, Who is at the right hand of God actually pleading as He intercedes for us?" (Rom. 8:33-34). So be encouraged this morning and know that Jesus is on your side pleading your case to the Father, so you can enjoy His grace and mercy and live according to His will, Word, and way. Sharpen your relationship with Jesus, know Him like never before. Spend time praying for others as Jesus is praying for you.

"Simon, Simon (Peter), listen! Satan has asked excessively that [all of] you be given up to him [out of the power and keeping of God], that he might sift [all of] you like grain, but I have prayed especially for you [Peter], that your [own] faith may not fail; and when you yourself have turned again, strengthen and establish your brethren" (Luke 22:31, 32).

Challenge of the day: Do not grow weary when under attack; Jesus is praying that your faith will fail not, and when it is all said and done, return stronger than ever and strengthen those around you.

To God be the glory! Many blessings and have a powerful day standing on the promise that Jesus is praying for you.

Day 338

I pray that all is well with you and your family. Start your day off with God knowing that you must faint not in well-doing. Do not give up when you are doing what is right in the presence of God. Hold fast to your faith. Things will get difficult and even challenging, but do not lose heart; God has everything under control. "And let us not lose heart and grow weary and faint in acting nobly and doing right, for in due time and at the appointed season we shall reap, if we do not loosen and relax our courage and faint" (Gal. 6:9). So be encouraged this morning and do not give up or give in, but keep the faith in God and do what is right.

> "Therefore, my beloved brethren, be firm (steadfast), immovable, always abounding in the work of the Lord [always being superior, excelling, doing more than enough in the service of the Lord], knowing and being continually aware that your labor in the Lord is not futile [it is never wasted or to no purpose]" (1 Cor. 15:58).

Challenge of the day: Be about the work of the Lord, and know that your labor will not go unnoticed and will produce good fruit.

To God be the glory! Many blessings to you and have a grand day serving the Lord with a strong heart of endurance.

Day 339

I pray that all is well with each of you. Start your day off with God knowing that you must worship Him with an open heart. Allow your worship to the only wise Lord God to flow from the inside out. Your connection to Jesus starts with the heart, which will be moved by the presence of the Lord as you usher the Spirit of God in your daily communion with Him through true worship. "And all the angels were standing round the throne and round the elders [of the heavenly Sanhendrin] and the four living creatures, and they fell prostrate before the throne and worshiped God. Amen! (So be it!) they cried. Blessing and glory and majesty and splendor and wisdom and thanks and honor and power and might [be ascribed] to our God to the ages and ages (forever and ever, throughout the eternities of the eternities)! Amen! (So be it!)" (Rev. 7:11, 12). So be encouraged this morning and worship the Lord God as the heavenly being lay prostrate before Him and magnify His Holy name.

"O come, let us worship and bow down, let us kneel before the Lord our Maker [in reverent praise and supplication]" (Ps. 95:6).

Challenge of the day: Set aside some time to bow before the King of Kings and Lord of Lords, Jesus Christ. Lie before Him and reverence Him in true worship.

To God be the glory! Many blessings and have a powerful day of worship and basking in the presence of the risen Savior.

Day 340

I pray that all is well with you and your family. Start your day off with God, knowing that God desires that you be whole and complete in Him . . . not broken, not distraught, but full of love, compassion, and in good health mentally, spiritually, emotionally, and physically. "And Peter said to him, Aeneas, Jesus Christ (the Messiah) [now] makes you whole. Get up and make your bed! And immediately [Aeneas] stood up" (Acts 9:34). So be encouraged this morning and arise from this dormant life. You can be whole in Christ Jesus; believe and trust in God to do what He promised He would do in your life. Do not hold back your conversation with God, but speak life, health, and enjoy the things of God.

> "But Peter said, Silver and gold (money) I do not have; but what I do have, that I give to you: in [the use of] the name of Jesus Christ of Nazareth, walk!" (Acts 3:6).

Challenge of the day: You no longer have to sit by at the gate of the temple called Beautiful begging for alms. Rise and walk in Christ Jesus and share your testimony about the greatness of Christ.

To God be the glory! Many blessings and have a powerful day proclaiming Christ as the One who made you whole and complete in all areas of your life.

Day 341

I pray that all is well with you and your household. Start your day off with God knowing that you must give out of a kind heart. When you give someone something, do it with love and kindness. By giving in this attitude, you will display the love of Jesus Christ. "Let each one [give] as he has made up his own mind and purposed in his heart, not reluctantly or sorrowfully or under compulsion, for God loves (He takes pleasure in, prizes above other things, and is unwilling to abandon or to do without) a cheerful (joyous, 'prompt to do it') giver [whose heart is in his giving]" (2 Cor. 9:7). So be encouraged this morning and enjoy giving of yourself (your time, talents, and treasures), as God moves upon your heart to give in a loving manner. After all, God gave His only Son in a loving manner, so why should we hold back or give with an ill and unwilling attitude?

"He who has a bountiful eye shall be blessed, for he gives of his bread to the poor" (Prov. 22:9).

Challenge of the day: Observe the needs of others and give to them as God has blessed you.

To God be the glory! Many blessings and have a powerful day sharing in the love of Christ through giving to those in need.

Day 342

I pray that all is well with you and your family. Start your day off with God, knowing that God will comfort you and give you peace in life. No matter how hard things may seem or what situations you are going through, God will comfort you. He will be there to carry you through and to hold you in the midst of the trials and tribulations of life. "Blessed be the God and Father of our Lord Jesus Christ, the Father of sympathy (pity and mercy) and the God [Who is the Source] of every comfort (consolation and encouragement), Who comforts (consoles and encourages) us in every trouble (calamity and affliction), so that we may also be able to comfort (console and encourage) those who are in any kind of trouble or distress, with the comfort (consolation and encouragement) with which we ourselves are comforted (consoled and encouraged) by God" (2 Cor. 1:3-4). So be encouraged this morning and know that you are comforted by God and also learn to comfort and encourage one another.

"I, even I, am He Who comforts you. Who are you, that you should be afraid of man, who shall die, and of a son of man, who shall be made [as destructible] as grass" (Isa. 51:12).

Challenge of the day: Go with God and be not afraid, because He will give you comfort throughout your life.

To God be the glory! Many blessings to you and have a peaceful day in all that you do.

Day 343

I pray that you and your family are well. Start your day off with God knowing that you must do the will of God. You must drink the cup of life that is given to you as God's will. The cup may be heavy and even challenging, but nevertheless, allow God's will to be done in your life, as Jesus did. "And He was saying, Abba, [which means] Father, everything is possible for You. Take away this cup from Me; yet not what I will, but what You [will]" (Mark 14:36). So be encouraged this morning and surrender to do the will of God. He will never leave you or forsake you as you drink from the cup of life. Jesus will be there to see you through; hold on and never give up.

"The Lord has opened My ear, and I have not been rebellious or turned backward" (Isa. 50:5).

Challenge of the day: Hear God's will for your life. Do not run or hide or even turn back. But go forward in God and He will give you peace.

To God be the glory! Many blessings and have a powerful day discovering what God's will is for your life, so you can drink the cup of life He has given you in peace and love.

Day 344

I pray that all is well with you and your family. Start your day off with God knowing that Jesus is Lord over your life. You cannot truly live and enjoy life without Christ Jesus. You must learn to surrender the issues of life to Jesus Christ and not worry or fret about them, but live the life that Jesus Christ intends for you to live. "The thief came only in order to steal and kill and destroy. I came that they may have and enjoy life, and have it in abundance (to the full, till it over-flows)" (John 10:10). So be encouraged this morning and live knowing that the death of Jesus Christ on the cross was for you, so that you can live your life according to the will of God (in abundance). Be at peace; Jesus is Lord over life and death. He can remove even the dead weight in your life, as you surrender it to Him.

"For with You is the fountain of life; in Your light do we see light" (Ps. 36:9).

Challenge of the day: Drink from the fountain that will give you abundant and everlasting life. After you drink, you cannot help but to walk in His light.

To God be the glory! Many blessings and have a powerful day knowing that Jesus is Lord over life.

Day 345

I pray that all is well with you and your family. Start your day off with God knowing that you must yield to the Spirit of God. Hear what God is saying to you and listen attentively and follow His leading. Being guided by the Holy Spirit will prove fruitful and refreshing. Be in tune with what is going on within your surroundings. "Do not continue offering or yielding your bodily members [and faculties] to sin as instruments (tools) of wickedness. But offer and yield yourselves to God as though you have been raised from the dead to [perpetual] life, and your bodily members [and faculties] to God, presenting them as implements of righteousness" (Rom. 6:13). So be encouraged this morning and submit your entire being to the Lord. Yield to God and walk in the righteousness thereof.

"SO, SINCE Christ suffered in the flesh for us, for you, arm yourselves with the same thought and purpose [patiently to suffer rather than fail to please God]. For whoever has suffered in the flesh [having the mind of Christ] is done with [intentional] sin [has stopped pleasing himself and the world, and pleases God], so that he can no longer spend the rest of his natural life living by [his] human appetites and desires, but [he lives] for what God wills" (1 Pet. 4:1, 2).

Challenge of the day: Live by God's rule and do not give into the fleshly desires or temptations.

To God be the glory! Many blessings to you and have a powerful day yielding to doing what God desires you to do.

Day 346

I pray that all is well with you and your family. Start your day off with God knowing that you are redeemed through the blood of Christ Jesus. You no longer have to allow your past to keep you in bondage. Jesus Christ paid for your past sins and even your future ones. "Christ purchased our freedom [redeeming us] from the curse (doom) of the Law [and its condemnation] by [Himself] becoming a curse for us, for it is written [in the Scriptures], Cursed is everyone who hangs on a tree (is crucified)" (Gal. 3:13). So be encouraged this morning and shout with a grateful heart, because you are redeemed from your past sins. Shout and know that Jesus Christ loves you more than you know. Do not hold on to your past or your sins; Jesus has paid the price for them all. He is the risen Savior. Rejoice and be glad in it.

"For great is Your mercy and loving-kindness toward me; and You have delivered me from the depths of Sheol [from the exceeding depths of affliction]" (Ps. 86:13).

Challenge of the day: Walk in your deliverance, because you have been redeemed and God's love and mercy are near you.

To God be the glory, many blessings, and have a powerful day walking as one who has been redeemed by Jesus Christ.

Day 347

I pray that all is well with you and your family. Start your day off with God knowing that you have staying power—power to stay close to the Lord and triumph over the enemy. The enemy does not have free reign over you or your life. God has given you power to walk over him. "Behold! I given you authority and power to trample upon serpents and scorpions, and [physical and mental strength and ability] over all the power that the enemy [possesses]; and nothing shall in any way harm you. Nevertheless, do not rejoice at this, that the spirits are subject to you, but rejoice that your names are enrolled in heaven" (Luke 10:19, 20). So be encouraged this morning and walk in the power and authority that God has given you. Do not be fearful but rejoice that your name is written in the Book of Life.

"[For my determined purpose is] that I may know Him [that I may progressively become more deeply and intimately acquainted with Him, perceiving and recognizing and understanding the wonders of His Person more strongly and more clearly], and that I may in that same way come to know the power outflowing from His resurrection [which it exerts over believers], and that I may so share His suffering as to be continually transformed [in spirit into His likeness even] to His death, [in the hope]" (Phil. 3:10).

Challenge of the day: Know more about Jesus and the power that He has given you through His resurrection.

To God be the glory, many blessings, and have a powerful day walking in the power and authority that is upon your life.

Day 348

I pray that all is well with you and your family. Start your day off with God knowing that you must be the leader that God has called you to be. Lead where you are assigned. Set the tone for yourself, your home, and even your occupation. "The Lord shall open to you His good treasury, the heavens, to give the rain of your land in its season and to bless all the work of your hands; and you shall lend to many nations, but you shall not borrow. And the Lord shall make you the head, and not the tail; and you shall be above only, and you shall not be beneath, if you heed the commandments of the Lord your God which I command you this day and are watchful to do them" (Deut. 28:12, 13). So be encouraged this morning and go forth and be the leader: the head and not the tail, the lender and not the borrower. Keep the commandments of the Lord and receive His blessings.

"For all who are led by the Spirit of God are sons of God" (Rom. 8:14).

Challenge of the day: Follow God's leading through His Spirit, and He will guide you in your leadership role. Without God's guidance, how can one truly lead?

To God be the glory! Many blessings to you and have a powerful day following God's leading as a son or daughter of God.

Day 349

I pray that all is well with you and your family. Start your day off with God knowing that you are indeed a part of the largest family ever. There is a spiritual family that you must tap into. Do not disregard its love and power. Nor should you consider yourself insignificant. You are of royalty and joint heirs with Christ Jesus. "For [the Spirit which] you have now received [is] not a spirit of slavery to put you once more in bondage to fear, but you have received the Spirit of adoption [the Spirit producing sonship] in [the bliss of] which we cry, Abba (Father)! Father! The Spirit Himself [thus] testifies together with our own spirit, [assuring us] that we are children of God. And if we are [His] children, then we are [His] heirs also; heirs of God and fellow heirs with Christ [sharing His inheritance with Him]; only we must share His suffering if we are to share His glory" (Rom. 8:15-17). So be encouraged this morning knowing that you are in the family of Christ Jesus. Rejoice and be glad, share in the love with your family. And receive your inheritance.

"For you have been granted [the privilege] for Christ's sake not only to believe in (adhere to, rely on, and trust in) Him, but also to suffer in His behalf" (Phil. 1:29).

Challenge of the day: You are privileged to know Christ; trust Him to guide you in all that you do.

To God be the glory! Many blessings and have a powerful day getting to know your spiritual family better, especially knowing Christ Jesus like never before.

Day 350

I pray that all is well with you and your family. Start your day off with God knowing that God desires that we share in the oneness with Him and our Lord Jesus Christ. There must be a sense of harmony, with fellowship across the nation and world for that matter. You must strive to be one and have the mindset of Jesus Christ. You must recognize the common bond of Jesus Christ in your life, as well as in others that you come across. "And [now] I am no more in the world, but these are [still] in the world, and I am coming to You. Holy Father, keep in Your name [in the knowledge of Yourself] those whom You have given Me, that they may be one as We [are one]" (John 17:11). So be encouraged this morning and live to discover the oneness of God in you, as well as in others.

> "And when Jesus heard it, He said to him, One thing you still lack. Sell everything that you have and divide [the money] among the poor, and you will have [rich] treasure in heaven; and come back [and] follow Me [become My disciple, join My party, and accompany Me]" (Luke 18:22).

Challenge of the day: Come and be one with Christ, join His team, and fellowship with others, so that they can see Christ in you.

To God be the glory! Many blessings to you and have a powerful day being one with Christ and other believers.

Day 351

I pray that all is well with you and your family. Start your day off with God knowing that you must leave an inheritance for your children's children. God is a generational God: He does things that will have an lasting impact on generations to come. Just as you are blessed through Abraham, you are to bless others (particularly your family). "A good man leaves an inheritance [of moral stability and goodness] to his children's children, and the wealth of the sinner [finds its way eventually] into the hands of the righteous, for whom it was laid up" (Prov. 13:22). So be encouraged this morning and prepare to set your family up for success, as God did for Abraham, Isaac, and Jacob. It is the Lord who has put you in a position to be successful, as well as your great-grandchildren, to partake in the inheritance thereof.

"Whoever despises the word and counsel [of God] brings destruction upon himself, but he who [reverently] fears and respects the commandment [of God] is rewarded" (Prov. 13:13).

Challenge of the day: Do not despise the Word and counsel of God, but pass it on to your children and their children. Teach them the ways of the Lord and they will reap the rewards of eternal life through Jesus Christ our Lord.

To God be the glory! Many blessings to you and have a powerful day preparing the next generation in the service of the Lord.

Day 352

I pray that all is well with you and your family. Start your day off with God knowing that you must be quick to listen and slow to speak. Listen to what God is saying unto you and then follow through. Sometimes you just have to get by yourself in a quiet spot and listen to the voice of God. Often you can hear something and run off shouting, but forgot to get the rest of the story. Listen to the whole story first, gather some insight, and speak the truth. "Understand [this], my beloved brethren. Let every man be quick to hear [a ready listener], slow to speak, slow to take offense and to get angry" (James 1:19). So be encouraged this morning and find time to listen to God. Be even-tempered; do not be in a hurry to get upset about things over which you have no control.

"He who has knowledge spares his words, and a man of understanding has a cool spirit" (Prov. 17:27).

Challenge of the day: Use your words wisely and remain calm at all times. No need to bring your blood pressure up; Jesus died on the cross so that you can live and not die. Be at peace within yourself and speak life-changing words in all of your situations.

To God be the glory! Many blessings to you and have a powerful day spending quiet time with God and waiting to see what is next for your life.

Day 353

I pray all is well with each of you and your families. Start your day off with God, knowing that the latter rain will come; just hold on and trust in the one and only true and living God. Be patient and trust God for the harvest, because it's coming. Just make sure you have room enough to receive it in your heart and your very surroundings. "So be patient, brethren, [as you wait] till the coming of the Lord. See how the farmer waits expectantly for the precious harvest from the land. [See how] he keeps up his patient [vigil] over it until it receives the early and late rains" (James 5:7). So be encouraged this morning and wait with an expectant heart, for the rain is coming full of blessings and you shall reap in the harvest of your life. Trust the fact that Jesus Christ (the One who died for your sins) is coming back again; be ready and welcome the great return of our living Savior.

"Be glad then, you children of Zion, and rejoice in the Lord, your God; for He gives you the former or early rain in just measure and in righteousness, and He causes to come down for you the rain, the former rain and the latter rain, as before" (Joel 2:23).

Challenge of the day: Stand praising God for the former and latter rain in your life. Live righteously and receive the blessings that will overtake you and cause you to rejoice and be glad in the Lord your God—who gives you all things, even eternal life.

To God be the glory! Many blessings and have a powerful day of great expectation for the rain, the former and latter, to flow in and around your life.

Day 354

I pray that all is well with you and your family. Start your day off with God knowing that you must recognize God as the Potter. It is He who put you together, and you must allow the Spirit of God to mold and shape you into what He desires for you to be. "Yet, O Lord, You are our Father; we are the clay, and You our Potter, and we all are the work of Your hand" (Isa. 64:8). So be encouraged this morning and let God shape your life; do not resist the growing plan that God has for you. Everything that you go through will cause you to grow a little closer to the Lord.

"However, we possess this precious treasure [the divine Light of the Gospel] in [frail, human] vessels of earth, that the grandeur and exceeding greatness of the power may be shown to be from God and not from ourselves" (2 Cor. 4:7).

Challenge of the day: Know that you possess something great on the inside of you—for the glory of the Lord and not for your fame.

To God be the glory! Many blessings and have a powerful day recognizing the changes that the Potter is making in your life.

Day 355

I pray that all is well with you and your family. Start your day off with God, knowing that you must understand that Jesus Christ is the only way to get to the Father God. Without Jesus, you cannot see or comprehend who God really is. Jesus is the Bridge that leads the way directly to God. "Jesus said to him, I am the Way and the Truth and the Life; no one comes to the Father except by (through) Me. If you had known Me [had learned to recognize Me], you would also have known My Father. From now on, you know Him and have seen Him" (John 14:6, 7). So be encouraged this morning and recognize Jesus Christ as the only way to God; recognize Him as the Truth, because He knows all, sees all, and understands all. Finally, recognize Him as the Life, because you can live beyond your greatest dreams and have eternal life in Him.

"But earnestly desire and zealously cultivate the greatest and best gifts and graces (the higher gifts and the choicest graces). And yet I will show you a still more excellent way [one that is better by far and the highest of them all—love]" (1 Cor. 12:31).

Challenge of the day: When you seek love, earnestly desire to experience it and share it with others, so that they may know what love truly is and will see the love of Christ in you.

To God be the glory! Many blessings and have a powerful day telling others about the true way to God, which is through Jesus Christ.

Day 356

I pray that all is well with you and your family. Start your day off with God, knowing that you must recognize that fact that you were born to serve with a purpose. God did not just send you here just to be here. You have an assignment, a mission, and a purpose, and only you can discover it for yourself. Reach within the depths of your heart and find out what it is you are to be doing for the Lord while living here on earth. "If anyone serves Me, he must continue to follow Me [to cleave steadfastly to Me, conform wholly to My example in living and, if need be, in dying] and wherever I am, there will My servant be also. If anyone serves Me, the Father will honor him. Now My soul is troubled and distressed, and what shall I say? Father, save Me from this hour [of trial and agony]? But it was for this very purpose that I have come to this hour [that I might undergo it]" (John 12:26, 27). So be encouraged this morning and serve with purpose; do not be afraid of the trials of life. Recognize your purpose and assignment and know who you are in Christ, while serving the Lord to the best of your ability.

"Fill up and complete my joy by living in harmony and being of the same mind and one in purpose, having the same love, being in full accord and of harmonious mind and intention" (Phil. 2:2).

Challenge of the day: Pray that God will surround you with people who have purpose and like minds and spirits.

To God be the glory, many blessings, and have a powerful discovering how to serve with purpose.

Day 357

I pray that all is well with you and your family. Start your day off with God, knowing that it is God who provides you with the power to get wealth and not you yourself. God gave you a mind to be creative and hands with which to work your gifts. Do not get puffed up or prideful and forget about God. "But you shall [earnestly] remember the Lord your God, for it is He Who gives you power to get wealth, that He may establish His covenant which He swore to your fathers, as it is this day. And if you forget the Lord your God and walk after other gods and serve them and worship them, I testify against you this day that you shall surely perish" (Deut. 8:18, 19). So be encouraged this morning and know that you must not forget God and serve the other gods because you have wealth. Remember the covenant that really has the power.

"God has spoken once, twice have I heard this: that power belongs to God" (Ps. 62:11).

Challenge of the day: Hear the voice of God and recognize His authority and power!

To God be the glory, many blessings, and have a powerful day honoring the Lord and remembering His covenant relationship.

Day 358

I pray that all is well with you and your family. Start your day off with God knowing that you must not attempt to rebel against God. You will not win, you will be fighting a losing battle that God already has won. Stop and think about the consequences of your actions. "Only do not rebel against the Lord, neither fear the people of the land, for they are bread for us. Their defense and the shadow [of protection] is removed from over them, but the Lord is with us. Fear them not" (Num. 14:9). So be encouraged this morning and think about who has the upper hand, the Lord God, He is strong and mighty. Allow Him to fight your battles and do not rebel against Him; stay the course that He has laid before you.

"How often they defied and rebelled against Him in the wilderness and grieved Him in the desert!" (Ps. 78:40).

Challenge of the day: Do not defy or rebel against the Lord. He is the only One who can and will deliver you from the desert and wilderness period in your life.

To God be the glory, many blessings, and have a powerful day remembering the true deliver God

Day 359

I pray that all is well with you and your family. Start your day off with God knowing that you must look after those who are in need. Do not turn a blind eye, but see what the needs of those around are and ask God to give you the wisdom to assist them. Take care of God's people. Love them with the love of Jesus Christ. "For He delivers the needy whom he calls out, the poor also and him who has no helper. He will have pity on the poor and weak and needy and will save the lives of the needy. He will redeem their lives from oppression and fraud and violence, and precious and costly shall their blood be in His sight" (Ps. 72:12-14). So be encouraged this morning and reach out to those in need share the blessings of God, because He will never forget those who are in need and downtrodden.

"For the needy shall not always be forgotten, and the expectation and hope of the meek and the poor shall not perish forever" (Ps. 9:18).

Challenge of the day: Remember, reach back and rise up those in need.

To God be the glory, many blessings, and have a glorious day taking care of the needs of others.

Day 360

I pray that all is well with you and your family. Start your day off with God knowing that you must practice what you preach. Do not say one thing and then do another. Folk are watching you, because you say that you are a Christian. Being a Christian means being Christlike, therefore just live out the Word of God in your life. "And this is how we may discern [daily, by experience] that we are coming to know Him [to perceive, recognize, understand, and become better acquainted with Him]: if we keep (bear in mind, observe, practice) His teaching (precepts, commandments)" (1 John 2:3). So be encouraged this morning and observe always what you are doing, ensuring that you are doing things in a Christlike manner.

> "No one born (begotten) of God [deliberately, know-ingly, and habitually] practices sin, for God's nature abides in him [His principle of life, the divine sperm, remains permanently within him]; and he cannot practice sinning because he is born (begotten) of God. By this it is made clear who take their nature from God and are His children and who take their nature from the devil and are his children: no one who does not practice righteousness [who does not conform to God's will in purpose, thought, and action] is of God; neither is anyone who does not love his brother (his fellow believer in Christ). For this is the message (the announcement) which you have heard from the first, that we should love one another" (1 John 3:9-11).

Challenge of the day: Live what you preach and preach what you live.

To God be the glory, many blessings, have a powerful day living out the Word of God in action.

Day 361

I pray that all is well with you and your family. Start your day with God knowing that you must be willing to see the mercy of God upon your life. God shows mercy to the merciful, those who are kind and considerate of others. Those who have compassion and display a kind heart must show mercy and kindness, lifting up those who are down and out. "Blessed (happy, to be envied, and spiritually prosperous—with life-joy and satisfaction in God's favor and salvation, regardless of their outward conditions) are the merciful, for they shall obtain mercy!" (Matt. 5:7). So be encouraged this morning and show mercy and kindness to those around you and to those in need. Ask God to give you a discerning spirit to know how to minister to those in need.

> "BLESSED (HAPPY, fortunate, to be envied) is he who considers the weak and the poor; the Lord will deliver him in the time of evil and trouble" (Ps. 41:1).

Challenge of the day: Consider the weak and the needy and allow God to use you to be a blessing to them. Also remind them that it is God who will deliver them and set them free.

To God be the glory, many blessings, and have a powerful day. Strengthen and show compassion to those who are in need. Show them the love of Jesus Christ.

Day 362

I pray that all is well with you and your family. Start your day with God knowing that you must know who is holding your hand. God is carrying your through life. His guidance and wisdom are perfect. The Lord holds your hand through the good and not-so-good days. His counsel is wondrous and timely. Do not refuse the help and guidance of the Lord. "Who [is so blind as] not to recognize in all these [that good and evil are promiscuously scattered throughout nature and human life] that it is God's hand which does it [and God's way]? In His hand is the life of every living thing and the breath of all mankind" (Job 12:9, 10). So be encouraged this morning and see the powerful hand of God upon your life. Everything is in His hands.

"BEHOLD, THE Lord's hand is not shortened at all, that it cannot save, nor His ear dull with deafness, that it cannot hear" (Is 59:1).

Challenge of the day: The Lord can reach down and pull you up, even when you are at the lowest point in life, and save you. He even hears you when you call. Listen and be ready to grab hold of God's outstretched arm of love.

To God be the glory, many blessings, and have a grand day expecting God's hand to move upon your life.

Day 363

I pray that all is well with you and your family. Start your day with God knowing that you must tend to God's sheep. Do not leave them by themselves. Go after them with love and in the name of Jesus Christ. Take care of those the Lord has placed in your life. Your life is for those around you more than for yourself. "Again He said to him the second time, Simon, son of John, do you love Me [with reasoning, intentional, spiritual devotion, as one loves the Father]? He said to Him, Yes, Lord, You know that I love You [that I have a deep, instinctive, personal affection for You, as for a close friend]. He said to him, Shepherd (tend) My sheep" (John 21:16). So be encouraged this morning and look for the sheep, the young and the old. Tend to them and care for them; show them brotherly love. Be there for those who are your assignment.

"Then we Your people, the sheep of Your pasture, will give You thanks forever; we will show forth and publish Your praise from generation to generation" (Ps. 79:13).

Challenge of the day: Teach the praises of God to the sheep and they will sing God's praises from generation to generation.

To God be the glory, many blessings, and have a powerful tending to the people around you.

Day 364

I pray that all is well with you and your family. Start your day with God knowing that things are not over until God says they are over. God has the final decision in your life. He has everything under His control, so why frustrate yourself with things that are out of your control? Live in peace in your inner being, acceptable to God's decision. "For from Him and through Him and to Him are all things. [For all things originate with Him and come from Him; all things live through Him, and all things center in and tend to consummate and to end in Him.] To Him be glory forever! Amen (so be it)" (Rom. 11:36). So be encouraged this morning, living and enjoying the fact that God has your best interests in His mind and in His heart.

"O GOD, my heart fixed (steadfast, in the confidence of faith); I will sing, yes, I will sing praises, even with my glory [all the faculties and powers of one created in Your image]!" (Ps. 108:1).

Challenge of the day: When your heart is fixed on God, you will be at ease with the things around you. Build your faith up in God because He has the final say so in your life.

To God be the glory, many blessings, and have a powerful day being at ease; it is not over until God says it is over.

Day 365

I pray that all is well with you and your family. Start your day with God, knowing that when it is said and done you can answer the question: are you truly living as Jesus Christ desires you to live? Your life must be one of fruitfulness, love, harmony, and discipline with balance. You must be willing to serve others when no one else is willing to serve them. You must be willing to love those no one else is willing to love. You must be willing to go and share Jesus Christ with as many as you can, not only through words only but also through your lifestyle. Enoch was a great example of a close and serious relationship with God. He pleased God to a point that He did not see death. To me, he was available, willing, and able to serve and take care of the business of God. And you also must be willing to establish such a relationship with Christ, so that at the end of it all this will be said: "His master said to him, Well done, you upright (honorable, admirable) and faithful servant! You have been faithful and trustworthy over a little; I will put you in charge of much. Enter into and share the joy (the delight, the blessedness) which your master enjoys" (Matt. 25:21). So be encouraged this day and be the servant, disciple, friend, and believer that the Lord Jesus has created you to be.

> "And Enoch walked [in habitual fellowship] with God; and he was not, for God took him [home with Him]" (Gen. 5:24).

Challenge of the day: Go back to the basics and make fellowship and living for God a habit.

To God be the glory! Many blessings to you and enjoy pleasing the Lord Jesus Christ with your life.

LaVergne, TN USA
22 November 2009
164896LV00004B/3/P